Literacies of Power

THE EDGE: Critical Studies in Educational Theory
Series Editors   Joe L. Kincheloe, Peter McLaren, and Shirley Steinberg

Literacies of Power: What Americans Are Not Allowed to Know
Donaldo Macedo

FORTHCOMING

Teachers as Cultural Workers: Letters to Those Who Dare Teach
Paulo Freire

Literacies of Power

What Americans Are Not Allowed to Know

Donaldo Macedo

Foreword by Paulo Freire

Westview Press
Boulder • San Francisco • Oxford

The Edge: Critical Studies in Educational Theory

Cover and frontispiece: THE NEW YORK SCHOOL, painting by George Deem, oil on canvas, photographed by Edward Peterson, Jr., Anonymous Collection. An earlier version of Chapter 1 was published as Macedo, Donaldo P., "Literacy for Stupidification: The Pedagogy of Big Lies," *Harvard Educational Review* 63, no. 2 (Summer 1993), pp. 183–206. Copyright © 1993 by the President and Fellows of Harvard College. All rights reserved. Excerpt from "Dream Deferred," from *The Panther and the Lash* by Langston Hughes, copyright 1951 by Langston Hughes, reprinted by permission of Alfred A Knopf Inc. "What Did You Learn in School Today?" words and music by Tom Paxton, copyright © 1962 Cherry Lane Music Publishing Company, Inc. (ASCAP). International copyright secured all rights reserved. Excerpt from "#37" in *The People, Yes* by Carl Sandburg, copyright 1936 by Harcourt Brace & Company and renewed 1964 by Carl Sandburg, reprinted by permission of the publisher. Conversation with Paulo Freire excerpted from Paulo Freire and Donaldo Macedo, *Literacy: Reading the Word and the World* (Granby, MA: Bergin & Garvey, 1987). Copyright © 1987 by Bergin & Garvey Publishers, Inc., an imprint of Greenwood Publishing Group, Inc., Westport, CT. An earlier version of Chapter 4 was published in Boston University's *Journal of Education* 173, no. 2 (1991). Reprinted by permission. Portions of *All Things Considered,* "Ghetto Life 101," originally aired June 8, 1993, by National Public Radio, used by permission.

Published in 1994 in the United States of America by Westview Press, Inc., 5500 Central Avenue, Boulder, Colorado 80301-2877, and in the United Kingdom by Westview Press, 36 Lonsdale Road, Summertown, Oxford OX2 7EW

Library of Congress Cataloging-in-Publication Data
Macedo, Donaldo P. (Donaldo Pereira), 1950–
    Literacies of power : what Americans are not allowed to know /
Donaldo Macedo.
        p.   cm.—(The edge, critical studies in educational theory)
    Includes bibliographical references and index.
    ISBN 0-8133-2252-9.—ISBN 0-8133-2253-7 (pbk.)
    1. Critical pedagogy—United States.   2. Literacy—Political
aspects—United States.   3. Discrimination in education—United
States.   4. Minorities—Education—United States.   5. Educational
change—United States.   I. Title.   II. Series.
LC196.5.U6M23   1994
370.11'5'0973—dc20   94-3375
                                                                                         CIP

Printed and bound in the United States of America

The paper used in this publication meets the requirements
of the American National Standard for Permanence of Paper
for Printed Library Materials Z39.48-1984.

10   9   8

To my wonderful daughters,
Vanessa and Erica, whose
love, loyalty, and dreams
give me hope for a
more humane and truthful world

Contents

Foreword, PAULO FREIRE   xi

Series Editors' Foreword, JOE L. KINCHELOE,
   PETER MCLAREN, & SHIRLEY STEINBERG   xiii

Acknowledgments   xvii

Introduction   1

1   **Literacy for Stupidification: The Pedagogy
    of Big Lies**   9

    The Instrumentalist Approach to Literacy, 16
    The Barbarism of Specialization, or the
       Specialization of Barbarism, 19
    The Illiteracy of Literacy of the Gulf War, 25

2   **Our Common Culture: A Poisonous Pedagogy**   37

    Western Heritage Versus Multiculturalism, 49
    What All Americans Need to Know, 65

3   **Our Uncommon Culture: The Politics of Race,
    Class, Gender, and Language**   91

4   **English Only: The Tongue-Tying of America**   125

    The Role of Language in the Education
       of Linguistic-Minority Students, 131
    A Democratic and Liberatory Education for
       Linguistic-Minority Students, 133

5   **Educational Reform: Literacy and Poverty Pimps**   137

    Educational Reforms That Deform, 152

The Choiceless Choice, 165
The Method: Fetish of Reform, 173

Notes   185
About the Book and Author   197
Index   199

Foreword

      I have read with great enthusiasm Donaldo Macedo's book *Literacies of Power: What Americans Are Not Allowed to Know.* And I congratulate all those who will encounter this excellent book, for not only is it timely but also it meticulously unveils the truths that have been astutely hidden through myriad ideological manipulations so as to make us accommodate to big lies.

From beginning to end, *Literacies of Power* is intellectually unquieting, rejecting the inertia that has often chained us, preventing us from comprehending our world. Donaldo Macedo's book convincingly demonstrates that a critical reading of the world is intimately related to a historical and cultural reading of the world. Such a reading allows us to make linkages and comparisons, arrive at conclusions, and speak in relation to the world both theoretically and practically. In so doing, human beings become truly capable of reading the world and, in turn, able to intervene in such a way as to effect positive change. Never is it possible to have intervention without full comprehension of the complex sets of circumstances that have shaped one's immediate context. Therefore, the comprehension of an object that does not trigger change ends up being an obstacle in the process of intervention.

The world may be read and expressed in spoken words, but sooner or later the speech needs to be complemented through writing. It is for this reason that there cannot be reading of text without reading the world, without reading the context. And the reading of the world that omits the reading of the text implies a rupture of the inherent cycle that involves thinking, action, language, and world. This is one of the violences that illiteracy engenders—a violence that incapacitates the conscious, speaking body of women and men who are forbidden to read and write; this is done in order to limit their capacity to read the world, write about its reading, and, in the process, rethink their prior reading of the world.

It is because of these relations that as long ago as the 1960s I was insisting that literacy is an act of knowing, a creative act that should view learners as subjects in the reading process and not as objects of the educator's action. To view learners as subjects and to engage in critical dialogue with learners leads to "conscientization," the process of becoming critically conscious of the sociohistorical world in which one intervenes or pretends to intervene politically. The same is true of comprehension of a text: It requires the reader's invention, even though the reader must also respect the work produced, in this case, by the author. In reality, there is no educational practice that is not an act of knowing and not the transference of knowledge—an act of knowing of which the learner is always a critical subject.

One of the neoliberal entrapments that progressive educators almost always fail to resist, particularly after witnessing the downfall of socialism, and that makes many of them into reactionaries, is "pragmatism." This pragmatism, while decreeing the death of ideologies and utopias, celebrates an educational practice based on immediacy and selfish interests. For educational pragmatists, there are no more dreams. Likewise, there is no more reading of the world. The new educational pragmatism embraces a technical training without political analysis, because such analyses upset the smoothness of educational technicism. Simply put, we are witnessing the assertion of an educational technicism that urges us not to burden students with political thoughts and to leave them alone so that they can best focus on their technical training. To the educational pragmatist, other social and critical preoccupations represent not just a waste of time but a real obstacle in their process of skills banking. In reacting indignantly, but always critically, against these neoliberal entrapments and big lies, in energetically defending the rights of human beings to unveil the world, to make the truth known, and to intervene, Donaldo Macedo, with this excellent book, takes his place among the best of the postmodernist progressive thinkers.

Literacies of Power is a book not only for those who are concerned with literacy and the critical reading of the word and the world. It is crucial reading as well for all women and men who oppose the struggle for critical knowledge of the world. I have no doubt that Donaldo Macedo's book will serve as the foundation for transformation, for a better understanding of the world, and for more active intervention in the world, both for those who resist and for those who think critically.

Paulo Freire

Series Editors' Foreword

Our teacher education students and the general public often have great difficulty understanding that schools may *not* always serve to make students "smarter." Indeed, schools frequently dispossess students of their ability to make sense of how the world works. With the publication of *Literacies of Power,* Donaldo Macedo has made our teaching task a little easier. Few books illustrate so clearly the ways that schools, the media, and other social institutions perpetuate ignorance. As schools, for example, fragment knowledge and deny contextual understanding, students find their ability to make connections between school information; their lived worlds; and social, cultural, and institutional relations of power and privilege more and more difficult. Yet school leaders continue to send data down the industrial conveyor belt into students' minds. Rarely do such leaders consider whether such a mechanistic pedagogy contributes to a cogent comprehension of the world and is a necessary precondition for transforming it.

Although Macedo speaks to our students and their school experience, this book transcends the boundaries of schooling. Sense making is not a central feature of the social landscape of the late twentieth century. Contextualization is a foreign concept to the nightly news and the morning newspaper, where current events are presented as fragments of unrelated facts removed from the settings that provide meaning to those who "consume" them. Thus, Macedo speaks to education in a broader sense that views pedagogy as a total social process shaping our way of seeing the world. Democracy depends on its citizens' ability to understand this process, to appreciate the ways that power works to undermine the common good.

Macedo's use of the word "stupidification" captures the imagination. When the word is used in our classes, our students' ears perk up like those of a greyhound spotting a rabbit. Schooling as a process of stupidification opens a new conceptual world, an alternative education universe where the halos of the "good guys" cannot resist tarnish. The "specialized ignorance" of the expert who has little or no conception of the most elementary concepts outside her or his field is sobering. We move then to a recognition of those teachers who understand the notion of the traditional teacher education model of the "anticipatory set" but have never considered the question of school purpose. We experience a profound anxiety as educational technicians violate the dignity of our students, pushing them into a conceptual corner with "wait time," "time on task," and the removal of the teaching act from the culture, power relations, and discourse communities that situate and inform the subjectivities of the learners. If there ever was such a thing, this is stupidification. "What do you mean, educational acts hold political implications?" the technicians ask. Their attempt to quash the thinking demanded by political analysis is part of a larger technicist effort to promote a ubiquitous sociocognitive de-skilling. Such a reality begs for the interdisciplinary contextualization provided by cultural studies. Contextualize or stupidify, Brothers and Sisters.

Stupidification fits quite nicely with the antidemocratic impulses of the public conversation about education at the end of the twentieth century. The voices of the dominant culture have assured us that democratic education is incompatible with quality and excellence. Democracy is a valuable concept only to the point that it does not interfere with capitalism, the interests of profit, and the aesthetics of the commodity form. Let us make sure, educational experts tell us, that we avoid such concepts as power and social struggle in education. Indeed, the demands of stupidification dictate that questions of power vis-à-vis socioeconomic-class relations, gender dynamics, and racial discrimination be discouraged. "What does class analysis have to do with education when we live in a classless society?" Diane Ravitch asks. "Race, class, and gender studies are inappropriate in our schools," William Bennett proclaims. Even Arthur Schlesinger Jr. creates an ideology that proclaims that multicultural education causes divisiveness between cultural groups. All these ideas lead to the Orwellian E. D. Hirsches, who happily move in with a "Core Knowledge"—*what everyone should know.* When we, as critical teacher educators, lobby for the inclusion of issues such as power and social structure in professional teacher education, we are too often met with a technical lexicon that calls for a practical teacher training that "adjusts students to the realities of public schooling."

Cynically we (Kincheloe and Steinberg) recall a faculty meeting of late 1993 called to discuss the ramifications of Florida International University's failing to meet National Committee for the Accreditation of Teacher Education (NCATE) standards. As colleagues debated the true mission and direction of the college and discussed the procedures and philosophy inherent in social change, a senior professor remarked that she was tired of hearing about social change, that everyone knew that the only purpose of a college education was to teach students to survive in the present school system. *Social change had nothing to do with a college education.* In an earlier meeting, the cochair of the Foundation Department stated that he was tired of all this "philosophy stuff" and urged the department to "get on" with the business of "training teachers to survive." Stupidification and petrification become synonymous.

The technobabble of many educational leaders conveniently ignores questions of ethics. Is it ethical in a democratic society to educate students for stupidification? Is it ethical to separate the struggle for a more just and democratic society from the reform of education? Defenders of the status quo invest in a magical philosophy of education. It is a Disneyesque theory that states that all we have to do is fill students' heads with particular bits of knowledge and presto—the poverty and violence of their everyday lives disappear. As Snow White sings *"Someday my prince will come,"* the happy students emerge from school as good citizens, educated and socialized by their contact with Euro-data. The credits roll and the movie ends—all is right with the world. The "bankruptcy" of the culture of the dispossessed has been replaced with "traditional values"—values based on a historical myth of the "good old days," when students learned how to become good members of society with strong family values.

Such a halcyon fairy tale is out of touch with the stark urban landscape of contemporary America. Indeed, the editors of such a film were victims of a metaphorical drive-by shooting on their way to the studio. The dispossessed students who are forced to watch it day after day, year after year, know something is wrong; they viscerally understand that it is out of touch with their everyday reality. But there is no time for such reflection on the part of teachers and students—they are much too busy running a maze of technical procedures. The industrial model of school in the late twentieth century requires students who are good team players, respect authority, value the work ethic, follow directions, and are passive. Students who might question a "core" fairy tale, who might prefer Picasso's *Guernica* to Norman Rockwell's *First Haircut*, are suspect; they have "an attitude." The postindustrial, or informationist, model of society that is making its appearance is constructing a cybernetic citizenry driven by the postmodern logic of production, consumption, distribution, and the imperialist project of transnational capitalism. In the era of the cultural logic of late capitalism, new systems of intelligibility are required by multinational corporate interests, which are linked to the disorganization and reorganization of late capitalism, the flexibility and mobility of industrial capital, the expansion of the informal economy and service sectors, the changing ethnic and gender composition of the labor force, the exportation of large segments of industrial production to the Third World, the instantaneous creation of new products whose image value takes precedence over their use value, and the disappearance of the social into the surface of an image-driven regime. Of course, schools become the ideological vehicles for the multinational corporate interests and are largely successful in creating voracious consumers whose designer identities will help usher in the global citizen-as-consumer. The logic of market exchange informs the new principles of historical agency as the pedagogy of stupidification joins hands with bureaucratic capitalism and the aestheticization of everyday life—all of which is homologous to conservative and neoliberal politics. Macedo's development of critical literacy brushes directly against the grain of such a politics, enacting a politics of liberation for the postmodern era.

Like so many critical teachers, Macedo has his personal story: At Boston English High, his guidance counselor advised him to become a TV repairman. Shirley Steinberg was informed that it wasn't ladylike to speak out in class; Joe Kincheloe's guidance counselor assured him that since he wasn't college material, piano tuning was an appropriate vocational choice; in Peter McLaren's doctoral studies program, his professor tried to discourage his development of a radical pedagogy, claiming that he was too emotionally immature to complete his degree. In our stories, we recognize many themes that serve as corollaries to commodity logic and that are tied to neoliberalism. Underlying such themes is the fear of difference in its many forms, such as those that appear in the social relations of race, class, and gender. There is a fear of oppositional challenges to the status quo, of the development of counter-hegemonic forms of advocacy that confront elite groups and their leadership strata and contest the perpetual assertion of their own values and systems of privilege. Yet when we examine our stories in light of our present circumstances, we realize that we are the lucky ones. This book demands an underground railroad for those less fortunate.

Joe L. Kincheloe
Peter McLaren
Shirley Steinberg

Acknowledgments

This book could not have been written without the support of my family, friends, and colleagues. I am immensely grateful to Nita and Paulo Freire for their friendship, guidance, and intellectual inspiration. I would like to express my gratitude to Henry Giroux for his mentorship and friendship. I owe a deep debt to Candace Mitchell for her insightful comments, her many readings and copyediting of the manuscript, and her support and friendship. My thanks also go to Joe Kincheloe, Shirley Steinberg, and Peter McLaren for inviting me to publish my book in their series and their total support throughout the preparation of the manuscript.

I thank my colleagues and friends Neal Bruss, Jack Bereton, Ellie Kutz, Judy Goleman, Jim Gee, Duncan Nelson, Maggie Hawkins, and Tim Seiber for their strong support of my work. I am grateful to Lilia Bartolomé for her careful reading of my work, for inviting me to test my ideas during the conceptualization of this book with her graduate students at Harvard, and for her strong support. I would also like to thank Arthur Lomba, who believes in me and gave me my first academic job. My thanks also go to Barbara Graceffa, who makes it possible to pursue academic interests beyond administration of our graduate program. I am also grateful to Fernando Colina for his tremendous help with the manuscript. Finally, I am deeply indebted to my parents, Silvia and Alceu, whose courage, hard work, and dignity taught me what it means to live in truth.

Donaldo Macedo

Introduction

IN AN IRONIC TWIST OF FATE, I feel obliged in this introduction to acknowledge two former educators whose pedagogy of exclusion nearly made me join the ranks of those who, by virtue of their race, ethnicity, culture, and language are greeted in school with an unwelcome-carpet treatment that steers them away from the classroom and toward the exit door. I vividly remember when, seeking help with my college application, I approached my guidance counselor at Boston English High School. He somberly looked me in the eye and said: "I honestly think that the best thing for you to do is to apply to Franklin Institute and become a TV repairman. You have been in this country only two years and you will never develop the necessary vocabulary to compete with the American-born who have been speaking English all their lives." What my guidance counselor failed to recognize is that I was already fluent in three languages and that I had scored over 600 in both my Spanish and my French Achievement Tests. What my guidance counselor did was equate my English-language development with my intellectual capacity. If the same diagnostic standards were to be applied to equate my American peers' foreign-language ability (including some of the foreign-language teachers themselves) with their intellectual capacity, they would all be referred to special education classes. Perhaps my guidance counselor was not really operating from a deficit-orientation model but was, instead, responding to a need for bilingual TV repairmen.

I left the counselor's office devastated but somewhat determined to prove him wrong. I stopped at the Arlington train station, walked to the Admission Office of the University of Massachusetts at Boston to get an application form. Weeks later I applied and eventually got accepted.

In September 1969, I euphorically began my studies at UMass/Boston. My enthusiasm was drastically short-lived because of my Freshman English professor, who, ironically, is a colleague of mine in the English Department where I teach today. This professor wanted us to read six novels and to keep a journal that we were to hand in at the end of the semester. The length, he emphasized, was to be forty-five pages. After the second class, I went into his office and explained that I had been in the country a relatively short time and that my major goal was to learn how

1

to write well in English so that I could succeed in my studies. I also told him that I had little difficulty understanding his lectures but found it more difficult to express myself in English. I asked if I could meet with him periodically to go over my journal assignment to guide me in the process. His guidance would not only teach me about the fundamentals of writing, but it would also allow me to avoid turning in a forty-five-page journal written over a semester without any feedback in the interim. When I finished voicing my concerns, he professorially rose from his chair, adjusted his eyeglasses and said, "Sonny, you should go learn English, then come to take my class."

Feeling the pressure of soon becoming classified as 1-A and subject to being drafted to go to Vietnam, I reached inward for strength to fight off the disconfirmation of my reality due to a temporary language barrier. I recalled the courage that my parents had demonstrated in leaving the comfort of their homeland to arrive at Logan Airport with seven children and five suitcases so we could all be educated. For this reason alone, I could not let them down. I also recalled the stoicism with which my parents had confronted the loss of their human dignity as we walked from apartment to apartment in search of a home, only to be told that the apartment had been rented, even though it had not. My parents faced the humiliation of being turned away time and time again just because they were perceived as "Spics" in the wrong neighborhood. I had to show the same strength my parents demonstrated when they walked my little brother to school so he would not be spat upon by kids who yelled "Spic, Spic," even though he and my parents did not understand the invective in English.

Instead of allowing these educators to disconfirm my lived experiences and history, I forced myself to reach inward for the strength to struggle against constant symbolic and real psychological violence. I had to juggle a thirty-six-hour-a-week job as a mechanic with the demands of the university and the attitudes of some professors who had little patience with culturally diverse students. The guidance counselor and English professor also unknowingly helped destroy the myths I had been inculcated with the previous two years in the Day School for Immigrants, where I was originally sent to learn English. There, for four hours every day, I learned how to recite the Pledge of Allegiance, memorized long vocabulary lists, and read from *Dick and Jane*. After six months I was upgraded to a more advanced English class where the teacher thought that the best way to learn English was through singing. So I learned all the patriotic songs—the "Star Spangled Banner," "America the Beautiful," and so forth.

My experiences, however, showed me that there was an enormous gulf between the patriotic slogans of "liberty," "freedom," "equality,"

'69 insensitivity

and "democracy" and the treatment that I was receiving once I had been typecast as a "Spic" in the neighborhood and in school. This initial disjunction between myths and the behavior of these two educators toward me made me become more critically aware of my reality and, at the same time, more vigilant and more determined not to fulfill their prophecy.

Fortunately, not all educators subscribe to the deficit-orientation model and invest in a pedagogy of exclusion. More and more educators are calling for radical changes in the school reality, changes that celebrate rather than disconfirm cultural and language diversity. One such educator was John O'Bryant, the first African-American elected to the Boston Public School Committee. John O'Bryant was a guidance counselor at Boston English High School when I was a student there. When he heard what I had been told by my guidance counselor, he approached me and said: "Pay no attention to him. You are going to college. I'm mad, didn't he look at your grades? Come to see me in my office after school—you are going to college." Whenever I faced difficulty in my studies, I would always be reminded of John O'Bryant's determination as he said to me: "You are going to college." He understood very well that guaranteeing equal access to unequal educational structures and unequal treatment in school would never lead to equality of education. For this reason he committed most of his life to changing the unequal structures of the Boston public schools so that minority students would be treated with the respect and dignity they deserve.

Unfortunately, John O'Bryant died unexpectedly without even seeing his dream of changing the schools realized. In fact, most of the changes he fought for are rapidly reverting to the same kind of asymmetry of treatment and education along the lines of race, ethnicity, gender, class, and language that he fought against. The mayor of Boston dismantled the elected school committee and appointed his own people. The dropout rate remains unacceptably high—with two out of five students not graduating. The figure for minority students is significantly higher, ranging from 50 to 65 percent. The hard-won integration of Boston schools is slowly reverting to new forms of segregation. The many school reforms have, in fact, led to the maintenance of the status quo, as an ex-member of the school committee, John Nucci, aptly noted, "The more things change, the more they stay the same."

I am also reminded of an excellent English professor, Marjorie Collins, who accepted me into her English class after I had been told to "go learn English." In our many tutoring sessions, Marjorie realized that not only did I understand Dickens but that I was able, as a reader, to critically move beyond mere description of the text. She understood that as a human being, I had ideas, desires, and dreams all bottled up in a temporary language barrier. Instead of using language as a gate to keep me from her class, she provided me with the necessary language instruction to transcend my linguistic difficulties. Marjorie's pedagogy was one of hope informed by tolerance, respect, and solidarity. Without Marjorie Collins and John O'Bryant I would probably have fallen victim to the discriminatory educational system that parades under the veil of democracy.

It was against this backdrop of discrimination that I wrote this book, *Literacies of Power*. It was not written merely to engage in the ever-present heated debate over multiculturalism. In my view, *Literacies of Power* is a wake-up call to those who have blindly accepted the empty slogans of "freedom," "liberty," "equality," and "democracy" as givens, as by-products of the struggle for democracy that our society has already won. My book is a wake-up call to the extent that it points to the enormous contradictions inherent in the many myths that sustain our fragile democratic reality. *Literacies of Power* also represents, for me, what it means to "come to voice." The writing of this book enabled me to understand the tensions, contradictions, fears, doubts, hopes, and dreams involved in the process of making meaning of one's role and responsibility in the world. The writing of *Literacies of Power* taught me about the arduous and complex process of coming to voice, a process of conscientization, which always involves pain and hope. During the writing of this book, I became fully aware that the development of subjectivity cannot be reduced to facile propositions such as: "We need to empower minorities" or "We need to give them voice." First of all, I became keenly aware that voice is not something to be given by those in power. Voice requires struggle and the understanding of both its possibilities and limitations. The most educators can do is to create structures that would enable submerged voices to emerge. It is not a gift. Voice is a human right. It is a democratic right.

I also realized through writing this book that many liberals and neoliberals who proselytize about "empowering minorities" and "giving them voices" feel somewhat uncomfortable when these minorities, in fact, develop their own voices and move from object to subject position. These same liberal educators begin to create new mechanisms to muffle the minority voices, particularly if these voices threaten their own class and privileged positions. Thus, when I speak at conferences, I regularly hear the following: "I agree with everything you said but I was put off by your tone." I gave a lecture at Harvard last year and the professor who had invited me said to me weeks later, "The students really enjoyed your talk, though some of them just could not understand why you are so angry."

Labeling the expression of anger an inappropriate act is yet another form of discourse sanitation. This became evident when one of the reviewers of this manuscript praised the book but found that the tone was somewhat sarcastic. The reviewer added, "though I do understand why the author is concerned and extremely angry with society and schools." When I discussed this review with the editor with whom I was attempting to negotiate a contract for the book, she admitted, "Donaldo, to be honest with you I was also taken aback by the rough edges of your discourse." She recommended that I tone down the "stridency" of my language in the book proposal before she submitted it to the editorial board for approval. This I did. Some time later, an editor friend of mine, upon reading the first chapter of this book and the edited prospectus called me and asked, "Why did you make the language in your prospectus so flat: I hope you are planning to keep the energy of your language in the first chapter throughout the book." The difference between my friend and the editor concerned about "stridency" indicates the political clarity that my friend possessed. My friend accepts the existence of a multiplicity of discourses rather than a monolithic way of writing. My friend also understands that the energy and passion that are often confused with stridency constitute the very soul of the author's voice.

Another pernicious mechanism used by academics who suffocate discourses different from their own is the blind and facile call for clarity. Such a call often ignores how language is being used to make social inequality invisible. A graduate student of mine pointed out to me in class that politically she agreed with almost all the issues I raised but she could not understand why I use such complex and sometimes inaccessible language when I write. Her position points out that one can have a high level of political clarity and yet be undermined by other forms of ideology that insidiously betray one's political positions. For example, two ideological forms come to mind: taste and style. If we consider taste to be outside the ideological symbolic evaluation systems, we can easily understand how someone is able to deconstruct the ideology of oppression while at the same time insist that the only way to achieve that deconstruction is through a discourse that involves what academics characterize as language clarity.

When I was working on *Literacy: Reading the Word and the World*, which I coauthored with Paulo Freire, I asked a colleague whom I considered to be politically progressive and to have a keen understanding of Paulo's work to read the manuscript. Yet, during a discussion we had of the book, she asked me, a bit irritably: "Why do you and Paulo insist on using this Marxist jargon? Many readers who may enjoy reading Paulo may be put off by the jargon." I was at first taken aback but proceeded to calmly explain to her that the equation of Marxism with jargon did not fully capture the richness of Paulo's analysis. In fact, Paulo's language was the only means through which he could have done justice to the complexity of the various concepts dealing with oppression. For one thing, I reminded her, "Imagine that instead of writing the *Pedagogy of the Oppressed*, Paulo Freire had written the *Pedagogy of the Disenfranchised*." The first title utilizes a discourse that names the oppressor, whereas the second fails to do so. If you have oppressed, you must have oppressor. What would be the counterpart of disenfranchised? The *Pedagogy of the Disenfranchised* dislodges the agent of the action while leaving in doubt who bears the responsibility for such action. This leaves the ground wide open for blaming the victim of disenfranchisement for his or her own disenfranchisement. This example is a clear case in which the object of oppression can be also understood as the subject of oppression. Language such as this distorts reality.

And yet, mainstream academics seldom object to these linguistic distortions that disfigure reality. I seldom hear academics on a crusade for "language clarity" equate mainstream terms such as "disenfranchised" or "ethnic cleansing," for example, to jargon status. On the one hand, they readily accept "ethnic cleansing," a euphemism for genocide, while, on the other hand, they will, with certain automatism, point to the jargon quality of terms such as "oppression," "subordination," and "praxis." If we were to deconstruct the term "ethnic cleansing" we would see that it prevents us from becoming horrified by Serbian brutality and horrendous crimes against Bosnian Muslims, such as the killing of women, children, and the elderly. The mass killing of women, children, and the elderly and the rape of women and girls as young as five years old take on the positive attribute of "cleansing," which leads us to conjure a reality of "purification" of the ethnic "filth" ascribed to Bosnian Muslims, in particular, and to Muslims the world over, in general.

I also seldom heard any real protest from these same academics who want "language clarity" when, during the Gulf War, the horrific blood bath of the battlefield became a "theater of operation" and the violent killing of over one hundred thousand Iraqis, including innocent women, children, and the elderly by our "smart bombs" was sanitized into a technical military term, "collateral damage." I can go on and on giving such examples to point out how academics who argue for language clarity not only seldom object to language that obfuscates reality but often use that same language as part of the general acceptance that the standard discourse is a given and should remain unproblematic. Although these academics accept the dominant standard discourse, they aggressively object to any discourse that both fractures the dominant language and bares the veiled reality in order to name it. Thus, a discourse that names it becomes, in their view, imprecise and unclear, and wholesale euphemisms such as "disadvantaged," "disenfranchised," "educational mortality," "theater of operation," "collateral damage," and "ethnic cleansing" remain unchallenged since they are part of the dominant social construction of images that are treated as unproblematic and clear.

I am often amazed to hear academics complain about the complexity of a particular discourse because of its alleged lack of clarity. It is as if they have assumed that there is a monodiscourse that is characterized by its clarity and is also available equally to all. If one begins to probe the issue of clarity, we soon realize that it is class specific, thus favoring those of that class in the meaning-making process.

The following two examples will bring the point home: Henry Giroux and I gave a speech at Massassoit Community College in Massachusetts to approximately three hundred unwed mothers who were part of a GED program. The director of this program later informed us that most of the students were considered functionally illiterate. After Henry's speech, during the question and answer period, a woman got up and eloquently said: "Professor Giroux, all my life I have felt the things you talked about. I just didn't have a language to express what I have felt all my life. Today I have come to realize that I do have a language. Thank you." And Paulo Freire told me a story of what happened to him at the time he was preparing the English translation of *Pedagogy of the Oppressed*. He gave an African-American student at Harvard a chapter of the book to read to see how she would receive it. A few days later, Freire asked the woman if she had read it. She enthusiastically responded: "Yes. Not only did I read it but I gave it to my sixteen-year-old son to read. He read the whole chapter that night and in the morning said: 'I want to meet the man who wrote this. He is talking about me.'" The question that I have for all those highly literate academics who find Giroux's and Freire's discourse so difficult to understand is, Why is it that a sixteen-year-old boy and a poor, semiliterate woman could so easily understand and connect with the complexity of Giroux's and Freire's language and ideas, and the academics, who are the most literate, find the language incomprehensible?

I believe that the answer has little to do with language and all to do with ideology. That is, people often identify with representations that they are either comfortable with or that help deepen their understanding of themselves. The call for language clarity is an ideological issue, not merely a linguistic one. The sixteen-year-old and the semiliterate poor woman could readily connect with these authors' ideology, whereas the highly literate academics are "put off" by some dimensions of the same ideology. It is, perhaps, for this reason that a university professor I know failed to include the work of Freire in a graduate course on literacy she taught. When I raised the issue with her, she explained that students often find his writing too difficult and cumbersome. It could also be the case that although the Divinity School at Harvard University offers a course entitled "Education for Liberation," where students study

Paulo Freire and James Cone extensively, no such opportunities are available at Harvard's School of Education.

For me, the mundane call for language simplicity and clarity represents yet another mechanism to dismiss the complexity of theoretical issues, particularly if these theoretical constructs interrogate the prevailing dominant ideology. It is for this very reason that Gayatri Spivak correctly pointed out that the call for "plain prose cheats." I would go a step further and say: The call for plain prose not only cheats, it also bleaches.

Literacy for Stupidification:
The Pedagogy of Big Lies

> *The great masses of people ... will more easily fall victims to a big
> lie than to a small one.*
> —Adolf Hitler

MOST AMERICANS WOULD CRINGE at the thought that they have
repeatedly fallen victim to big lies told by their government. In fact, they
would probably instinctively point out that the manipulation of people
through big lies only occurs in totalitarian, fascist governments such as
Hitler's. In the same breath, they might remind us that their ancestors
gave their lives in the great wars so that we could enjoy the freedom and
democracy we now have. They might also hasten to recite slogans such
as "live free or die," "freedom of speech," and "freedom of information."
While busily calling out slogans from their patriotic vocabulary memory
warehouse, these same Americans dutifully vote, for example, for Ronald Reagan, giving him a landslide victory when he ran on a platform
that promised to balance the budget, cut taxes, and increase military
spending. This "unreason of reason" led George Bush to characterize
Reagan's economic plan as voodoo economics—even though he himself
later became entranced by the big lie of this same voodooism.

What U.S. voters failed to do was to demand that Reagan tell the whole
truth and nothing but the truth. In other words, they failed to require
that Reagan acknowledge that, in order for his proposition to be true
(and not a lie), the voters would have to give him and Bush a blank credit
card with $4.3 trillion in deficit credit to create the false sense of eco-
nomic prosperity enjoyed under their leadership. I say a false sense not
only because of the present economic malaise but also because the
Reagan economic boom was a bust. According to Samuel Bowles, David
M. Gordon, and E. Thomas Weisskopf: "Output growth did not revive
during the 1980's cycle. Far from stimulating investment through mas-
sive tax cuts and concessions to the wealthy, Reagan-Bush economic
policy has dealt investment a blow; compared with the previous busi-

ness cycle, the pace of real net productive investment declined by a quarter during the most recent business cycle."[1]

Despite concrete evidence indicating that the Reagan-Bush economic plan was a failure, U.S. voters swept Bush into office in 1988 with the same voodoo trickle-down economics, now ornamented with a thousand points of short-circuited lights. These same voters ascended to Bush's morally high-minded call to apply international laws against Saddam Hussein's tyranny and his invasion of Kuwait. The great mass of voters who rallied behind Bush, pushing his popular approval rating beyond 90 percent during the Gulf War, failed to realize that these same international laws had been broken by Bush a year or so before in Panama and by his predecessor in Grenada, Libya, and Nicaragua. This leads to the question why we supposedly highly literate and principled citizens of a great democracy frequently demonstrate the inability to separate myth from reality. This inability pushes us to perpetual flirtation with historical hypocrisy. However, not all Americans suffer from the inability to separate myths from reality, to read the world critically. For example, David Spritzler, a twelve-year-old student at Boston Latin School, faced disciplinary action for his refusal to recite the Pledge of Allegiance, which he considered "a hypocritical exhortation to patriotism" in that there is not "liberty and justice for all." According to Spritzler, the pledge is an attempt to unite the "oppressed and the oppressors. You have people who drive nice cars, live in nice houses and don't have to worry about money. Then you have the poor people, living in bad neighborhoods and going to bad schools. Somehow the Pledge makes it seem that everybody's equal when that's not happening. There's no justice for everybody."[2]

Spritzler was spared disciplinary action only after the American Civil Liberties Union wrote a letter on his behalf, citing a 1943 case, *West Virginia State Board of Education versus Barnett,* in which the U.S. Supreme Court upheld a student's right not to recite the Pledge of Allegiance and to remain seated.

What remains incomprehensible is why a twelve-year-old boy could readily see through the obvious hypocrisy contained in the Pledge of Allegiance, while his teachers and administrators, who have received much higher levels of education, cannot. As Noam Chomsky pointed out in reference to a similar situation, these teachers' and administrators' inability to see through the obvious represents "a real sign of deep indoctrination [in] that you can't understand elementary thoughts that any 10-year-old can understand. That's real indoctrination. So for him [the indoctrinated individual] it's kind of like a theological truth, a truth of received religion."[3] These teachers and administrators should know that history shows us convincingly and factually that the United States has systematically violated the Pledge of Allegiance, from the legalization of slavery, the denial of women's rights, and the near-genocide of Native Americans to the contemporary discriminatory practices against people who, by virtue of their race, ethnicity, class, or gender, are not treated with the dignity and respect called for in the pledge.

If we did not suffer from historical amnesia, we would easily recall that, once upon a time, the Massachusetts legislature promulgated a law that provided monetary rewards for dead Indians: "For every scalp of a male Indian brought in ... forty pounds. For every scalp of such female Indian or male Indian under the age of twelve years that shall be killed ... twenty pounds."[4] Even the abolitionist President Abraham Lincoln did not truly uphold the U.S. Declaration of Independence propositions of equality, life, liberty, and the pursuit of happiness when he declared: "I will say, then, that I am not, nor ever have been in favor of bringing about in any way the social and political equality of the white and black races. ... I as much as any other man am in favor of having the superior position assigned to the white race."[5]

One could argue that the above-cited incidents belong to the dusty archives of our early history, but I do not believe that we have learned a great deal from historically dangerous memories, considering that our leaders continue to incite racial tensions, as evidenced in the issue of Willie Horton in the presidential campaign or in Bush's opposition to job quotas on the pretext that they were a renewed invitation to racial divisiveness. This racial divisiveness actually has served the Republican Party's interest of splitting voters along class, racial, and ethnic lines. Our perpetual flirtation (if not marriage) with historical hypocrisy becomes abundantly clear if we imagine the juxtaposition of students reciting the Pledge of Allegiance in Charlestown High School in 1976, in classrooms ornamented with copies of the Declaration of Independence hanging alongside racial epithets scrawled on the walls: "Welcome Niggers," "Niggers Suck," "White Power," "KKK," "Bus is for Zulu," and "Be illiterate, fight busing."[6]

Our inability to see the obvious was never more evident than when a predominantly White jury found the four White policemen who brutally beat Rodney King "not guilty." Even though the world was shocked beyond belief by the raw brutality and barbarism of the Los Angeles law enforcers, the jurors who saw the actual video shots of King struggling on his hands and knees while being hit repeatedly by the policemen's batons concluded that "Mr. King was controlling the whole show with his action."[7] The racist ideology of Simi Valley, California, blinded these jurors to such an extent that they could readily accept the savage beatings they had seen on the video to have been, as the defense attorneys claimed, nothing more than a "controlled application of fifty-six batons" in order to contain King, who had been portrayed as a dangerous "animal," like "gorillas in the mist."[8] However, one of the jurors did not fully accept the view of reality suggested by the defense attorneys: "I fought so hard to hang on, and hang on to what I saw on the video. ... There was no way I could change the others. They couldn't see what I saw. ... [But] they could not take away from what my eyes saw."[9]

The real educational question and challenge for us is to understand why most of the jurors either could not see, or refused to see, what their eyes and the eyes of the entire world saw on television. Unfortunately, in the present setup of our educational system, particularly in our schools of education, it is very difficult to acquire the necessary critical tools that would unveil the ideology responsible for these jurors' blinders. A critical understanding of the savage beating of Rodney King and the subsequent acquittal of the four White police officers necessitates the deconstruction of the intricate interplay of race, ethics, and ideology—issues that schools of education, by and large, neglect to take on rigorously. Courses that deal with issues such as race relations, ethics, and ideology are almost absent from the teacher-preparation curricula. This serious omission is, by its very nature, ideological and constitutes the foundation for what I call the pedagogy of big lies.

At this juncture, I can easily frame my argument to demonstrate that many, if not all, of David Spritzler's teachers and administrators are either naïve victims of a big lie or are cognizant of the deceptive ideological mechanisms inherent in the pledge and consciously reproduce them, even if it means violating the very rights the oath proclaims. I argue that the latter is true. Even if we want to give such educators the benefit of the doubt, their naïveté is never innocent, but ideological. It is ideological to the degree that they have invested in a system that rewards them for reproducing and not questioning dominant mechanisms designed to produce power asymmetries along the lines of race, gender, class, culture, and ethnicity.

Those teachers who refuse such investments in the dominant ideological system usually think more critically, thus recognizing the falsehoods embedded in the various myths created by the dominant class. Critical teachers of this sort, instead of sending David to the principal's office, would seize the pedagogical moment to engage the entire class in a consciousness-raising exercise that would be in line with both the democratic ideals of the Pledge of Allegiance and the development of critical thinking skills. For instance, the teacher could have given David the opportunity to have his voice heard as he discussed the enormous contradictions inherent in the Pledge of Allegiance. The teacher could also have engaged the other students by asking them if they agreed or disagreed with David's position. The teacher could have asked the following: "Do you agree that the pledge is a 'hypocritical exhortation to patriotism'? Explain why." This question would enable other students to voice their opinions regarding their perception of the Pledge of Allegiance. Students could also be asked whether David was right in asserting that the Pledge of Allegiance is a mere attempt to unite the "oppressed and the oppressors," since "you have people who drive nice cars, live in nice houses and don't have to worry about money. Then you have the poor people, living in bad neighborhoods and going to bad schools." The teacher could continue to encourage an open dialogue by asking students if they knew people who were poor, "living in bad neighborhoods and going to bad schools." If many students were to confirm David's position, then the teacher could raise the following questions: "Why do you think that we have so many poor people living in bad neighborhoods? Do you think that poor people choose to live in bad neighborhoods? Who is responsible for the present inequality? Would you like to live in a bad neighborhood and go to a bad school? What would you do if you were forced to live in poverty and to go to a bad school?"

I am sure that a multiplicity of responses would have been given by the students, according to their own social class and race position as well as their different levels of political awareness. This exercise could have provided great insights into the students' personal narratives. It would also help the students to understand that the Pledge of Allegiance cannot fulfill its ideals in light of the social disparities and inequalities in our society. This exercise would also have provided the students the opportunity to reflect on the meaning of the proposition "liberty and justice for all." This reflection could also have prepared these students to understand their civic responsibility and their role in a society that, although it promises "equality, liberty and justice for all," is replete with inequality and injustice for those groups of people who are from different racial, class, and ethnic backgrounds.

The above exercise is one of the many constructive and creative ways that a critical teacher could begin to problem-pose with the class, as together they engage in a pedagogical process to deconstruct the myth sustained by the Pledge of Allegiance. However, in order to do so, the teacher has to be not only critical but also willing to take great risks, including losing his or her job, since the doctrinal system does not reward dissent. This risk became obvious when Jonathan Kozol was fired from the Boston Public Schools in 1964 for having his all-Black segregated fourth-grade class read Robert Frost and Langston Hughes. The reason for his dismissal was that he did not follow the curriculum. Kozol wrote that according to school officials, "Robert Frost and Langston Hughes were 'too advanced' for children of this age. Hughes, moreover, was regarded as 'inflammatory.'"[10] It did not matter that "one of the most embittered children in the class began to cry when she first heard the words of Langston Hughes."

What happens to a dream deferred?
Does it dry up
like a raisin in the sun?[11]

It did not matter to the Boston school officials that this fourth-grade girl was touched by the poem and went "home and memorized the lines." What mattered to them in 1964 when they fired Jonathan Kozol and in 1992 when they attempted to expel David Spritzler for refusing to say the Pledge of Allegiance was to deny the fourth grade the opportunity to answer and understand "what happens to a dream deferred" and to prevent David Spritzler from exposing the hypocrisy embedded in the Pledge of Allegiance. Boston school officials and educators of this sort have chosen to "live within a lie" to protect their privileged positions and the rewards the doctrinal system provides them.

What I have described so far points to an intricate and complex web of lies that functions to reproduce the dominant ideology through cultural literacy. This will become clearer in my analysis of the role of literacy in cultural reproduction, an analysis in which I will show how collective experiences function in the interest of the dominant ruling elites rather than in the interest of the oppressed groups that are the object of the policies of cultural reproduction.

Literacy for cultural reproduction uses institutional mechanisms to undermine independent thought, a prerequisite for the Orwellian "manufacture of consent" or "engineering of consent." In this light, schools are seen as ideological institutions designed to prevent the so-called crisis of democracy, another Orwellian concept, meaning the beginnings of democracy.[12]

In fact, this very perspective on schools was proposed by the Trilateral Commission, whose members—among them Jimmy Carter—belonged to the international and essentially liberal elite. This commission was created in response to the general democratic participation of masses of people in the Western world in questioning their governments' ethical behavior. Its major purpose, as many understand it, was to seek ways to maintain the Western capitalist cultural hegemony. The Trilateral Commission referred to schools as "institutions responsible for the indoctrination of the young."[13] Noam Chomsky stated it simply: The Trilateral Commission argued that schools should be institutions for indoctrination, "for imposing obedience, for blocking the possibility of independent thought, and they play an institutional role in a system of control and coercion."[14] This becomes clear in the conservative call for the control of the so-called excess of democracy. For example, according to Henry Giroux, Boston University President John Silber, who prided himself on being an education "expert," "has urged fellow conservatives to abandon any civility toward scholars whose work is considered political."[15] What Silber failed to realize is that the very act of viewing education as neutral and devoid of politics is, in fact, a political act. In order to maintain schools as sites for cultural reproduction and indoctrination, Silber preferred an educational system that brooks no debate or dissent. This is apparent in his urging of "his fellow conservatives to name names, to discredit educators who have chosen to engage in forms of social criticism (work that the New Right considers political) at odds with the agenda of the New Right's mythic conception of the university as a warehouse built on the pillars of an unproblematic and revered tradition."[16]

Although it is important to analyze how ideologies inform various literacy traditions, in this chapter I limit my discussion to a brief analysis of the instrumentalist approach to literacy and its linkage to cultural reproduction. I also argue that the instrumentalist approach to literacy does not only refer to the goal of producing readers who meet the basic requirements of contemporary society but also includes the highest level of literacy found in disciplinary specialism and hyperspecialization.

Finally, I analyze how the instrumentalist approach to literacy, even at the highest level of specialism, functions to domesticate the consciousness via a constant disarticulation between the narrow reductionistic reading of one's field of specialization and the reading of the universe within which one's specialism is situated. This inability to link the reading of the word with the world, if not combated, will further exacerbate already feeble democratic institutions and the unjust, asymmetrical power relations that characterize the hypocritical nature of contemporary democracies. The inherent hypocrisy in the actual use of the term "democracy" is eloquently captured by Noam Chomsky in his analysis of the United States. Chomsky wrote:

> "Democracy" in the United States rhetoric refers to a system of governance in which elite elements based in the business community control the state by virtue of their dominance of the private society, while the population observes quietly. So understood, democracy is a system of elite decision and public ratification, as in the United States itself. Correspondingly, popular involvement in the formation of public policy is considered a serious threat. It is not a step towards democracy; rather, it constitutes a "crisis of democracy" that must be overcome.[17]

The Instrumentalist Approach to Literacy

The instrumental literacy for the poor, in the form of a competency-based skills-banking approach, and the highest form of instrumental literacy for the rich, acquired through the university in the form of professional specialization, share one common feature: They both prevent the development of the critical thinking that enables one to "read the world" critically and to understand the reasons and linkages behind the facts.

Literacy for the poor is, by and large, characterized by mindless, meaningless drills and exercises given "in preparation for multiple choice exams and writing gobbledygook in imitation of the psycho-babble that surrounds them."[18] This instrumental approach to literacy sets the stage for the anesthetization of the mind, as poet John Ashbery eloquently captured in "What Is Poetry":

> *In School*
> *All the thoughts got combed out:*
> *What was left was like a field.*[19]

The educational "comb," for those teachers who have blindly accepted the status quo, is embodied in the ditto sheets and workbooks that mark and control the pace of routinization in the drill-and-practice assembly line. Patrick Courts correctly described the function of these workbooks and ditto sheets:

> Either you must fill in the blank (or does the blank fill you in?—they have lots of blanks) or you must identify the correct or incorrect answer by circling it, underlining it, or drawing an X through it. In addition to all this, students will find that learning to spell involves copying the same word five times and copying the definition; and learning the meaning of the word involves looking it up in the dictionary and copying the definition; and learning to write involves writing a sentence or two using the word they copied five times and looked up in the dictionary. Much of what they read in the first four or five grades, they will read-to-read: That is, they will be practicing reading in order to show that they can read, which much of the time means that they will be involved in "word-perfect" oral-reading activities, grouped as Cardinals (if they are good at it), or Bluebirds (if they are not). They will learn that reading has one of two functions: Either you read orally to show that you can "bark at print" well (delighting your teachers and boring your peers), or you read silently in order to fill in those blanks in the workbook.[20]

One would hope the students grouped as Cardinals, who survived reading-and-writing drill boot camp to become fully literate, were empowered with some sort of ability for independent critical analysis and thought. Unfortunately, these Cardinals continue in their literacy practices to experience the same fragmentation of knowledge, albeit with more sophistication. The fragmentation of knowledge via specialization produces an intellectual mechanization that, in the end, serves the same function as the fragmentation of skills in the literacy for the poor. It is not a coincidence that the defense lawyers for the White policemen in the Rodney King trial insisted on showing the jurors the video frame by frame over and over again, instead of running the video at the normal speed. The fragmentation of the Rodney King beating served two important functions: (1) By being shown each frame separately, the jurors were not allowed to see and experience the total impact of the violence applied in the beatings, and (2) by repeating the frames over and over again, the defense lawyers were able to anesthetize the sensibilities of the jurors and routinize the action captured in each frame.

Although the fragmentation of skills and bodies of knowledge is not the same as the fragmentation of the video into separate frames, the underlying principle serves the same function: On the one hand, it creates the inability to make linkages, and on the other hand, it deadens the senses. This process leads to a de facto social construction of not seeing. My colleague Robert Greene[21] noted that this once again proves the old proverb, The eyes do not see; they only record while the mind sees. To the extent that the mind can be ideologically controlled, it filters in order to transform what the eyes record, as was the case in the transformation of Rodney King's brutal beating to a "systematic application of fifty-six batons." However, an African-American colleague, Pancho Savery, correctly pointed out to me[22] that the defense attorney's machinations to prevent linkages and to deaden the jurors' senses could work only if jurors were already invested in the doctrinal system that imposed a willful blindness to realities that contradicted or questioned the system. In other words, the success of the ideological manipulation depends on the degree to which one invests in the doctrinal system and expects rewards from it. Savery argued that the fragmentation of the video frames and the playing of them over and over again would not deaden the senses of most African-Americans. On the contrary, the more they were to see the video of King's beating, even in fragmented frames, the more enraged they would become, as they are not invested in the racist doctrinal system of which they are the victims.

For some, the instrumentalist approach to literacy may have the appeal of producing readers who are capable of meeting the demands of our ever more complex technological society. However, such an approach emphasizes the mechanical learning of reading skills while sacrificing the critical analysis of the social and political order that generates the need for reading in the first place. Seldom do teachers require students to analyze the social and political structures that inform their realities. Rarely do students read about the racist and discriminatory practices that they face in school and the community at large. The instrumentalist approach has led to the development of "functional literates" groomed primarily to meet the requirements of our contemporary society. The instrumentalist view also champions literacy as a vehicle for economic betterment, access to jobs, and increase in the productivity level. As was clearly stated by UNESCO: "Literacy programs should preferably be linked with economic priorities. [They] must impart not only reading and writing, but also professional and technical knowledge, thereby leading to a fuller participation of adults in economic life."[23]

This notion of literacy has been enthusiastically incorporated as a major goal by the back-to-basics proponents of reading. It has also contributed to the development of neatly packaged reading programs that are presented as the solution to difficulties students experience in reading job application forms, tax forms, advertisement literature, sales catalogs, product labels, and the like. In general, the instrumentalist approach views literacy as meeting the basic reading demand of an industrialized society. As Henry Giroux pointed out:

> Literacy within this perspective is geared to make adults more productive workers and citizens within a given society. In spite of its appeal to economic mobility, functional literacy reduces the concept of literacy and the pedagogy in which it is suited to the pragmatic requirements of capital; consequently, the notions of critical thinking, culture and power disappear under the imperatives of the labor process and the need of capital accumulation.[24]

A society that reduces the priorities of reading to the pragmatic requirements of capital necessarily has to create educational structures that anesthetize students' critical abilities, in order to "domesticate social order for its self-preservation."[25] Accordingly, it must create educational structures that involve "practices by which one strives to domesticate consciousness, transforming it into an empty receptacle. Education in cultural action for domination is reduced to a situation in which the educator as 'the one who knows' transfers existing knowledge to the learner as 'the one who does not know.' "[26]

Paulo Freire's concept of banking refers to this treatment of students as empty vessels to be filled with predetermined bodies of knowledge, which are often disconnected from students' social realities. This type of education for domestication, which borders on stupidification, provides no pedagogical space for critical students like David Spritzler, who question the received knowledge and want to know the reasons behind the facts. His defiance of the rigid bureaucracy, his refusal to surrender his civil rights, is rewarded by a threat of disciplinary action. In other words,

- Do thing for you if liked ! - in Society
- Get along -

APPROPRIATELY CRITICAL

according to Freire, the real rewards go to the "so-called good student who repeats, who renounces critical thinking, who adjusts to models, … [who] should do nothing other than receive contents that are impregnated with the ideological character vital to the interests of the sacred order."[27] A good student is the one who piously recites the fossilized slogans contained in the Pledge of Allegiance. A good student is the one who willfully and unreflectively accepts big lies, as described in Tom Paxton's song:

What did you learn in school today, dear little boy of mine?
What did you learn in school today, dear little boy of mine?
I learned that Washington never told a lie,
I learned that soldiers seldom die,
I learned that everybody's free,
And that's what the teacher said to me.
That's what I learned in school today,
That's what I learned in school.
I learned that policemen are my friends,
I learned that justice never ends,
I learned that murderers die for their crimes
Even if we make a mistake sometimes.
I learned our government must be strong,
It's always right and never wrong
Our leaders are the finest men
And we elect them again and again.
I learned that war is not so bad.
I learned about the great ones we have had.
We've fought in Germany and in France,
And someday I may get my chance.
That's what I learned in school today
That's what I learned in school.[28]

The Barbarism of Specialization, or the Specialization of Barbarism

Long before the explosion of hyperspecialization and the tragedies of the Holocaust and Hiroshima, Spanish philosopher José Ortega y Gasset cautioned us against the demand for specialization so that science could progress. According to Ortega y Gasset, "The specialist 'knows' very well his own tiny corner of the universe; he is radically ignorant of all the rest."[29] I am reminded of a former classmate of mine in linguistics, whom I met while doing research work at MIT. When she learned that I was working with pidgin and creole languages, she curiously asked me, "What's a pidgin language?" At first I thought she was joking, but soon I realized that her question was in fact genuine. Here we had a perfect case of a technician of linguistics doing the highest level theory available in the field without any clue about historical linguistics. It is not difficult to find other examples of such limited specialization because, more and more, specialists dominate institutions of learning and other institutional structures of our society. The social organization of knowledge via rigidly defined disciplinary boundaries further contributes to the formation of the specialist class, that is, engineers, doctors, professors, and so on. This sort of specialist is "only acquainted with one science, and even of that one only knows the small corner in which he is an active investigator. He even proclaims it as a virtue that he takes no cognizance of what lies outside the narrow territory specially cultivated by himself, and gives the name 'dilettantism' to any curiosity for the general scheme of knowledge."[30]

This "dilettantism" is discouraged through the mythical need to discover absolute objective truth. I remember vividly when I gave my linguist friend at MIT articles to read on pidgins and creoles. I later questioned her as to whether she had found the readings interesting and informative. Half apologizing but with a certain pride in her voice, she told me: "If I want to be a great theoretical linguist, I just can't be reading too much outside theoretical linguistics. I can't even keep up with all the reading in syntax alone." Obviously there are exceptions to this attitude, Noam Chomsky, bell hooks, Howard Zinn, Gayatri Spivak, and Henry Giroux being prime examples. However, it is quite frequent in specialization to divorce science from the general culture within which it exists.

Not only does specialization represent a rupture with philosophies of social and cultural relations, but it also hides behind an ideology that creates and sustains false dichotomies rigidly delineated by disciplinary boundaries. This ideology also informs the view that "hard science," "objectivity," and "scientific rigor" must be divorced from the messy data of "soft science" and from the social and political practices that generate these categories in the first place. For example, those linguists and psycholinguists who "believe that what they study has little to do with social values or politics in any sense"[31] fail to realize that their research results are "the product of a particular model of social structures that gear the theoretical concepts to the pragmatics of the society that devised ... the model to begin with."[32] That is, if the results are presented as facts determined by a particular ideological framework, "these facts cannot in themselves get us beyond that framework."[33] Too often, the positivistic overemphasis on "hard science" and "absolute objectivity" has given rise to a form of "scientism" rather than science. By "scientism" I refer to the mechanization of the intellectual work cultivated by specialists, which often leads to the fragmentation of knowledge, as accurately understood by Ortega y Gasset: "A fair amount of things that have to be done in physics or in biology is mechanical work of the mind which can be done by anyone, or almost anyone ... to divide science into small sections, to enclose oneself in one of these, and leave out all consideration of the rest."[34] Specialists of this sort have often contributed to a further fragmentation of knowledge because of their reductionistic view of the act of knowing. They have repeatedly refused to admit to themselves that their very claim of objectivity is, in fact, an ideological act. Objectivity always contains within it a dimension of subjectivity; thus, it is dialectical.

Almost without exception, traditional approaches to literacy do not escape the fragmentation of knowledge and are deeply ingrained in a positivistic method of inquiry. This has resulted, in effect, in an epistemological stance in which scientific rigor and methodological refinement are celebrated, whereas "theory and knowledge are subordinated to the imperatives of efficiency and technical mastery, and history is reduced to a minor footnote in the priorities of 'empirical' scientific inquiry."[35] In general, this approach abstracts methodological issues from their ideological contexts and consequently ignores the interrelationship between the sociopolitical structures of a society and the act of reading and learning. In part, the exclusion of social, cultural, and political dimensions from literacy practices gives rise to an ideology of cultural reproduction that produces semiliterates. My linguist friend at MIT, who reads only the theoretical work in syntax and dismisses relevant literature that links linguistics to the social and historical context, serves as a prime example of the highest level of instrumental literacy. In other words, at the lowest level of instrumental literacy, a semiliterate reads the word but is unable to read the world. At the highest level of instrumental literacy achieved via specialization, the semiliterate is able to read the text of his or her specialization but is ignorant of all other bodies of knowledge that constitute the world of knowledge. This semiliterate specialist was characterized by Ortega y Gasset as a "learned ignoramus." That is to say, "He is not learned, for he is formally ignorant of all that does not enter into his speciality; but neither is he ignorant, because he is a 'scientist' and 'knows' very well his own tiny portion of the universe."[36]

Because the "learned ignoramus" is mainly concerned with his or her tiny portion of the world, disconnected from other bodies of knowledge, he or she is never able to interrelate the flux of information so as to gain a critical reading of the world. A critical reading of the world implies, according to Freire, "a dynamic comprehension between the least coherent sensibility of the world and a more coherent understanding of the world."[37] This means, for example, that medical specialists in the United States, who have contributed to a great technological advancement in medicine, should have the ability to understand and appreciate why over 30 million Americans do not have access to this medical technology and why we still have the highest infant mortality rate of the developed nations. (The United States in 1989 ranked twenty-fourth in child mortality rate as compared to other nations.)[38]

The inability to make linkages between bodies of knowledge and the social and political realities that generate them is predominant even among those who recognize that a coherent comprehension of the world cannot be achieved through fragmentation of knowledge. For example, at a recent professional meeting, a concerned environmental scientist decried the absence of critical perspectives in his field of study. He eloquently called for an interdisciplinary approach to world environmental problems, particularly within the developing countries. His present research is linked with environmental concerns in Mexico. With a certain amount of pride he emphasized that his research breakthrough could be used as a commodity in Mexico, since that country is becoming more and more rigorous with respect to environmental laws. He failed, however, to ask a fundamental question: How can the United States package environmental technology for Mexico while it is establishing factories there that pollute the country because they can operate with less government regulation than at home? This environmentalist was baffled that such a question should even be raised.

Although specialization may lead to a high level of literacy acquisition in a particular subfield of knowledge, it often produces a disarticulation of this same knowledge by dislodging it from a critical and coherent comprehension of the world that informs and sustains it. This disarticulation of knowledge anesthetizes consciousness, without which one can never develop clarity of reality. As suggested by Frei Betto, clarity of reality requires that a person transcend "the perception of life as a pure biological process to arrive at a perception of life as a biographical, and collective process."[39] Betto viewed his concept as "a clothesline of information." In other words, "on the clothesline we may have a flux of information and yet remain unable to link one piece of information with another. A politicized person is one who can sort out the different and often fragmented pieces contained in the flux."[40] The apprehension of clarity of reality requires a high level of political clarity, which can be achieved by sifting through the flux of information and relating each piece to another one so as to gain a global comprehension of the facts and their raison d'être.

We can now see the reasons why David Spritzler's teachers and administrators, who had attained a higher level of literacy through a banking model of transference of knowledge, could not makes connections between the pieces of this knowledge to separate the mythical dimension of the Pledge of Allegiance from factual reality. Part of the reason lies in the fact that the teachers, who, like most specialists, have accepted the dominant ideology, are technicians who, by virtue of the specialized training they receive in an assembly line of ideas and aided by the mystification of this transferred knowledge, seldom reach the critical capacity of analysis to develop a coherent comprehension of the world. In reality, there is little difference between the pedagogy for schoolchildren described in Tom Paxton's song and the prevalent pedagogy in universities as described by Freire:

> Today at the university we learned that objectivity in science requires neutrality on the part of the scientist; we learned today that knowledge is pure, universal, and unconditional and that the university is the site of this knowledge. We learned today, although only tacitly, that the world is divided between those who know and those who don't (that is, those who do manual work) and the university is the home of the former. We learned today that the university is a temple of pure knowledge and that it has to soar above earthly preoccupations, such as mankind's liberation.
>
> We learned today that reality is a given, that it is our scientific impartiality that allows us to describe it somewhat as it is. Since we have described it as it is, we don't have to investigate the principal reasons that would explain it as it is. But if we should try to denounce the real world as it is by proclaiming a new way of living, we learned at the university today that we would no longer be scientists, but ideologues.
>
> We learned today that economic development is a purely technical problem, that the underdeveloped peoples are incapable (sometimes because of their mixed blood, their nature, or climatic reasons).
>
> We were informed that blacks learn less than whites because they are genetically inferior.[41]

In short, this type of educational training makes it possible for us to rally behind our political leaders, who ritualistically call for the protection of human rights all over the world, without our recognizing these same leaders' complicity in the denial of rights of human beings who live under dictatorships that we support either overtly or covertly. The selective selection of our strong support for human rights becomes glaringly clear in the case of Haitians. In fact, the *Boston Globe*, confident of readers' inability to link historical events, published a front-page article on the U.S. Supreme Court decision that allowed the administration to repatriate thousands of Haitian refugees. On page 2 of the same issue, the *Boston Globe* also ran a story about groups organized in Miami to search for and assist Cuban boat people to reach their final destination in Florida.[42]

Although U.S. foreign policy is so glaringly contradictory, most Americans are unable or unwilling to see it. For example, on the one hand, the United States has had a macho-man policy of nonnegotiation with Cuba, Nicaragua under the Sandinistas, and Libya. On the other hand, the United States has engaged in endless negotiations with the Haitian military. According to Derrick Z. Jackson of the *Boston Globe,* the vacillating policy toward Haiti was evident when a U.S. naval vessel carrying military engineers was not able to dock at Port-au-Prince. However, the same naval force was fully equipped and ready to intercept and send back any Haitian refugees it encountered in the open sea. We now have learned from Representative Robert Torricelli, a Democrat from New Jersey who is a member of the House Intelligence and Foreign Affairs Committee, that from the mid 1980s until the overthrow of the democratically elected Jean-Bertrand Aristide, the Central Intelligence Agency made payments to Aristide's top military opponents. Jackson reported that Torricelli defended the payments as if they were scholarships sponsored by the Cub Scouts: "The U.S. government develops relationships with ambitious and bright young men at the beginning of their careers and often follows them through their public service ... [it] should not surprise anyone that these include people in sensitive positions in current situations in Haiti."[43]

"Sensitive positions" in the official discourse is a euphemism for death squads directed by Port-au-Prince Chief of Police Michel François and Raoul Cedras who were responsible for over three thousand deaths during a period of two years since the coup. The callous U.S. insensitivity toward human misery and overlooking of massacres when convenient for its policies led Jackson to conclude that it "should not surprise anyone why the United States developed relationships with ambitious and bright young men whose idea of 'public service' was the overthrow of democracy. The United States was never comfortable with Aristide, Haiti's first democratically elected leader."[44]

Whereas the United States is most comfortable with brutal totalitarian leaders like the Duvaliers and the El Salvador military leaders, who have records of barbarous massacres, it is often very uncomfortable with any democratic movement whose major purpose is the institutionalization of a democratic vision that emphasizes agrarian reform, education, less military spending, and more spending on social programs such as health care and social security. Contrary to the U.S. proselytizing about democracy in the Third World, a closer analysis of its foreign policy reveals a sad truth: the U.S. fatal attraction to undemocratic and cruel military dictatorships.

It is this lack of connectedness that helped Bush to prevail in erasing the public's historical memory file of foreign policy in order to garner support for his fabricated high-tech war in the Gulf. In what follows, I use the Gulf War as an example of how questions of literacy and ideology can be used to separate events from their historical contexts. This fragmentation serves to create a self-serving history that feeds the recontextualization of a distorted and often false reality, leading (sometimes) to a specialization of barbarism ipso facto. In other words, the high-tech management of the Gulf War celebrated technical wizardry while it dehumanized the tens of thousands of people who were victims of specialized technical prowess.

The Illiteracy of Literacy of the Gulf War

It is not a coincidence that during the Gulf War we were saturated with information around the clock in the comfort of our homes, and yet we remained poorly informed. It is also not a coincidence that George Bush categorically and arrogantly stated there would be "no linkage" in any possible diplomatic settlements in the Gulf crisis. Bush's insistence on "no linkage" served to eclipse historicity so as to further add to a total social amnesia. How else could we explain that a highly developed society that prides itself on its freedom of information and high democratic values could ignore the clarity of the obvious? I say the "clarity of the obvious" because it is a well-known fact that the Reagan-Bush decade was characterized by a total disdain for the United Nations. The Reagan-Bush administration stopped paying the U.S. membership contribution to the United Nations and threatened to withdraw from the world body because the rest of the world was not, in their view, subservient enough to U.S. interests. And yet, during the Gulf crisis, the same George Bush found it convenient to hail the United Nations as the theater where "civilized" nations uphold international laws and high principles.

If it had not been for the denial of linkage and the social amnesia, we could have easily referred to Daniel Patrick Moynihan's role as the ambassador to the United Nations. In his memoir, *A Dangerous Place*, Moynihan discussed the invasion of East Timor by Indonesia and shed light on his role as the U.S. ambassador to the United Nations: "The U.S. government wanted the United Nations to be rendered ineffective in any measures that it undertook. I was given this responsibility and I filled it with no inconsiderable success."[45] Moynihan later recounted his success when he stated that "within two months, reports indicated that Indonesia had killed about 60,000 people. That is roughly the proportion of the population that the Nazis had killed in Eastern Europe through World War II."[46] By not linking these historical events, the Bush administration was able to claim the moral high ground in the defense of international laws and the sanctity of national borders during the Gulf crisis.

The U.S. defense of high principles and international laws that led to the Gulf War could only have moral currency if we were to obliterate our memory of recent history. Before proceeding, let me make it clear that Saddam Hussein's invasion of Kuwait was brutal, cruel, and unforgivable. The violation of international laws and borders by other nations, including the United States, is no small matter. According to Noam Chomsky, the irony of the U.S. opposition to such violation and defense of high principles can be seen in reviewing recent U.S. actions:

- The U.S. invasion of Grenada.
- The U.S. invasion of Panama, where the United States installed a puppet regime of its choice with U.S. military advisors running it at every level.
- The U.S. mining of the Nicaraguan harbor. The World Court found the United States guilty, and the U.S. reaction was to arrogantly dismiss the World Court.
- The Turkish invasion and virtual annexation of northern Cyprus that killed several hundred people and drove out thousands more. The United States was in favor of the action.
- The Moroccan invasion of the western Sahara, also supported by the United States.
- The Israeli invasion of Lebanon, where the United States vetoed a whole series of resolutions in the Security Council, which was trying to terminate the aggression. In human terms, at least 20,000 were killed, mostly civilians.
- The Indonesian invasion of East Timor in which 60,000 people were massacred. The Carter administration provided 90 percent of the armaments to the invaders.[47]

Against this landscape of violation of international laws and aggression perpetrated by the United States or by other countries with U.S. support, how can we explain the ease with which Bush convinced a supposedly highly literate and civilized citizenry that Saddam Hussein's invasion of Kuwait was an isolated case of aggression against a weaker nation and had nothing to do with the historical record? The inability to link and treat the "clothesline" of the Gulf War had to do with ideological obstacles that too often obfuscate political clarity. We need to develop a more critical literacy along Freirian lines where, "as knowing subjects (sometimes of existing knowledge, sometimes of objects to be produced), our relation to knowable objects cannot be reduced to the objects themselves. We need to reach a level of comprehension of the complex whole of relations among objects."[48] In his book *The Social Mind*, Jim Gee elegantly demonstrated that "to explicate the 'internal working' of the 'machine,' and not the uses to which the machine is put in the world of value conflicts and political action," is to treat each piece of the "clothesline" separately so as to never allow us to reach a level of comprehension of the complex whole of relations among objects.[49] This functions as a form of illiteracy of literacy, in which we develop a high level of literacy in a given discourse while remaining semiliterate or illiterate in a whole range of other discourses that constitute the ideological world in which we travel as thinking beings.

In an era in which we are more and more controlled by ever-increasing technological wizardry—ephemeral sound bites, metaphorical manipulations of language, and prepackaged ideas void of substance—it becomes that much more urgent to adhere to Gee's proposal that we acquire literacies rather than literacy. Given our tendency as humans to construct "satisfying and often self-deceptive 'stories,' stories that often advantage themselves and their groups," the development of a critical comprehension between the meaning of words and a more coherent understanding of the meaning of the world is a prerequisite to achieving clarity of reality. As Freire suggested, it is only "through political practice [that] the less coherent sensibility of the world begins to be surpassed and more rigorous intellectual pursuits give rise to a more coherent comprehension of the world."[50] Thus, in order to go beyond a mere word-level reading of reality, we must develop a critical comprehension of psychological entities such as "memories, beliefs, values, meanings, and so forth ... which are actually out in the social world of action and interaction."[51] We must first read the world—the cultural, social, and political practices that constitute it—before we can make sense of the word-level description of reality.

The reading of the world must precede the reading of the word. That is to say, to access the true and total meaning of an entity, we must resort to the cultural practices that mediate our access to the world's semantic field and its interaction with the word's semantic features. Since meaning is, at best, very leaky, we have to depend on the cultural models that contain the necessary cultural features responsible for "our stories" and "often self-deceptive stories."[52] Let's look at the Gulf War again to see how the role of cultural practices not only shapes but also determines metaphorical manipulations of language, which are facilitated by the electronically controlled images and messages through "the strategic use of doublespeak to disguise from television viewers the extent of the real terror and carnage of the military campaign against Iraq."[53] According to William Lutz, doublespeak "is a language that avoids or shifts responsibility, language that is at variance with its real or purported meaning. It is a language that conceals or prevents thought; rather than extending thought, doublespeak limits it."[54]

The Gulf War coverage represented the production of doublespeak par excellence. The media's and the government's successful use of euphemisms to misinform and deceive can be seen in the transformation of the horrible carnage of the battlefield into a "theater of operation," where the U.S. citizenry became willfully mesmerized by the near-precision zapping of "smart bombs" during the aseptic "surgical strikes." The "theater of operation" positioned viewers to see "human beings become insentient things while weapons become the living actors of war. 'Smart' weapons that have eyes and computer 'brains' make decisions when and where to drop seven and a half tons of bombs, taking away the moral responsibility of the combatants themselves."[55]

The effective outcome of the doublespeak during the Gulf War not only gave primacy to sophisticated weaponry with its newly acquired human attributes; the doublespeak also functioned as a means to dehumanize human beings by removing them from center stage. The preoccupation of reporters and so-called experts was to point out zealously the "accuracy" of the "smart bombs" while showing over and over again Star Wars–like images of "surgical strikes." What these reporters did not show was that of the roughly 82,000 tons of bombs dropped, 92.6 percent were not "precision guided ordinances." Even the "smart bombs," which made up 7.4 percent of the total that were dropped during the war, had a widely varied reliability rate of between 20 percent and 90 percent.[56] However, it would be considered unpatriotic and un-American to question the Pentagon-controlled deceit of the U.S. public. In fact, after the Gulf War had all but faded in our national consciousness, the Pentagon ordered Theodore Postal, an MIT professor and leading critic of the Patriot missile, "to cease all public discussion of his critique or face disciplinary action."[57] The Pentagon's gag order was summarized by Postal himself: "The Army and Raytheon are now using DIS [Defense Investigation Service] which appears to be more than an unwitting partner to suppress my speech on the subject of Patriot performance in the Gulf."[58] So much for independent thought, critical thinking, and freedom of speech.

What the U.S. citizenry was less concerned with was the terror of war and the horrible carnage caused by the 82,000 tons of "delivered packages" that ended up as de facto carpet bombings. But then, the U.S. television viewers and newspaper readers had already been positioned in a "theater of operation" context as passive observers seduced and fascinated by the wizardry of exciting precision-guided missiles. The "theater ... overfloweth with computer graphics, night-vision lenses, cruise missiles and, best ever, the replay of the impact of laser guided bombs."[59] Missing from the "theater" center stage were the horrified human faces of tens of thousands of Iraqis, including women and children, who were decimated by the unparalleled bombing "sorties." The U.S. public's feelings were steered away from the reality of over 100,000 Iraqi casualties to the degree that the electronic management of the Gulf War vulgarly reduced human suffering and casualties to mere "collateral damage."

In "Media Knowledges, Warrior Citizenry, and the Postmodern Literacies," Peter McLaren and Rhonda Hammer accurately characterized the Gulf War as "a gaudy sideshow of flags, emblems, and military hardware—a counterfeit democracy produced through media knowledge able to effectively harness the affective currency of popular culture such that the average American's investment in being 'American' reached an unparalleled high which has not been approximated since the years surrounding the post World War II McCarthy hearings."[60] This unparalleled patriotism was cemented by the signifier yellow ribbon that functioned effectively to suffocate any truly democratic dialogue. The yellow ribbon ideologically structured the Gulf War debate so as to brook no dissent or dialogue. Criticizing the Bush administration's policies was viewed as not supporting the troops. In fact, the yellow ribbon did more to ideologically cage the American mind than all the speeches given by politicians. One could easily argue that the yellow ribbon patriotically tied American minds by making them sufficiently complacent so that they would comply with the manufacture of consent for a fabricated war.

The complexity of networks of relations in our present telecratic society is making our sensibilities of the world increasingly less coherent—leading to a real crisis of democracy, to the extent that the present "propaganda approach to media coverage suggests a systematic and highly political dichotomization in news coverage based on serviceability to important domestic interests. This should be observable in dichotomized choices of story and in the volume and quality of coverage."[61] This political dichotomization became flagrantly obvious when, on the one hand, George Bush, in the style of John Wayne, rallied "civilized" nations to uphold high moral principles against aggression when Saddam Hussein invaded Kuwait. On the other hand, Bush sheepishly watched and allowed thousands of Kurds, whom he had incited to revolt, to be exterminated by the same forces of aggression. So much for high moral principles. What is at stake here is our ability as democratic citizens and thinking beings to see through the obvious contradictions and discern myth from reality. However, our level of critical consciousness is being rapidly eroded to the degree that "today's cultural and historical events bombard our sensibilities with such exponential speed and frequency, and through a variety of media forms, that our critical comprehension skills have fallen into rapid deterioration."[62]

The deterioration of Americans' critical comprehension of the world became self-evident when they readily rallied behind the "Pentagon's vacuous military briefings, lists of aircraft types, missions, and losses [that became] the sterilized equivalent of body counts recited in Saigon. Far more important elements—human and political—[were] lost."[63] It is indeed a sad statement about the inability of the U.S. citizenry to make the necessary historical linkages so as to develop a rigorous comprehension of the world when, with the exception of a small minority, only Vice President Dan Quayle was able to read the Gulf War correctly by describing it as "a stirring victory for the forces of aggression."[64] President Bush became entrapped in a similar Freudian slip during an interview with Boston's Channel 5 TV news anchor, Natalie Jacobson. Referring to the Gulf War, Bush said, "We did fulfill our aggression," instead of the no doubt intended, "We did fulfill our mission."[65]

The seemingly misspoken words by both Bush and Quayle denude the pedagogy of big lies to the extent that their statements more accurately capture the essence of Ortega y Gasset's proposition that civilization, if "abandoned to its own devices" and put at the mercy of specialists, would bring about the rebirth of primitivism and barbarism.[66] In many instances, the attainment of a high level of technical sophistication has been used in the most barbaric ways, as evidenced in the gassing of the Jews and the bombing of Hiroshima. It is certainly not an enlightened civilization that prides itself in reducing Iraq to a preindustrial age—killing tens of thousands of innocent victims, including women and children, while leaving Saddam Hussein, our chief reason for war, in power and with unreduced capacity to perpetuate genocide against his own people. Ask the Africans who endured the chains of slavery, the Indians who were victims of a quasi-genocide, the Jews who perished in the Holocaust, or the Japanese who experienced firsthand the destructive power of science to measure our so-called advanced Western civilization. If they apply the same rigorous, objective standards of science, intellectual honesty, and academic truth in their inquiry, their response would have to be that Western civilization is unequivocally primitive and barbaric. Ortega y Gasset could not have been more insightful on this issue when he wrote:

> It may be regrettable that human nature tends on occasion to this form of violence, but it is undeniable that it implies the great tribute to reason and justice. For this form of violence is none other than reason exasperated. Force was, in fact, the "ultima ratio." Rather stupidly it has been the custom to take ironically this expression, to methods of reason. Civilization is nothing else than the attempt to reduce force to being the "ultima ratio." We are now beginning to realize this with startling clearness, because "direct action" consists in inventing the order and proclaiming violence as "prima ra-

tio," or strictly as "unica ratio." It is the norm which proposes the annulment of all norms, which suppresses all intermediate process between our purpose and its execution. It is the Magna Carta of barbarism.[67]

Ortega y Gasset's profound thoughts enable us to deconstruct Bush's policy of violence parading under the veil of reason and justice. In fact, Bush successfully made force not only the "ultima ratio" but also the "unica ratio." His total disregard for a multitude of proposals to negotiate a settlement in the Gulf characterized the "norm which proposes the annulment of all norms, which suppresses all intermediate process between our purpose and its execution."[68] Flip-flopping from a defensive stance to the protection of our oil and the invocation of international laws and the sanctity of national borders, Bush simply refused to negotiate. When Saddam Hussein proposed to withdraw from Kuwait with the condition that an international conference be held to discuss the Middle East situation, Bush flatly refused the offer, which, incidentally, was very much in line with the UN General Assembly vote that had called for an international peace conference in the Middle East. It was just such a conference that Bush and his administration aggressively promoted after the execution of the violence and terror that reduced Iraq to a preindustrial age. Had Bush accepted Saddam's condition for an international conference, he would have avoided the carnage that cost over a hundred thousand lives and an ecological disaster of enormous proportions. Bush's insistence on force led his administration to a constant double standard, which the uncritical citizenry, including the media and the intelligentsia, failed to see and question. Bush, although he often referred to the UN resolution of November 29, 1990, which gave "the U.S. a green light to use military means to expel Iraqi troops from Kuwait," totally rejected a "U.N. General Assembly resolution, passed a week later by a vote of 142 to 2, which called for an international peace conference on the Middle East."[69] Bush's convenient selective selection of the United Nations as a forum for international dispute resolution and justice points to a systematic gunboat diplomacy that views force as the "unica ratio" in our foreign policy. We do not have to dig too far in our historical memory files to understand that, over and over again, the United States resorts to force to promote its so-called national interest, which is, more appropriately, the interest of capital and the ruling elite. When we mined the Nicaraguan harbor and supported the Contras as our proxy army and were censored by the World Court, we arrogantly dismissed the much-hailed world body, the theater of justice, and the Mecca of international disputes and settlements. It is this same arrogance of power and force that justified and rationalized Desert Storm. And closer to home, it is this same arrogance of power and force that continues to justify and rationalize our war on drugs.

In order for us to better understand how our rationalization process works to transform force and violence into methods of reason, I will create two hypothetical scenarios. The first finds its parallel in the Gulf War, the second in the war on drugs. To begin the first scenario, let's imagine that the African countries decided to call the UN General Assembly to session to ask for permission to send a defensive armed force led by Ethiopia to the Canadian and Mexican borders with the United States to protect and guarantee the flow of grain in order to prevent the death of the more than 20 million people who die of hunger in Africa every year. These African countries would argue that the United States, being a major producer of food, should stop burning grain and paying farmers not to produce so that prices remain stable and crops be profitable. The Africans would also passionately point out that the burning of grain and the limitation on production constitute a crime against humanity, and that the 20 million Africans who are at risk of dying of hunger should be protected by international laws that view allowing hunger to be a human rights violation. If this hypothetical scenario were to occur in reality and a half-million African troops were dispatched to the U.S. borders with Canada and Mexico, most of us would find the move so ridiculous as to be laughable.

Well, Bush's initial rationale to send troops to Saudi Arabia was to protect the flow of oil that otherwise would disrupt the economies of the developed and industrialized nations. Even though Bush later recanted his earlier position by claiming that the fight was not about oil but about naked aggression, all evidence points to oil as the reason for the Gulf War. If Bush were defending the world order from naked aggression, he would first have to bomb Washington, D.C., since we had recently been engaged in a number of naked aggressions, mainly the invasion of Panama, the war against Nicaragua via a proxy army, the bombing of Libya, the invasion of Grenada—to mention only a few of the most recent violations of the same international laws that Bush so passionately wanted to protect during the Gulf War. In fact, the oil rationale made infinitely more sense, given the architecture of our foreign policy throughout history. The question that we should now ask of ourselves is, Would it be ridiculous for the African nations to send an army to protect the flow of grain that would save the lives of millions of people who may die of hunger, but not ridiculous for the United States to send a half-million troops to the Gulf to protect the flow of oil so industrialized nations would avoid economic chaos?

Let's turn to the second scenario, which finds its parallel rationale in the war on drugs. Let's imagine that the developing countries, composed mainly of Latin American nations but including some African nations as well, were to call for a regional summit where a decision was made to send troops to the United States to put a halt to the steady supply of armaments to support what they have characterized as the death industry in their countries. By "death industry" these nations are referring to the money spent arming their military forces. Many developing countries, because of the never-ending military rule, often supported by the Western powers, spend between 25 and 50 percent of their GNP on armaments. This militarization of their societies is not only destroying their economies but also leading to the killing of great numbers of people every year. Thus these developing countries would send their troops to strategically selected locations in the United States where research and production of destructive armaments are contributing to economic chaos in their own countries and the killing of millions worldwide. Their troops would be trained to bomb and destroy all research laboratories and armament factories—such as Raytheon, General Dynamics, Boeing—in the hope of stopping the flow of arms to their countries. All of this would have international approval, since this measure would be in the national interests of these countries. If this hypothetical scenario were to be enacted, we could readily imagine the panic of all of those highly trained specialists who would be jobless once their factories and research laboratories had been destroyed. We could imagine as well the chaos that would ensue when these same specialists were left without a livelihood and abandoned to luck or perhaps to some form of social welfare. A turn to the latter for support would entail a reliance on a social structure that they no doubt had fought most of their lives to destroy, or at least to curtail to a bare minimum.

I see little difference in what we are doing to fight the drug war. The United States has militarized many Latin American countries, including Colombia, Peru, Bolivia, and Guatemala, to fight and destroy coca fields and drug laboratories, which constitute the only means of economic survival for millions of natives in these countries. By randomly destroying these people's only means of economic support in already-poor countries with feeble economies, we are sentencing these native people to hunger and possibly death. However, we seldom think about the consequences and implications of the arrogance of power in the design of our drug war policy. That is to say, if we switch contexts and focus on our hypothetical scenario, we can clearly see through the infantile dimension and the lack of logic behind the imagined destruction of workplaces devoted to the production of armaments. I am arguing that it is the same infantile, illogical policy that we support when we ratify Bush's war on drugs. The only effective way to fight the war on drugs is to decrease demand. Even law enforcement officials and officials of these Latin countries have admitted that they are losing the drug war. In fact, by focusing only on the destruction of drug production while ignoring the social causes that breed a high demand for drugs, we are contradicting even our principle of capitalism. In other words, the best way to control production is to control demand. If we try to destroy production while leaving demand unchecked, producers will find markets elsewhere—as is the case with drugs produced in Latin America that are reaching markets in Europe and safe ports elsewhere.

These contradictions and instances of the unreason of reason are rarely understood and just as rarely questioned. If, by coincidence, we come to understand the blatant contradictions and question them, the ideological machine will force us immediately into line. That is what happened to a reporter in San Antonio, Texas, who incessantly questioned Bush about the obvious failure of his drug war. He was immediately fired for being insistent and impolite to the president. Here politeness functioned as yet another mechanism to eliminate the possibility of publicizing the truth. Since our society functions more and more on a pedagogy of lies, it depends on ideological institutions, such as schools and the media, to reproduce cultural values that work to distort and falsify realities so as to benefit the interest of the power elite. If schools were really involved in the development of critical thinking to arm students against the orchestrated distortion and falsification of reality, they would have to teach the truth and teach how to question. That includes, obviously, the deconstruction of the Pledge of Allegiance to bare its hypocrisy and the rewriting of history books to keep alive unpleasant memories: Then slavery, the Holocaust, genocide, and Hiroshima could not be repeated under the guise and protection of Western civilization.

I believe that we can now return, with greater understanding, to our original question: Why is it that David Spritzler, a twelve-year-old boy, could readily see through the hypocrisy in the Pledge of Allegiance, while many of his teachers and administrators could not? According to Chomsky, when he was discussing other educational situations, these teachers and administrators, having been indoctrinated by schools, are unable to understand elementary thoughts that any ten-year-old can understand.[70] The indoctrination process imposes a willful blindness to facts and contradictions. However, the more educated and specialized individuals become, the more interest they have vested in the system that provides them with special privileges. For this reason, we often see people whose consciousness has not been totally atrophied, yet they fail to read reality critically and they side with hypocrisy. In most cases, these individuals begin to believe the lies, and in their roles as functionaries of the state, they propagate the lies. That is why, for example, according to Noam Chomsky, the majority of the educated population supported the war in Vietnam while it was being waged, whereas in 1982, according to a Gallup poll, over 70 percent of the general population said that the Vietnam War was "fundamentally wrong and immoral, not a mistake."[71] This is another example that supports the contention that more education does not necessarily entail a greater ability to read reality.

As I have tried to demonstrate, both the competency-based skills-banking approach to literacy and the highest level literacy acquisition via specialization fail to provide readers with the necessary intellectual tools to denude reality that is often veiled through the ideological manipulation of language. It is safe to assume, given the way the educated class more often than not supports "theological truths" (or unquestioned truths), that the less educated one is, in the reproductive dominant model, the greater the chances that one can read the world critically. Chomsky accurately captured this form of illiteracy of literacy when he stated:

> The less educated ... tend to be more sophisticated and perceptive about these matters, the reason being that education is a form of indoctrination and the less educated are less indoctrinated. Furthermore, the educated tend to be privileged and they tend to have a stake in the doctrinal system, so they naturally tend to internalize and believe it. As a result, not uncommonly and not only in the United States, you find a good deal more sophistication among people who learn about the world from their experience rather than those who learn about the world from a doctrinal framework that they are exposed to and that they are expected as part of professional obligation to propagate.[72]

It is indeed ironic that in the United States, a country that prides itself on being the first and most advanced within the so-called First World, over 60 million people are illiterate or functionally illiterate. If Jonathan Kozol was correct, the 60 million illiterates and functional illiterates whom he documents in his book *Illiterate America* do not constitute a minority class of illiterates.[73] To those 60 million we should add the sizable groups who learn how to read but who are, by and large, incapable of developing independent and critical thought. In 1985, the United States was in 49th place among the 128 countries of the United Nations in terms of literacy rate. This ranking applies basically to the reading of the word and not the world. Our ranking, if applied to the reading of the world, would indeed be much lower. Although the literacy statistics given are nine years old, the literacy problem has gotten worse. According to a comprehensive literacy study done by the U.S. government, "an estimated 90 million adults ... cannot write a brief letter explaining an error on a credit card bill, [or] figure out a Saturday departure on a bus schedule."[74]

Against this high illiteracy landscape, we can begin to wonder why a country that considers itself a model of democracy can tolerate an educational system that contributes to such a high level of illiteracy and failure. I am increasingly convinced that the U.S. educational system is not a failure. The failure that it generates represents its ultimate victory to the extent that large groups of people, including the so-called minorities, were never intended to be educated. They were never intended to be part of the dominant political and economic spheres. How else can we explain why we sit idly by and tolerate dropout rates of minorities that exceed 60 percent in many urban cities, with New York City at 70 percent?[75] I believe that, instead of the democratic education we claim to have, we really have in place a sophisticated colonial model of education designed primarily to train state functionaries and commissars while denying access to millions, which further exacerbates the equity gap already victimizing a great number of so-called minority students. Moreover, the education provided to those with class rights and privileges is devoid of the intellectual dimension of teaching, since the major objective of a colonial education is to further de-skill teachers and students so as to reduce them to mere technical agents who are destined to walk unreflectively through a labyrinth of procedures. What we have in the United States is not a system to encourage independent thought and critical thinking. Our colonial literacy model is designed to domesticate in order to enable the "manufacture of consent." The Trilateral Commission members could not have been more accurate when they referred to schools as "institutions responsible for the indoctrination of the young." I see no real difference between the more or less liberal Trilateral Commission position on schooling and Adolf Hitler's fascist call against independent thought and critical thinking. As Hitler noted, "What good fortune for those in power that people do not think."

2 Our Common Culture: A Poisonous Pedagogy

Reporter: Mr. Gandhi, what do you think of modern civilization?
Ghandi: That would be a good idea.

IN CHAPTER 1, I DISCUSSED how institutions, particularly schools, reproduce the dominant ideology through a web of lies that distort and transfigure reality. Central to this cultural reproductive mechanism is the overcelebration of myths that inculcate us with beliefs about the supremacy of Western heritage at the same time as the dominant ideology creates other instruments that degrade and devalue other cultural narratives along the lines of race, ethnicity, language, and gender. That is why it has become necessary to launch a frontal attack on the 1960s experiments in cultural democracy that questioned these myths. Many conservatives viewed the democratic experiments of the 1960s as an "excess of democracy." It is for similar reasons that conservative scholars such as Allan Bloom reacted so aggressively against what they perceived to be "the pernicious influence of German philosophy from Nietzsche to Heidegger as refracted through the mindless relativism of modernizers."[1] Since cultural relativism not only questions the notion of a Western cultural heritage but also provides us with critical tools that reveal that the myth of a Western cultural heritage "has often been employed as a weapon against those who would democratize institutions, who would change relations of power,"[2] the preservation of these myths becomes imperative and requires a subtle and poisonous pedagogy to prevent us from ever knowing the truth.

In the context of the Western cultural heritage, myths constitute a barrier to a true reading of reality. According to John F. Kennedy, "The greatest enemy of the truth is very often not the lie, deliberate, continued and dishonest—but the myth—present, persuasive, and unrealistic."[3] Therefore, the proponents of "our common" Western cultural heritage must fully understand the power of propagation of myths to muffle the manifestation of a truly cultural democracy and maintain the present cultural hegemony. As correctly pointed out by Barbara Flores, myths "are persistent because they often are not questioned; they are persuasive because they offer a simplistic view of a complex reality; and they are unrealistic because they disguise the truth."[4]

As we unpack the ideological content of myths, we begin to understand better why David Spritzler's teacher and principal, who had invested heavily in the dominant doctrinal system, went to great lengths to sacrifice the very principles of the Pledge of Allegiance in order to prevent David Spritzler from "living in truth." Vaclav Havel argued that those individuals who want to "live in truth" represent a real threat to the dominant doctrinal system and must be weeded out or, at the least, neutralized. Thus the Boston school official's imposition of the Pledge of Allegiance in an open "democratic" society such as the United States has the same ideological function as the greengrocer in a closed communist society who displays "among the onions and carrots, the slogan: 'Workers of the world, unite.'"[5] According to Vaclav Havel, the greengrocer puts slogans on the window of his shop "simply because it has been done that way for years, because everyone does it, and because that is the way it has to be. If he were to refuse, there could be trouble."[6] Havel argued that if the greengrocer were forced to display the slogan "'I am afraid and therefore unquestionably obedient,' he would not be nearly as indifferent to its semantics, even though the statement would reflect the truth. The greengrocer would be embarrassed and ashamed to put such an unequivocal statement of his own degradation in the shop window, and quite naturally so, for he is a human being and thus has a sense of his own dignity."[7]

For this reason, the Boston teacher and principal who attempted to expel David Spritzler from school would be ashamed and embarrassed to admit that they acted so because they were afraid and therefore unquestionably obedient. Thus, to overcome this complication, Vaclav Havel pointed out that the greengrocer's "expression of loyalty must take the form of a sign which, at least on its textual surface, indicates a level of disinterested conviction. It must allow the greengrocer to say, 'What's wrong with the workers of the world uniting?'"[8] In the same vein, David Spritzler's teacher and principal must also show an expression of loyalty to the slogan in the Pledge of Allegiance, at least at "a level of disinterested conviction." They must say to themselves, "What is wrong with 'justice and liberty for all?'" Like the greengrocer, David Spritzler's teacher and principal allow signs and slogans to conceal from themselves "the low foundations of [their] obedience, at the same time concealing the low foundations of power. It hides them behind the façade of something high. And that something is ideology."[9]

It is precisely because of ideology that conservative educators such as Diane Ravitch, Arthur Schlesinger Jr., John Silber, and E. D. Hirsch try to keep the political nature of education hidden and outside the public debate. By so doing, on the one hand, they attempt to maintain the pillars of the system of lies, as did the communist leaders that Havel wrote about, on "its unstable foundation,"[10] and on the other hand, they seek to prevent the revealing of reality as it is, for such a revelation would open the possibility of living in truth. Because living in truth represents a fundamental threat to a system of lies, it is not surprising that academic discourse goes to great lengths to develop a discourse based on euphemism. Academic discourse becomes, then, a de facto discourse of not naming the euphemism for what it is. It is for this reason that Allan Bloom and E. D. Hirsch, among others, attack multiculturalism, as it calls into question Western cultural hegemony and the barbarism Western cultures committed against other cultural groups in the name of "civilizing" the "barbaric" other. As I will discuss later in this chapter, it is not a mere coincidence, nor is it an innocent accident of nomenclature, that the destruction of entire villages in Vietnam that resulted in the killing of women, children, and the elderly was called by the United States a "pacification operation." Nor is it a coincidence that the last invasion of Panama was named "Operation Just Cause." The latter was an invasion that killed thousands of innocent victims in order to arrest a head of state—a thug created and supported by the U.S. government as a paid CIA informant who was considered "friendly" until he began to act too independently for our "democratic" taste. The arrest of a head of state through an invasion also violated the same international laws we claimed to protect during the Gulf War.

It is through the manipulation of language that the ideological doctrinal system is able to falsify and distort reality, making it possible for individuals to accommodate to life within a lie. It is for this very reason that Chomsky argued that schools become "institutions for indoctrination, for imposing obedience, for blocking the possibility of independent thought, and [that] they play an institutional role in a system of control and coercion. Real schools ought to provide people with techniques of self-defense, but that would mean teaching the truth about the world and about society, and schools couldn't survive very long if they did that."[11]

Therefore, in order to guarantee their survival, schools must perpetuate the dominant ideology based on a web of lies so as to provide individuals with "the repository of something 'supra-personal' an objective [that] enables people to deceive their conscience and conceal their true position and their inglorious modus vivendi, both from the world and from themselves."[12] By refusing to acknowledge that schools are ideological sites (their refusal is a lie in itself), conservative educators such as E. D. Hirsch, Diane Ravitch, and John Silber attempt to impose a pedagogy that robs students of the necessary critical tools to understand the "veil behind which human beings can hide their own 'fallen existence,' their trivialization, and their adaptation to the status quo."[13]

Once citizens are adapted to the status quo and rewarded by it, it becomes increasingly less difficult for them to live within a lie and ignore the true reality, even when faced with documented historical evidence. Nowhere is this more evident than in a debate between John Silber and Noam Chomsky. When Chomsky proceeded to expose the contradictions and hypocrisy of the U.S. policy in El Salvador, by citing the wholesale slaughter of El Salvadorans by ultra-right-wing death squads supported and trained by the United States, John Silber angrily demonstrated the nonrational nature of his rationality:[14]

CHOMSKY:
If we had the slightest concern with democracy, which we do not, and never have, we would turn to countries where we have influence like El Salvador. Now in El Salvador, they don't call the archbishop bad names: what they do is murder him. They do not censor the press, they wipe the press out. They send the army out to blow out the church radio station. The editor of the independent newspaper was found in a ditch mutilated and cut to pieces with a machete.

SILBER:
Don't … [interrupting Chomsky].

CHOMSKY:
May I continue? I did not interrupt you …

SILBER:
[interrupting Chomsky] Don't you ever want to put a true fact on anything you say? You just simply want to lie systematically on television.

CHOMSKY:
I am talking about 1980 …

SILBER:
[interrupting Chomsky] You are a systematic liar.

CHOMSKY:
Did these things happen?

SILBER:
These things did not happen in the context you suggest at all. You are a phony and it's time people heard you correctly.

CHOMSKY:
It's clear why you want to divert me from the discussion …

SILBER:
[interrupting Chomsky] No, it's not. It's entirely rubbish.

In the above exchange, John Silber was once again the mouthpiece of the system mouthing off the party line. In fact, he conformably and arrogantly could ignore the historical facts since, according to Chomsky, "if you're following the party line you don't have to document anything; you can say anything you feel like. … That's one of the privileges you get for obedience. On the other hand, if you're critical of received opinion, you have to document every phrase."[15] By supporting a party line that is more often than not laced with lies and deceit, John Silber is considered by the media and many educators a great educator and a philosopher even though, to my knowledge, he has never published any substantive work in either field. During his campaign for governor of Massachusetts, he was queried about his scholarship; he stated that his major book manuscript in philosophy was accidentally burned in a house fire. Yet, the system has characterized him as a leader (sometimes a controversial one) and unquestionably portrayed him as a great educator and philosopher without any evidence to support such claims.[16] On the other hand, Noam Chomsky, who was called "arguably the most significant intellectual alive" in the *New York Times*,[17] and has published extensively and exerted considerable influence in various fields, including linguistics, education, philosophy, and psychology, is at the same time marginalized and his political work dismissed because he speaks the truth. Is it not hypocritical that our democratic system has elevated John Silber to the category of educational leader when he publicly stated on national television that universities cannot be run democratically: "The more democratic the university becomes, the lousier it becomes"?[18] Under his leadership, Boston University has not allowed the poststructuralists or deconstructionists to "take over" the English Department. He argued that the university refused to offer dance therapy "because we don't understand the theory of it." Silber also prided himself on the fact that Boston University has resisted revisionist history and the Frankfurt School of Critical Theory in the Philosophy Department. Silber's blatant disregard for academic freedom is best illustrated by his own words:

> We have resisted the official dogmas of radical feminism. We have done the same thing with regard to gay and lesbian liberation, and animal liberation. We have refused to introduce condom machines into University buildings and thereby compete with drugstores. We refuse to believe that students at Boston University need a college education in how to perform the sex act. We believe that students in America who haven't figured that out before they get to college are too dumb to come to college. And we have no wish to share any responsibility whatsoever for what they do with their knowledge. We will not serve as procurers or facilitators of sexual liaisons.
>
> We have resisted the fad of Afro-centrism. We have not fallen into the clutches of the multi-culturists. We recognize that Western culture, so-called, is in fact a universal culture. Western mathematics is the mathematics of the world; Western science is the science of the world; and the Western culture has been philosophically oriented from the start toward finding the truth, and starting to approach it as closely as possible. It was in the Western cultural tradition that people began to develop courses in anthropology, in the history of foreign countries and in comparative religions. Buddhism, for example, was brought into German universities by Kant and by Hegel. This is a part of the very meaning of Western culture and civilization—not to be parochial, but to be universal in one's concern.[19]

I believe that a great deal can be learned from a democratic system that supports lies and suffocates truths. We now have learned from the UN Truth Commission the truth that Chomsky has been trying to tell us all along.[20] We now have documented evidence that Bishop Romero's assassination was ordered by Roberto D'Aubuisson, the man who was given the red carpet treatment in Congress by Jesse Helms and other ideologues who supported, and still support, unimaginable atrocities in Latin America in general and in El Salvador in particular. Yet there is no mechanism to make individuals like John Silber accountable for their intellectual dishonesty and moral irresponsibility. Because there is no accountability requirement if one supports the party line, John Silber could continue not only to lie about the atrocities committed in El Salvador with the support of the United States but also to arrogantly and systematically lie about his personal gains in unethical investments in Seradyn stocks that gave him a profit of $386,700. When Ed Bradley of *60 Minutes* showed Silber a copy of his income tax return (which Silber promised the voters when he ran for governor in 1990 but never made public), Silber replied, "I had forgotten that."[21] Because Silber is part of a system that "is captive to its own lies," he can arrogantly falsify everything and be rewarded and promoted by the system to the status of leader, educator, and philosopher with little, if any, evidence to support such status.

We are now beginning to see that the greater the investment in the dominant doctrinal system, the greater the rewards received and the more dogmatic the defense of the doctrinal system becomes. For example, within the past decade, many books, articles, and media editorials have been published attacking curricular diversity and multiculturalism. However, the debate that has emerged tends to recycle old assumptions and values regarding the meaning and usefulness of cultural literacy. The notion that cultural literacy is a matter of learning the values of our "common" Western cultural heritage still informs the vast majority of schools and universities and manifests its logic in the renewed emphasis on the romanticized "good old days" of our Western heritage.

One old, yet false, assumption is the theory of the melting pot, which contributed to "the creation of a brand-new national identity, carried forward by individuals who, in forsaking old loyalties and joining to make new lives, melted away ethnic differences."[22] This process is succinctly captured in the following description of a performance by elementary school students:

> On the stage was represented an immigrant ship. In front of it was a huge melting pot. Down the gangplank came the members of the class, dressed in their national garb and carrying luggage such as they carried when they landed in this country. Down they poured into the melting pot and disappeared. Then the teachers began to stir the contents of the pot with long ladles. Presently the pot began to boil over and out came the men dressed in their best American clothes and waving American flags.[23]

What is seldom discussed is that the melting pot theory represents a second stage of quasi-genocide designed to enable the dominant cultural group to consolidate its cultural hegemony. As correctly pointed out by Amilcar Cabral, the ideal for a cultural domination can be reduced to the following: The dominant cultural group (1) liquidates practically all the population of the dominated country, thereby eliminating the possibilities for cultural resistance; or (2) succeeds in imposing itself without damage to the culture of the dominated people—that is, harmonizes economic and political domination of these people with their cultural personality.[24]

The first strategy was used to a great extent by European colonizers in their quasi-genocide of Native Americans. The second strategy provides the basis for the melting pot theory, which differs little from "the imperialist colonial domination [that] tried to create theories which, in fact, are only gross formulations of racism, and which, in practice, are translated into a permanent state of siege on the indigenous population."[25] In other words, the melting pot theory, or the "progressive assimilation of the native populations[,] ... turns out to be only a more or less violent attempt to deny the culture of the people in question."[26] It is this racist dimension of the melting pot theory that needs to be fully understood instead of allowing it to obfuscate the binaristic position of Western heritage versus multiculturalism. The issue is not Western heritage versus multiculturalism: The real issue is cultural domination and racism. In fact, it is an oxymoron to speak of American democracy and our "common culture" in view of the quasi-apartheid conditions that have predominated in the United States. It is precisely because of the power inherent in a return to the cultural source that apologists such as Arthur Schlesinger Jr. became concerned that a "cult of ethnicity has arisen both among non-Anglo whites and among nonwhite minorities to denounce the idea of a melting pot, to challenge the concept of 'one people' and to protect, promote, and perpetuate separate ethnic and racial communities."[27] Schlesinger's position not only was dishonest but also served to alarm the public regarding what he referred to as the "multiethnic dogma [that] abandons historic purposes, replacing assimilation by fragmentation, integration by separatism. It belittles Unum, and glorifies Pluribus."[28] A more honest account of history would highlight the fact that African-Americans did not create laws so they could be enslaved; they did not promulgate legislation that made it a crime for them to be educated; nor did they create redlining policies that sentenced them to ghettos and segregated neighborhoods. Unless Arthur Schlesinger Jr. is willing to confront the historical truth, his concern for the disuniting of America is yet another veil to mask White-male-supremacy values that place the discriminatory policies in the United States beyond analysis—thus, beyond scrutiny. What Schlesinger failed to recognize was that there was never a "common culture" in which people of all races and cultures equally participated. The United States was founded on a cultural hegemony that privileged and assigned control to the White patriarchy and relegated other racial, cultural, and gender groups to a culture of silence.

Peter McLaren made this point when he analyzed conservative attacks on multiculturalism from the perspective of what he and others called critical multiculturalism. McLaren wrote:

> Viewed from the perspective of critical multiculturalism, conservative attacks on multiculturalism as separatist and ethnocentric carry with them the erroneous assumption by White Anglo constituencies that North American society fundamentally constitutes social relations of uninterrupted ac-

cord. The liberal view is seen to underscore the idea that North American society is largely a forum of consensus with different minority viewpoints simply accretively added on. We are faced here with the politics of pluralism which largely ignores the workings of power and privilege.[29]

Because subordinate groups, through discriminatory policies, were made invisible and absent from history (i.e., blocked from equal access to education and the economic high echelon), their voices were either muffled or silent. This culture of silence served, by and large, to create the impression of a mythical common culture and to deny the existence of cultural difference. This position is akin to that of the Portuguese dictator Antonio Salazar, who, in attempting to defend his colonist policies in Africa, "affirmed that Africa does not exist."[30]

The present historical context points to a changing world where White patriarchal supremacy, designed to silence and subjugate other cultural and racial groups, is no longer working. At least it is not working as effectively as it did in the past. Hence, we are not presently experiencing the breakdown of our "common culture" or the disuniting of America. What we are in fact experiencing is that submerged cultural voices have emerged to protest loudly against centuries of discriminatory policies that legally kept those voices from being present in history and thus heard. The White supremacy borders that kept ethnic, racial, and cultural groups in reservations (a euphemism for concentration camps), ghettos, and segregated neighborhoods are beginning to collapse. However, this progressive collapse of White supremacy should not constitute a basis for conservatives such as Arthur Schlesinger Jr. to berate the new "cult of ethnicity," the "multiethnic dogma," or the "militants of ethnicity [who] now contend that a main objective of public education should be the protection, strengthening, celebration, and perpetuation of ethnic origins and identities [that breeds] separatism ... nourishes prejudices, magnifies differences and stirs antagonisms."[31]

Even Schlesinger's choice of terminology such as the "cult of ethnicity" or the "multiethnic dogma" points to his own cultural biases. His treatment of these cultural issues would have been more objective if he had also exercised the same word choice in his discussion, for example, of the "White supremacy cult" or the "White racist dogma." If Schlesinger and his conservative cohorts really believed that African-Americans and other racial minorities are separatists, they should look Cornel West straight in the eye and explain to him why, after all of his intellectual accomplishments as a major scholar in the United States, New York City taxi drivers refuse to pick him up as a paying passenger. West painfully recounted the insidious racism that permeates the day-to-day life in the United States: "I waited and waited and waited. After the ninth taxi refused me, my blood began to boil. The tenth taxi refused me and stopped for a kind, well-dressed, smiling female fellow citizen of European descent. As she stepped in the cab, she said, 'This is really ridiculous, is it not?' "[32]

The day-to-day racism in the United States is not limited to the streets of New York but is alive and well in the ivory tower of academia, as noted by Henry Louis Gates Jr., a professor at Harvard University, when discussing his experience at Duke University: "It was the most racist experience I ever had in my professional life. ... No matter what kind of car I drove or house I had, it was assumed it was a gift from the university. It was all a 'where did that nigger get that Cadillac?' kind of thing."[33]

Unfortunately, racism is not limited to Duke University. In her discussion "on being black at Yale," bell hooks argued that the failure of Yale University to "transform ... both in terms of racial makeup of students and faculty ... promotes an atmosphere of demoralization, alienation, and despair among concerned, aware students and faculty, especially black students and faculty."[34]

Arthur Schlesinger Jr. and other conservative scholars who believe in academic honesty and the pursuit of objective truth need to understand that the perceived ethnic and racial separatism is nothing more than a reaction to a de facto White separatism protected historically by laws and other cultural mechanisms designed to "consign certain human beings to the margin of society, if not painful lives and early deaths."[35] What Schlesinger and other conservative scholars have wrongly designated as "separatism" is really an expression of resistance to the extent that asymmetrical cultural differences generate ideologies that produce both discrimination and resistance. However, it is the dominant cultural group that always generates discriminatory practices while the subordinate groups often look inward for cultural seeds that will enable them to offer resistance to cultural dominance. The fact that Cornel West unveiled "ugly racial memories" did not constitute discrimination or any type of separatist behavior. Nor has pointing out that "race matters" and deconstructing racist ideology necessarily made Cornel West, bell hooks, Henry Louis Gates Jr., among others, separatists. Only those who are privileged for being White neglect to understand the violence of being a criminal suspect just because of the color of one's skin. What can the great books of our Western heritage tell Cornel West about being stopped on phony charges because the color of his skin? As West recounted: "Years ago, while driving from New York to teach at Williams College, I was stopped on fake charges of trafficking cocaine. When I told the police officer I was a professor of religion, he replied, 'Yeah, and I'm the Flying Nun. Let's go, nigger!' I was stopped three times in my first ten days in Princeton for driving too slowly on a residential street with a speed limit of twenty-five miles per hour."[36]

Against this landscape of violent racism one can begin to understand that the best solution for preventing the disuniting of America is to eradicate the racist ideology that constitutes the very fabric of our society. The emergence of submerged cultural voices does not "give way to the Tower of Babel" but represents the essence of a truly cultural democracy. Instead of being concerned with the disuniting of America, these conservative scholars should celebrate the present yearning of different cultural groups to democratize our institutions and our society.

A sure prescription for the disuniting of America rests mostly on the reproduction of the White racist ideology, which, sadly, did not end with the integration of schools, buses, and restaurants. In fact, racist outbreaks are becoming commonplace in our increasingly xenophobic society. As recently as April 1, 1993, six African-Americans "among 21 Secret Service agents who went for breakfast at the Denny's in Annapolis, Maryland ... after preparing for President Clinton's visit to the United States Naval Academy" were denied service at the restaurant. This episode led their lawyer, John Relman, to remark that although they were good enough to protect the president, "they were not good enough to get served a plate of eggs at Denny's."[37] If it were not for our historical amnesia, we could easily repeat John Relman's words when describing the African-Americans who sacrificed and risked their own lives in both world wars but were greeted at home with ordinances that relegated them to the back of the bus and kept them from White neighborhoods and schools. These ordinances may no longer be on the books, but the racist essence of our so-called common culture manifests itself in myriad ways, as Boston City Councilman Bruce Bollings personally experienced not too long ago when a White female taxi driver refused to take him to his home in Roxbury. When Bollings refused to leave the taxi, the driver summoned help and a White male driver forcibly dragged him out of the taxi while spouting racist invectives at Bollings. As we weave through the fabric of our "common culture" we can only conclude that no matter who you are and what position you hold in our society, if you are non-White you are often reduced to the status of half-citizen to the degree that you are not allowed to automatically and equally participate civically in all aspects of life. Instead of becoming enslaved by the rhetoric of our "common culture," we should embrace a multicultural curriculum in which we not only develop tolerance but we also learn to respect other cultures so as to be in solidarity with other fellow cultural beings. As Henry Louis Gates Jr. succinctly pointed out, "Beyond the hype and the high-flown rhetoric is a pretty lonely truth: there is no tolerance without respect and no respect without knowledge."[38]

In this chapter I will continue to argue that cultural literacy cannot be viewed as simply the acquisition of Western heritage values aimed at safeguarding our so-called common culture. This view endorses the reproduction of Western cultural hegemony. The notion of a "common" cultural Western heritage sustains an ideology that systematically negates, rather than makes meaningful, the cultural experiences of members of the subordinate cultural groups. For the notion of cultural literacy to become useful, it has to be situated within a theory of cultural production and viewed as an integral part of the way in which people produce, transform, and reproduce meaning. Cultural literacy must be seen as a medium that constitutes and affirms the historical and existential moments of lived experience that produce a subordinate or lived culture. Hence, it is an eminently political phenomenon and must be analyzed within the context of a theory of power relations and an understanding of social and cultural reproduction and production. By "cultural reproduction," I refer to the collective experiences that function in the interest of the dominant groups rather than in the interest of the oppressed groups that are victimized by the policies of the dominant ideology. I use the term "cultural production" to refer to specific groups of people producing, mediating, and confirming the mutual ideological elements that emerge from and reaffirm their daily lived experiences. In this case, such experiences are rooted in the interests of individual and collective self-determination.

This theoretical posture underlies my examination of how our "common culture" policies, carried out in the name of democracy, have in effect constituted a kind of a colonial legacy. These policies operate in a way that threatens to eradicate the cultural expressions of the members of those groups who, by virtue of their race, ethnicity, language, and gender are not treated with the dignity and respect warranted in a true cultural democracy. The colonial model of cultural literacy that is implicit in our "common culture" posture produces an educational system that is "discriminatory, mediocre, and based on verbalism. ... Divorced from the reality of the country, it [is], for this reason, a school system for a minority and thus against the majority."[39]

Peter McLaren, in his criticism of both liberal and conservative positions on diversity, observed:

> Too often liberal and conservative positions on diversity constitute an attempt to view culture as a soothing balm—the aftermath of historical disagreement—some mythical present where the irrationalities of historical conflict have been smoothed out. This is not only a disingenuous view of culture, it is profoundly dishonest. The liberal and conservative positions on culture also assume that justice already exists and needs only to be evenly apportioned. However, both teachers and students need to realize that justice does not already exist simply because laws exist. Justice needs to be continually created, constantly struggled for. The question that I want

to pose to teachers is this: do teachers and cultural workers have access to a language that allows them to sufficiently critique and transform existing social and cultural practices that are defended by liberals and conservatives as democratic?[40]

Nowhere is this colonial legacy more evident than in the arguments about curriculum diversity and multiculturalism that are raging in schools and universities across the United States. What follows is a glimpse into the explosive ideological fervor that informs the current debate over curriculum diversity and multiculturalism.

Western Heritage Versus Multiculturalism

Rare is the university or college that has escaped the debate over multiculturalism and diversity. In some schools, the issue has given rise to extraordinarily volatile and violent contexts where racism, anti-Semitism, antifeminism, and ethnic xenophobia characterize campus life. Student demonstrations such as the one witnessed at Harvard Law School, which led Derrick Bell to take a leave from his professorship until Harvard appointed and gave tenure to more people of color, have become commonplace occurrences on many campuses. Harvard University, as the bastion of Western heritage in the United States, did not allow its Law School faculty to be democratized and forced Bell to either violate his conscience and stop his protest or to forsake his tenured position. Bell chose the latter, thus also electing to live in truth and to protect his dignity as an African-American. Had Bell chosen the former, which required that he invest in the doctrinal system and remain silent, he would have been rewarded with the continuance of his tenured position and perhaps more. Harvard's reward system again became evident when the university invited General Colin Powell to deliver the 1993 commencement address even after General Powell had unabashedly voiced his homophobic attitudes.

The White-male doctrinal reward system effectively worked also when the almost-all-White-male U.S. Senate rallied behind Clarence Thomas, who had been accused of sexual harassment by Anita Hill and who showed questionable intellectual and experiential credentials to serve as a Supreme Court justice. However, intellectual capacity and competence matter little when pitted against the reproduction of an ideology of White-male supremacy. This was clearly understood when the same White-male-dominated Congress (this time including liberal senators) rallied in opposition to President Bill Clinton's nomination of Lani Guinier, a professor at the University of Pennsylvania Law School, to head the Justice Department's Civil Rights Division. When the nomination of Clarence Thomas, who had worked aggressively under Reagan and Bush to weaken and dismantle affirmative action, was challenged, President Bush did not abandon him. In contrast, when the nomination of Lani Guinier, who had successfully defended several affirmative action policies before the conservative Rehnquist Supreme Court, was in trouble, President Clinton backed down and thus denied her the opportunity to challenge before Congress the distortions and the assassination of her character by conservatives who oppose the implementation of civil rights laws. By withdrawing Lani Guinier's nomination, President Clinton prevented her from using the Senate confirmation forum not only as means to challenge the distortions of her writings by conservatives but also as a process to engage the entire nation in a public debate concerning the discriminatory "winner take all" legislative structures that, more often than not, reproduce White-supremacy values that continue to work against the interests of minority groups. The withdrawal of Guinier's nomination to head the Justice Department's Civil Rights Division also pointed to a problem area in our democracy where to dissent is tantamount to committing professional suicide: It is all right to have an opinion as long as that opinion coincides with the dominant ideology. The controversy over Guinier's nomination also demonstrated that for all practical purposes, our democracy is characterized by one dominant ideology that manifests itself in the two-party system. Ideologically speaking, what is the real difference between Democrats and Republicans? How can we honestly speak of democracy when it is almost impossible to have competing ideologies in our political system? Ours is a system that does not tolerate the presence of a truly socialist ideology and, God forbid, a Marxist representation, as is the case in other major industrial, democratic societies.

Lani Guinier's position pointed to the heart of the problem by showing that the working-class poor, African-Americans, and members of other minority cultural groups do not have representation in the present two-party system, where the White-male-dominated, capitalist ideology works aggressively against the interests of these groups. In essence, the present political structure that brooks no debate or dialogue among competing ideologies makes it impossible for the citizenry to understand the fallacy in the equation of capitalism with democracy; the present political structure, with its veiled McCarthyism, prevents any substantive debate on issues of national interest.

Like Lani Guinier, Johnnetta B. Cole, the president of Spelman College, a prestigious college for African-American women, was dropped for consideration as secretary of education, in her case when right-wing ideologues, in a red-baiting exercise, denounced her for her call for a more open-minded policy toward Cuba. The myopic and contradictory policy toward Cuba must remain beyond debate. If such policy contradiction were allowed to be debated, we could easily see the weakness of the U.S. position: We continually violate international laws to undermine Cuba because of its communist regime while we readily go to bed with China, which is far more oppressive than Cuba, as could be seen in the Tiananmen Square mass killings. However, because of our capitalistic interests in China's large market, we can sacrifice our democratic discourse and reward China with Most Favored Nation status in trade. This policy highlights the weak foundation of the equation of capitalism with democracy. We are concerned with democracy as long as it benefits our capitalistic interests. If our capitalistic interests are threatened, we can just as easily sacrifice our democratic values, as was the case in the coup we sponsored to unseat a democratically elected president in Guatemala in 1954. Since then, we have been supporting a series of cruel dictatorships that have no regard for freedom or human rights there, but do guarantee to our corporations easy control of the Guatemalan market. By the same token, if a communist market proves to be profitable, it matters little that this communist regime violates human rights and denies its citizens freedom and liberty, as is the case with China.

Multicultural issues intertwined with racial and gender realities are now dominating campus life across the United States. Hardly a day goes by when one does not read about yet another incident or racial skirmish at some school, college, or university. The following are just a handful of racial incidents on campuses that have captured national attention as outlined by *U.S. News* in an article entitled "Race on Campus."

- At the University of Massachusetts at Amherst [in fall 1992]— scene of some of the worst outbreaks of racial violence on campus in recent years—an African-American residential adviser was beaten up by a white visitor and feces were smeared on the door of his room. Enraged, scores of black students rampaged through a 22-story dormitory. Police had to warn residents not to leave their rooms.
- At the University of North Carolina at Chapel Hill [in April 1993], a group of students, continuing a lengthy campaign, staged a sit-in at the administration building to demand a more central location for a proposed black cultural center.
- At Michigan's Olivet College [in] April [1992], a racial brawl inspired by a white student's allegation of harassment resulted in the hospitalization of two students and the temporary withdrawal of almost all of the school's 60 black students.
- At Georgia State University in Atlanta [in fall 1992], 70 black students staged a sit-in at the office of President Carl V. Patton after unknown students scrawled racially insulting graffiti on a campus

trash can. They successfully demanded the creation of an African-American Studies Department.

➤ At campuses across the nation, the Anti-Defamation League of B'nai B'rith reports, "stridently anti-semitic" speakers like the Rev. Louis Farrakhan and rapper Sister Souljah are increasingly popular with black student groups.[41]

The increasing cultural, ethnic, and racial unrest across universities and college campuses in the United States has reflected our society's intensified xenophobia that culminated with the Los Angeles uprising and racial disturbances that followed the verdict of the first Rodney King trial. On some campuses, the division along race, ethnic, and gender lines is so serious that Christina Hoff-Sommers, a philosophy professor at Clark University, characterized it as "a little like Bosnia out there right now."[42] In response to the racial unrest at the University of North Carolina at Chapel Hill, Associate Chancellor Edith Wiggins, remarked: "It has been brutal. ... There is blood all over this campus."[43] Even on more progressive campuses where curriculum diversity has been more or less embraced, the diversity, in most cases, has given rise to the creation of centers, institutes, and programs that according to Hoff-Sommers, are "now organized into race/class/gender centers where you can nurse and nurture your anger. ... I think you're going to have very active groups, mobs in some cases, outraged and making a variety of demands."[44] Hoff-Sommers's reactionary position against campus diversity fails to recognize a more fundamental question: Why are groups along race, class, and gender lines angry and, in some cases, outraged? Partly, the response would have to point to the elitist Western cultural hegemony that has dominated university life, as well as the White patriarchy that has, in the past, relegated other cultural subjects along the lines of race, ethnicity, class, and gender to the margins of university life and, in some cases, to a culture of silence. Even in cases where centers, institutes, and programs have been created, such as women's studies, these units have remained at the margins of university life, leading to what a colleague and friend, Ramon Flecha, from the University of Barcelona, Spain, has called "diversity for inequality." In other words, instead of making diversity the core of university life, these centers, institutes, and programs are often relegated to the periphery. What conservative educators fail to acknowledge is that the present racial and cultural unrest on campuses is the enactment of history, although manifested in different forms. For instance, what is the underlying difference between the incident where an African-American student at the University of Massachusetts was beaten up by a White visitor and the incident on December 10, 1850, when Harvard students demanded the dismissal of Blacks from the classroom, stating that "the intermixing of white and black races in the lecture rooms ... was distasteful to a large portion of the class, and injurious to the interest of the school"?[45]

Against this landscape of racism and xenophobia on campuses, in particular, and in society, in general, I proposed to participants in the "Future of the University" seminar at a major public university that it would be to the university's benefit to create the structures needed to encourage and support rigorous studies in racial and cultural relations. By promoting racial and cultural relations as an area of rigorous inquiry, the university would not only be better equipped to deal with the racial unrest within its campuses, but it also would have the necessary understanding concerning race and cultural relations to contribute positively to the prevention of racial riots, as witnessed in schools across the United States. The university, through a more thorough understanding of race and cultural issues, could help create conditions so that universities and schools could become learning centers and not war zones, where students would not fear for their safety. During our discussion in our first meeting, I kept raising these issues, and at one point, a senior administrator interjected, "These issues may be true of your campus but here our student population is 94 percent white." I calmly asked him if he had been reading newspapers that had featured for several months the racial unrest at his campus. In fact, in a recent video dealing with racism on university campuses entitled "Racism 101," his institution was prominently featured.

By the end of our first meeting, the cochair of the "Future of the University" seminar asked me if I would agree to put my ideas on paper to be sent to all participants. Almost everyone agreed that my proposal would be the major item on the next meeting's agenda. The other item on the agenda for the next meeting was a colleague's recommendation to make the academic experience for students more friendly. In order to capture the spirit of my modest and mostly practical proposal, I will reproduce it here in toto. The reproduction of this memo also highlights how even a mild request to study race and cultural relations threatens the existing dominant order at universities. I should also mention that not all university leaders are reluctant to deal with issues of racism. For example, Sherry Penney, the chancellor at the University of Massachusetts at Boston, where I work, immediately embraced and supported the ideas contained in my modest proposal below:

To: Participants in the "Future of the University" Seminar
From: Donaldo Macedo

Re: Race Relation and Cultural Issues
Date: March 2, 1993

The idea for a Center for Race Relations and Cultural Studies grew out of an engaging discussion I had some time ago with Henry Giroux concerning the identification of intellectual endeavors that would enable the five campuses to collaborate so as to strengthen the present structural reality created by the merge. In addition to the development of a closer working relationship among the five campuses, the proposed Center for Race Relations and Cultural Studies would not only enhance the public mission of the University, but it would also create a new pedagogical space that could contribute immensely to the present heated debate in cultural studies.

In this proposal, the term cultural studies is used in its broadest sense to include the debate over the canon, multiculturalism, as well as the very faculty culture that may resist the creation of such a center. By studying the faculty culture, the proposed Center could provide new insights into how to best implement the recommendation to make the academic experience at the university more learner friendly. But the question that arises is how can we make the university more learner friendly toward the changing multiracial and multicultural makeup of the University if a significant percentage of the faculty may resist our curriculum diversity and multiculturalism? There are no easy answers to this question and our recent experiences at the university attest to that. Given the complexity of these issues, it behooves the University to create conditions that would enable interested faculty members to rigorously study these complex and important issues along the lines of race, gender, ethnicity, and culture. To do otherwise, is to recoil in an attempt to salvage traditional university structures that may no longer be able to provide the necessary conditions for understanding the ever-changing, multicultural world of the 21st century.

I offer this proposal as food for thought and as one of the many ideas which will be discussed in this important seminar. I am in total agreement with my colleague who eloquently encouraged us to let a hundred flowers bloom. The real challenge for us is to be receptive and open to the multiplicity of ideas that will certainly be generated by the seminar and to create structures that will enable us to find unity through diversity. This unity through diversity will prevent us from taking the position that certain race and cultural issues are not part of the reality of an individual campus. I contend that, if we are to be united as a system with five different campuses, what happens in one campus invariably affects the mission of the University.

The proposed Center for Race Relations and Cultural Studies at the University would function as a think-tank where rigorous research studies would combine a thorough understanding of contemporary race and cultural issues with the possibility of effectively addressing the pressing challenges that characterize the urban landscape. The proposed Center could highlight the importance of studying urban life while at the same time providing a new approach to developing ways of thinking, working and learning about life in urban settings.

The purpose of the Center would be to illuminate the ways in which knowledge, institutional structures, and human agency and culture manifest themselves around a number of problems and concerns regarding urban life.

The proposed Center for Race Relations and Cultural Studies will create the foundations for a community of scholars interested in race relations and cultural studies. Drawing upon faculty from all five campuses of the University, such a Center will promote research that draws upon different theoretical traditions and approaches to studying race relations and cultural conflicts. Such a Center will provide a vehicle for grounding the research and training of professionals as disciplinary and interdisciplinary endeavors. For this reason, the Center for Race Relations and Cultural Studies will be intimately linked with various academic departments such as Sociology, Anthropology, Linguistics, among others. In order for this collaborative academic venture to work, the Center should have a supra-campus structure directly linked to the President's Office.

This structural arrangement would, on the one hand, highlight the importance of the Center's work and, on the other hand, it would avoid the highly entrenched traditions of colleges and departments that often compartmentalize and fragment bodies of knowledge that are critical for a global understanding of the complex issues of race and cultural conflicts. The Center would combine a critical interest in urban issues within an interdisciplinary approach ascribing to the following goals and objectives:

GOAL I

It would argue for ways in which cultural processes can be understood so as to illuminate the goal of developing a new pedagogy that would inform the public about the purpose and meaning of living in a democratic ever-changing multicultural society;

GOAL II

It would analyze theory and practice of defining the ethical and social responsibilities of citizens who are part of a complex web of race, class, ethnic, gender, and cultural texts;

GOAL III

It would highlight cultural processes as forms of textual, social, political and racial analysis;

GOAL IV

It would offer analyses of the ways in which the urban populace constructs meaning out of the richly textured fabric of their diverse histories, languages and communities.

The proposed Center for Race Relations and Cultural Studies would combine historical, political, anthropological, linguistic and cultural analysis as part of its task of extending the meaning of participation in a diverse, democratic multiracial and multicultural urban setting. The Center would also fill an enormous void in the present state of the critical discourse on cultural studies and race relations in urban contexts. It would find a major audience in minority populations, sociologists, anthropologists, public policy makers, educators concerned with urban issues, and among individuals interested in cultural studies and race relations as well as among those interested in ways in which critical theory can be offered as a discourse of cultural change and pedagogical possibility to re-think what it means to educate people capable of a new vision, people who can rewrite the contemporary multiracial and multicultural narrative by developing a public philosophy capable of animating a democratic public culture, one which prepares citizens to enter the ever-changing, multiracial and multicul-tural world of the 21st century.

OBJECTIVES

1. To bring together both national and local scholars to pursue research which links society to wider cultural and racial processes.

2. To collect, document, produce, support and disseminate research in the ar-eas of cultural studies and race relations.

3. To create and enhance on-going discussions among faculty from various disciplines regarding the relationships between various cultural processes and race relations studies.

4. To conduct collaborative research concerning urban policies with various organizations in the state government and other agencies that work directly with a multiracial and multicultural population.

ACTIVITIES

The primary function of the Center will be to promote research in the area of culture and race relations, which builds upon and extends the discourses and methodological approaches that characterize work going on in the wider area of social, racial and cultural theory. To accomplish this goal several activities are envisioned.

1. The creation of regularly scheduled faculty seminars to review the most re-cently published research in cultural studies and to exchange information and criticism regarding our own on-going projects.

2. The creation of a documentation center that would collect and classify works on culture and race relations. The documentation center will become an international research archive on cultural studies and race relations. Moreover, through this documentation center, the program would establish contact with similar centers in Europe, Australia, Canada and South America.

3. The sponsoring of scholars for two and three day visits. The on-going pres-ence of such scholars would provide access to some of the most recent scholar-ship related to various aspects of cultural studies and race relations. Such visit-ing scholars would also provide both faculty and students the possibilities for dialogue and critique.

4. The pursuit of research funding from external funding agencies. Although much funding for research exists at the present time, these grants are difficult to obtain by individual faculty members generally isolated in their respective aca-demic disciplines. The presence of an organized center for research to seek such funds and to assist others in their search for funds should increase the success of attracting the support of external funding agencies.

A high profile Center at the University organized around the study of race and culture could be a first step in seriously addressing the crisis that currently besets the quality of life in our contemporary urban settings. The Center would promote studies which combine theory and practice through reflection and inquiry.

As a first step, this Center will provide a vehicle for the interdisciplinary study of race through the conceptual lens of cultural analyses. Through the study of urban institutions as fundamental cultural sites that both bear the influences of the larger society while simultaneously helping to shape it, we will be able to demonstrate the role that these institutions play in producing various forms of experience around the organization of particular forms of knowledge and social practices that make up everyday life within the cultural context of urban life.

The pay-off to the University would far surpass the small initial investment. One impact of this program would be to place the University near the top of major institutions in the United States for the study of race relations and culture. Furthermore, as students come to realize that the University houses some of the major scholars in race relations and cultural studies on a full-time basis and would also be attracting world-renowned scholars through various visiting scholar programs, there would also be an increase in graduate student enrollment. Moreover, student appeal would be generated through the possibility of being able to share in some of the most important and innovative work being done in race and culture theory and practice. The long-term benefits would accrue when the University-sponsored research and publications, the University-educated graduate students, and the University-influenced visiting scholars would help to establish the University's reputation throughout the nation and the world. Such a network would place the University in a leadership role in defining the direction of race and culture theory and practice in the crucial upcoming decades. In closing, it should be noted that programs of culture and race relations have been highly successful in countries such as England, Sweden, Brazil and Australia. The University needs to take the initiative in order to capitalize on these traditions and to develop them in the United States.

Also worth noting is that the University has an unusual number of faculty that work or are interested in race and cultural studies programs that link culture and race through an interdisciplinary approach. Many of these faculty have national reputations and would contribute to the prestige and importance of the work that would be conducted thorough a race relations and cultural studies program.

Some of the ideas discussed in that proposal also grew out of my long friendship and collaboration with Henry Giroux, whose work has pointed squarely to the need to democratize schooling in the United States. To my surprise, a few days after I sent my proposal on "Race Relations and Cultural Studies" to the participants in the "Future of the University" Seminar, I received a response from the cochair of the seminar that not only saddened me but also made me realize how polarized the question of diversity had become. Again, I will reproduce his memo in its entirety (including his bracketed comments) so as not to compromise its spirit.

---

6 March 1993
To: The Members of the Seminar on the Future of the University
From:
Subject: A Defense of the Tradition

Enclosed you will find a paper drafted by Donaldo for our next meeting, in which he proposes the establishment of a Center for Race Relations and Cultural Studies at the University. Believing, as I do, that old John Stuart Mill was right when he claimed that we must confront the arguments against our positions if we are to keep our ideas alive, I have decided to play Devil's Advocate for a bit. In this memorandum I am going to defend the traditional view of what ought to be taught in our universities. I believe that traditional view has much to recommend it, and that those of us who reject it must confront it head on, and not simply rely on the political climate of the time to excuse us from making an argument against it.

Let me consider, in turn, the major areas of instruction in the university, beginning with the core of Arts and Sciences.

1. The natural sciences are universal, objective, and culture-free, as is evidenced by the speed and ease with which the latest theories and discoveries of physics, chemistry, biology, or mathematics travel from country to country, culture to culture, language to language. When a Chinese physicist, an Indian biochemist, a Nigerian geneticist, a Japanese mathematician does his or her work, there is nothing to indicate the culture from which he or she comes, or the language in which he or she works. The fact that modern science developed in Western Europe and the United States, for the most part, is an irrelevant accident. So multicultural transformations are irrelevant to science. Universities ought simply to teach science, not Western science, Eastern science, Black science, Hispanic science, and so forth. With regard to this major component of the curriculum, the debate over multiculturalism is simply beside the point.

To be sure, one can engage in the practice of identifying the ethnic or racial origins of great scientists, but that has nothing to do with science *per se*. In certain Jewish American circles, it is quite common to hear people mutter, with a little wink or a knowing look, "unsere leute" ["our people"], when some prominent figure is mentioned. But that, surely, is not what the proponents of multiculturalism have in mind!

2. When we turn to the Social and Behavioral Sciences, we find that those disciplines that deal with objective social structures and laws are equally as universal as are the natural sciences and mathematics. That is why modern economic theory, for example, regardless of its origins in Western Europe and the United

States, has been adopted worldwide as the tool for analyzing economic phenomena and developments.

One can, of course, argue that Marx offers us a valid or even superior alternative to standard neo-classical theory [I happen to believe that myself], but Marx is as thoroughly a part of the Western European/American tradition as Keynes, Marshall, or Samuelson. It is worth recalling that Marx was the last of the great classical economists, self-consciously following in the tradition of Adam Smith and David Ricardo. The dispute between Marxian economic theorists and neo-classical economic theorists falls entirely within the one scientific tradition of Western economic theory [using the term "scientific" in its German acceptation—wissenschaftliche—to mean "pertaining to an organized, rational body of knowledge"].

There is no serious Islamic or Chinese or African economic theory worthy of the name. There are great economists from every part of the world, but they all work within the theoretical limits of the one science of economics.

Very much the same is true of Sociology, insofar as it achieves the status of knowledge, and of Anthropology and Psychology as well. Some of what passes for knowledge in these fields is not deserving of the title, of course [though that is always true, in any field of investigation]. But it is simple ignorant prejudice to accuse Max Weber of Western parochialism. No student of society has achieved a greater degree of objectivity, cross-cultural universality, or depth of insight into the causes and principles of social structure. All of the work currently being done by proponents of multiculturalism owes an enormous debt to the groundbreaking investigations of Weber, Durkheim, Mannheim, and the other towering European figures of late nineteenth and early twentieth century social science.

Should we teach their writings to our students, despite the fact that they are all dead white males? Of course we should. To deprive our students of their insights would be criminal—especially since it is their understandings of society that will enable our students to question the received pieties of current public discourse and achieve a genuinely independent, critical perspective on contemporary society. That is what those great thinkers sought to do in their own day, and there is no better way to learn how to do it in our day than to walk for a bit in their footsteps.

3. And so we come to the Humanities, where the call for multiculturalism began, and where it raises the most controversy. (It is no accident that the argument looks strongest precisely in the area where there is least claim to anything resembling knowledge.)

Let us consider, one by one, several of the major fields of study in the Humanities. Consider first History, which many humanists would identify as the core discipline of humanistic learning. History, as we know it, is in fact not very old, though there are major works of historiography, Herodotus, Thucydides, ibn-Khaldun, etc. dating back many centuries. The critical, scholarly, theoretically guided reconstruction of the past has achieved its present level of intellectual power only in the past century and a half, and that achievement has been the work, almost exclusively, of scholars in Western Europe and America. There is no tradition of scientific historiography in Islam, or in China, or in India, or in sub-Saharan Africa, or in Japan. The great historiographical work on those cultures was begun by Western historians, and is carried on now by indigenous scholars, insofar as it is at all, entirely within the methodology and theoretical framework developed in the West. Even the major critiques of established historiography from non-Western societies deploy the critical tools developed within Western culture as their weapons. (Think, for example, of the well-known work of Samir Amin, which would be inconceivable without the precedent of Marx and other Western thinkers.)

The same observations can be made concerning the scholarly and humanistic study of Oriental languages, African languages, Semitic languages, and so forth. Though the subject matter is, in a manner of speaking, "Third World," the techniques, the theories, the very conception of a scientific study of language, is a Western product. There is no indigenous tradition of scholarly study of Arabic in Arabic, or of Chinese in Chinese, or of Xhosa in Xhosa, or of Mayan in Mayan. These are the products of Western academic work, and ought to be taught as such to our students.

What shall we say of philosophy? Well, what we call "Western philosophy" is actually a tradition of thought and argument having its origins in the Eastern Mediterranean and Egypt, and developing, over more than two millennia, in Northern Africa, Southern Europe, Northern Europe, and then in America. It thus includes within itself a very broad spectrum of the speculative and argumentative traditions of a variety of cultures. There is, as it happens, an incredibly rich and ancient tradition of analytic philosophical writing in the languages of the Indian sub-continent, known to a few specialized Western scholars but generally speaking not incorporated into academic philosophy as it should be. But for the rest, what is referred to as "philosophy" in non-Western societies is usually religious writing of one sort or another, and has the failings, as intellectual work, that religious writing always has.

Which brings us, finally, to Literature, where all the fuss started. When one clears away the rubble, turns down the volume, and takes a long, hard look at the great multicultural debate, it turns out to be a neighborhood spat among professors of literature over which novels, plays, and poems to teach to undergraduates. A good deal of the heat [unaccompanied by light] was generated by the irritating claims of those in literary studies who think poetry is the height of human experience, and that fiction is a vulgar pursuit useful only as a middle class entertainment.

But there is a somewhat more magnanimous [i.e., larger-souled] view, frequently identified as the theory of the Great Conversation, that really has much to be said for it. Since my heart at least half belongs to this view, let me sketch it for you at some length.

When I was a boy, I found in my parents' attic, buried under a mound of ancient science textbooks, a slender volume entitle "Heavenly Discourses," by Charles Erskine Scott Wood. This consisted, as the title perhaps suggests, of a series of imaginary conversations in heaven among famous men and women who could not, under normal historical circumstances, have encountered one another here on earth. The book made an enormous impression on me—so much so that my very first college paper, written in the Fall of 1950, was an imaginary heavenly discourse, featuring John Stuart Mill, T. S. Eliot, Zarathustra, and Carl

Sandburg, on the issues posed by Ortega y Gasset's *Revolt of the Masses*. [As you might perhaps guess, Sandburg won.]

The ideal of the Great Conversation is merely an elaborate formalization of Wood's charming conceit [speaking anachronistically, of course, since the idea antedates his book.] Western Civilization is conceived as a perpetual debate about a number of timeless questions, conducted by the great minds of the Judeo-Christian, Greco-Roman tradition, with its medieval Arabic variants, through the medium of a small, but continuously growing, library of great works of philosophy, tragedy, poetry, fiction, history, political theory—and, more recently, sociology, anthropology, economics, and anthropology. [sic] Homer and the nameless authors of the Old Testament, Sophocles and Euripides, Plato and Aristotle, Herodotus, Thucydides, Cicero, Caesar, Paul and the Evangelists, Ovid, Sappho, Philo, Tertullian, Aquinas, Maimonides, Averroës, Avicenna, Erasmus, Luther, Chaucer, Calvin, John of Salisbury, Jean Bodin, Machiavelli, Hobbes, Bacon, Montaigne, Descartes, Spinoza, Shakespeare, Donne, Herbert, Locke, Galileo, Newton, Berkeley, Hume, Leibniz, Kant, Rousseau, Hegel, Fichte, Schelling, Herder, Marx, Smith, Bentham, Mill—on and on they come, quibbling, quarreling, drawing distinctions, splitting hairs, proving the existence of God, refuting the proofs for the existence of God, reading one another, referring to one another—a grand faculty seminar, captured for all time in no more than several hundred immortal books.

A liberal education—so this story has it—is a ticket of admission to the Conversation. At first, one is a mere auditor, much as I was when, as a boy of ten, I sat on the steps of the staircase leading from my parents' living room and listened to my parents, my uncles and aunts, and the neighbors debating politics, literature, and the bureaucratic insanity of the New York School System in which they worked, longing for the day when I too would be permitted to enter the discussion and make my voice heard with the others. Later, after one has read some of the books and deciphered their arguments, one offers one's first, hesitant, no-doubt badly-phrased opinions—"Mightn't it be that we can read Plato's Myth of the Metals ironically, as the pessimism of an idealist who knows too well that the Republic can never be instantiated?"

Eventually, an inspired few will actually enter the Conversation, and make to it contributions that will be taken up into the immortal lists of Great Books. But for the rest of us, it is enough that we have been initiated into its rituals and shibboleths. Throughout our lives, that eternal debate will be the intellectual accompaniment of our quotidian lives. In the evening, after dinner, we can sit quietly before the fire and turn once again the pages of *The Republic*, *The City of God*, *Macbeth*, *The Critique of Pure Reason* [well, perhaps not *The Critique of Pure Reason*], *Northanger Abbey*, *The Red and the Black*, or *Jane Eyre*.

What qualifies these books to be included in the Great Conversation? Unlike the Bible, these books do not come already labeled as divinely inspired and therefore deserving of special attention. Each text earned its way onto the list by its ability to sustain the penetrating examination of powerful minds over many centuries. Why do we include the *Republic* but not the dialogues written by Plato's great pupil, Aristotle? Because the *Republic* is beautifully written, powerfully written, challenging, provocative, persuasive. Because the Allegory of the

Cave and the Myth of Gyges stand up under repeated examination, critique, and reflection. Because ... the give and take between Socrates and Thrasymachus in Book I puts truly powerful arguments in Thrasymachus' mouth, so that the dispute between himself and Socrates becomes a genuine confrontation between two entirely opposed ideals of the good life. No doubt it is irritating to young scholars to find so long a list of great works trotted out before them as the wisdom of their forefathers; it is natural, and entirely healthy, that they should iconoclastically challenge the intellectual merit of those classics. By just such a process of generational challenge have new works of lasting value been identified and add to the canon.

Should we teach our students these great works? Why on earth not? Our students, let's face it, will read, during their undergraduate years, only a fraction of what they need to read, on any theory, to become educated. Since there are more truly great words than they can read in four undergraduate years, why not give them only great works? Why waste our time on works that are less than great? Keep in mind that while, for us, these works may be familiar, and therefore somewhat tiresome, for our students, they retain the power and freshness that earned them their place on the list originally. The first time you read the *Republic* or *Don Quixote* or *Hamlet* or *Bleak House*, it is like the first time you hear the B Minor Mass! With any luck, the heavens will open and you will, for a moment, know what it is to have a life of the mind.

4. What has already been said for the natural and social sciences holds true, *a fortiori*, for Engineering, Nursing, Food and Natural Resources, Management, Education, and the other professional schools and faculties. While the application of their knowledge is worldwide, the knowledge itself has its origin in Western practices and principles.

Thus, the call for multiculturalism is without rational foundation, and ought therefore to be rejected. Modern scientific knowledge is the product of an intellectual development in Western Europe and the United States some four centuries old. It is the product of early modern and Enlightenment Western thought, and is understood as such around the world. We owe it to our students to give them the best that has been thought and learned, and that is exactly what we are already doing in our faculties, departments, and courses. Change the racial and ethnic composition of the student body and faculty, by all means, but leave the substance of education alone! It is fine just as it is.

O.K. folks. There it is—the best case I can make for the traditional view. Let's have a substantive debate!

———

The spirit of this defense of Western tradition captures, par excellence, the essence of Allan Bloom's book *The Closing of the American Mind*, for "there can be no doubt that the reception which Bloom's book has enjoyed signifies that he has tapped the elitists' collective nerve."[46] The defense of the Western tradition in this memo also shows that "intellectuals are uneasy about their role as teachers because their own experiences, interests, and values seem profoundly at odds with the several generations they have taught since the 1960's."[47] Like Allan Bloom, my colleague's dismissal of multiculturalism as nothing "resembling knowledge" follows "the belief, common among natural scientists, that their disciplines yield the only 'real' knowledge."[48]

Conservative educators who provide a celebratory defense of a Western cultural heritage fail to acknowledge their roles as revisionist historians who present history "as if all members of history had a common interest which historians serve to the best of their ability."[49] According to Howard Zinn, "This is not intentional deception; the historian has been trained in a society in which education and knowledge are put forward as technical problems of excellence and not as tools for contending social classes, races, nations."[50] It is this overemphasis on technicism dislodged from the ideology that generates and shapes it that is now threatened by a new class of intellectuals who view education and knowledge "as tools for contending social classes, races, nations." Proponents of multiculturalism and curriculum diversity not only are engaged in the democratization of universities and societal structures but have also refused to "join in a classical evocation of a mythically integrated civilization that becomes the vantage point from which to utilize the current situation."[51]

The defense of the tradition espoused by Allan Bloom, who was no doubt influenced by purist philosophers like Ortega y Gasset, follows a rationale that "derives from the classical definitions of the well-educated man—thoroughly grounded in the classics, articulate in spoken and written expression, actively engaged in intellectual pursuit."[52] What Bloom and other conservative educators have failed to acknowledge is how the traditional approach to education has primarily served the interests of the elite classes, mostly White males. If they were to acknowledge the elitist, antidemocratic, and discriminatory nature of traditional approaches to learning, they would understand the perceived anger and demands from the members of those groups who have been denied access to the bastions of knowledge and power. In Bloom's view, education is the acquisition of predefined forms of knowledge that are organized around the study of Latin and Greek and the mastery of the great classical works. This traditional elitist approach to education is inherently alienating in nature. On the one hand, it ignores the life experience, history, culture, and language practices of students. On the other, it overemphasizes the mastery and understanding of classical literature and the use of great books as the only vehicle that enables one to search for the "Good and True."

The failure of the Western cultural heritage defenders to recognize that subordinate groups do not have the same cultural capital as those of members of the dominant groups guarantees the continuation of present-day asymmetrical power relations. This failure to address questions of cultural capital or various structural inequalities means that the traditional approach to education based solely on Western cultural values will invariably reproduce the cultural capital of the dominant class, to which traditional education is intimately tied. Tell the children of East St. Louis who are confronted with a cruel poverty and victimized by myriad oppressive conditions, as described by Jonathan Kozol in his book *Savage Inequalities,* that their human misery will immediately change upon reading Plato's *Republic.* Try to tell the residents of East St. Louis that "the first time you read the *Republic* or *Don Quixote* or *Hamlet* or *Bleak House,* it is like the first time you hear the B Minor Mass! With any luck, the heavens will open and you will, for a moment, know what it is to have a life of the mind." Try to tell the children of East St. Louis to ignore the hunger and malnutrition imposed by an average daily expenditure of $2.40 for each child. Try to tell them that what is important is not the quality of the physical life but the "life of the mind." Tell the children of East St. Louis who live in dilapidated and roach- and rat-infested houses that "throughout [their] lives, that eternal debate will be the intellectual accompaniment of [their] quotidian lives. In the evening, after dinner, [they] can sit quietly before the fire and turn once again the pages of *The Republic, The City of God, Macbeth, The Critique of Pure Reason, Northanger Abbey, The Red and the Black,* or *Jane Eyre.*"[53]

For that matter, ask the millions of homeless people in the United States to "sit quietly before the fire and turn once again the pages" of the Great Books and make believe they are comfortable in the warmth of their living rooms. Let's ask the defenders of the Western cultural heritage who pretend to "live in truth" to show the residents of East St. Louis how, by reading the Great Books, they can change their oppressive conditions, which Kozol described as follows:

> East St. Louis ... has some of the sickest children in America. Of 66 cities in Illinois, East St. Louis ranks first in fetal death, first in premature birth, and third in infant death. Among negative factors listed by the city's health directory are the sewage running in the streets, air that has been fouled by the local plants, the high lead levels noted in the soil, poverty, lack of education, crime, dilapidated housing, insufficient health care, unemployment.[54]

Without minimizing the importance and value of the Great Books, one can, however, say with near-certainty that the education one receives from studying them endorses the dominant values and meanings that are mostly responsible for the cruel and stark poverty and human misery that cities like East St. Louis exemplify. It is this type of cultural reproduction that underlies the blind reverence to Western cultural heritage; it willfully ignores the fact that "every achievement of civilization—the pyramids, great works of Greek philosophy and science, the wonderful representations of the human body and the soul that emerged during the Renaissance—has been built on the backs of slaves, on a faraway peasantry; in short, on a material foundation that undermines the notion of an uncomplicated marriage between high culture and humanism."[55]

One could easily argue, as Walter Benjamin reminded us, that "ignoring these facts ... helps to sustain the culture and civilization in general,"[56] even if it is on the backs of the present worldwide human exploitation, on the mass killings of elderly, women, and children by our Western-developed smart bombs, the mass rape and killing of women in Vietnam by our Western-educated GIs, the mass killing and mass rape of women, including children as young as five years old in Bosnia, as Western civilization watches from the sidelines. The selective selection of historical facts, with the omission of the memories of holocausts, past and present, the near-genocide of the Indians at the hands of Western civilizers, among other vicious atrocities, constitutes the foundation for the vast majority of educational programs that manifest their logic in an emphasis on the romanticized "good old days" of our Western heritage. It is thus not a coincidence that cultural legionnaires such as E. D. Hirsch have supported the notion that cultural literacy is a matter of acquiring the values of our "common culture." Thus springs his urgency in prescribing what all Americans need to know.

What All Americans Need to Know

In his celebrated book *Cultural Literacy: What Every American Needs to Know*, E. D. Hirsch provided a pointed attack on U.S. education, which he claimed had reduced learning to skills acquisition devoid of cultural content. As an alternative, Hirsch argued that schools should de-emphasize "process" and reemphasize "content," which is, according to Hirsch, rooted in our "common cultural" background knowledge. What Hirsch failed to recognize was that his treatment of "culture" was "descriptive rather than anthropological and political. ... Its meaning is fixed in the past, and its essence is that it provides the public with a common referent for communication and exchange."[57]

However, Hirsch's common cultural shared information is nothing less and nothing more than a veiled cultural information–banking model based on a "selective selection" of Western cultural features, a model that "dismisses the notion that culture has any determinate relation to the practices of power and politics or is largely defined as a part of an ongoing struggle to move history, experience, knowledge, and the meaning of everyday life in one's own terms."[58]

What is more pernicious than Hirsch's fossilized encyclopedia of "our common culture" background knowledge, is his selective omission of cultural facts that all Americans also need to know but are prevented from knowing. This is part of the ongoing "poisonous pedagogy" designed "to impart ... from the beginning false information and beliefs that have been passed on from generation to generation and dutifully accepted by the young even though they are not only unproved but are demonstrably false."[59] According to Alice Miller, to ensure that the received belief and value system is continually reproduced, the recipients "shall never be aware for their own good" of the mechanisms inherent in "poisonous pedagogy," which involve "laying traps, lying, duplicity, subterfuge, manipulation, 'scare' tactics, withdrawal of love, isolation, distrust, humiliation and disgracing [the recipient], scorn, ridicule, and coercion even to the point of torture."[60]

Although Alice Miller's work focused mostly on child-rearing practices, the mechanisms of "poisonous pedagogy" also inform our education and even our government. We do not have to look further than our newspaper headlines to identify explicit mechanisms of poisonous pedagogy in the behavior of our politicians. For instance, in a 1993 "Spotlight" investigation of corrupt politicians in the Massachusetts legislature, the *Boston Globe* concluded that "the Beacon Hill system often seems designed to obfuscate the truth, hinder public scrutiny and conceal the identity of special interests and their agents."[61] The prevalent behavior of lying and concealment of truths is part of our political culture and is best measured by the public's resignation to such lies. In Chapter 1, I discussed the inner workings of the pedagogy of big lies employed by our education system and our government. Anyone who followed the Iran-Contra investigation can affirm that both Presidents Reagan and Bush were less than truthful to the public and they were no more truthful about our complicity in concealing the truth about the carnage and crimes against humanity committed by the El Salvadoran army in the massacre of El Mozote in 1981, the vicious murders of the six Jesuit priests, and the rape and murder of the four American churchwomen. Yet the public resignation about such lies is so complete that there was little uproar when the *Boston Globe* headlined its report "The Truth Comes on a Dirty US War."[62] The same public resignation about lies and deceit by our public officials was evident when President Bush pardoned Caspar Weinberger, who was accused of lying to Congress in the Iran-Contra affair. It was the same public resignation that allowed the former secretary of state, Alexander M. Haig Jr., to be not accountable for his irresponsible assertion that the four churchwomen raped and murdered by the El Salvadoran army in 1980 might have been killed as they tried to run a roadblock.

The mechanisms of poisonous pedagogy are a part of our educational system that is designed to instill obedience so as to require students to "(1) willingly do as they are told, (2) willingly refrain from doing what is forbidden, and (3) accept the rules for their sake."[63] Thus, obedience becomes a pivotal tool for the reproduction of the dominant culture to the extent that independent thoughts and actions are regulated by the system and/or repressed by the individual who has submitted his or her will to the entrapment of poisonous pedagogy. The rule of obedience in eradicating critical thought and independent action was well understood throughout history:

> Obedience is so important that all education is actually nothing other than learning how to obey. It is a generally recognized principle that persons of high estate who are destined to rule whole nations must learn the art of governance by way of first learning obedience. *Qui nescit obedire, nescit imperare:* the reason for this is that obedience teaches a person to be zealous in observing the law, which is the first quality of a ruler. Thus, after one has driven out willfulness as a result of one's first labors with children, the chief goal of one's further labors must be obedience.[64]

Obedience, however is not easily instilled in individuals. It requires a sophisticated use of ingredients of poisonous pedagogy, including "scare" tactics, lies, manipulation, and other means designed to get individuals to submit to the rule of law and to accept what has been presented as sacred. All this must take place in a carefully crafted manner so that the individual won't notice and will therefore not be able to expose the lies. Hitler was fully aware of this fact when he stated: "It also gives us a very special, secret pleasure to see how unaware the people around us are of what is really happening to them."[65] I would argue that many of our own educators and politicians enjoy a "very special secret pleasure" in viewing how anesthetized we have become and how unaware we are of what is really happening to us.

Obedience is imposed not only through received false cultural information but also through the omission of cultural facts, such as the horrendous crimes that have been committed against humanity in the name of the Western heritage, in order to prevent the possibility of keeping dangerous memories alive. It is, then, not accidental that Hirsch's "shopping mall"[66] cultural literacy gives rise to a type of education based on the accumulation of selected cultural facts that are disconnected from the sociocultural world that generated these "facts" in the first place. Educators who adhere to Hirsch's perspective often contribute to the fragmentation of knowledge because of their reductionistic view of the act of knowing. The acquisition of what all Americans need to know in a fossilized encyclopedic manner prevents the learner from interrelating the flux of information so as to gain a critical reading of the world. The latter implies, obviously, the ability of learners to understand that Hirsch's view of "widely accepted cultural values" often equates Western culture with civilization, while leaving unproblematic Western culture's role in "civilizing" the "primitive" Others. In order to execute its civilizing tasks, those steeped in Western culture resorted to the most primitive barbarism so as to save the "Other" cultural subjects from their primitive selves. Ironically, Hirsch neglected to include in *Cultural Literacy: What Every American Needs to Know* information that would show how those steeped in Western culture, in the name of civilization and religion, subjugated, enslaved, and plundered Africa, Asia, and the Americas. If Hirsch's perspective on cultural literacy allowed readers to become critical so that they could apply the same "rigorous" standards of science, intellectual honesty, and academic truth in their inquiry that academics claim to employ, the readers would arrive at a much more complex response than is anticipated in the prevailing version of our "common cultural" literacy.

Critical readers would also question why Hirsch's *Dictionary of Cultural Literacy: What Every American Needs to Know* fails to inform American readers that "Indian towns and villages were attacked and burned, their inhabitants murdered or sold into foreign slavery."[67] These often-omitted historical facts were described by William Bradford, the governor of Plymouth Colony: "It was a fearful sight to see [the Indians] thus frying in the fire and the streams of blood quenching the same, and horrible was the stink and scent thereof; but the victory seemed a sweet sacrifice, and [the settlers] gave the praise thereof to God, who had wrought so wonderfully for them."[68]

Critical readers would also question why Hirsch's cultural literacy conveniently failed to discuss how history shows us convincingly and factually that the United States systematically violated the Pledge of Allegiance through the legalization of slavery, the denial of women's rights, the near genocide of Indians, to the contemporary discriminatory practices against those people who by virtue of their race, ethnicity, class, or gender are not treated with the dignity and respect called for in the pledge. If Hirsch, Arthur Schlesinger Jr., and others did not suffer from historical amnesia, they would have included in "our common cultural" literacy the following observation:

> If you were a colonist, you knew that your technology was superior to the Indians'. You knew that you were civilized, and they were savages. ... But your superior technology proved insufficient to extract anything. The Indi-

ans, keeping to themselves, laughed at your superior methods and lived from the land more abundantly and with less labor than you did. ... And when your own people started deserting in order to live with them, it was too much. ... So you killed the Indians, tortured them, burned their villages, burned their corn fields. It proved your superiority, in spite of your failures. And you gave similar treatment to any of your own people who succumbed to their savage ways of life. But you still did not grow much corn.[69]

One can now begin to see why Hirsch's information-banking model of cultural literacy is based on a selective form of history. His serious omission of important historical facts in his common cultural list that "every American needs to know" points to the ideological nature of his pedagogy and constitutes the foundation for what I have been calling the pedagogy of big lies. If we compare and juxtapose Hirsch's texts with the historical information he has left out of his cultural inventory list, we would begin to understand the importance of keeping readers from knowing the truth for their own good. The column on the left in the list that follows is taken from E. D. Hirsch's *Dictionary of Cultural Literacy: What Every American Needs to Know*.[70] The column on the right, "What every American needs to know but is prevented from knowing," represents an elaboration of historical facts that fills the gap between what should have been said but was conveniently omitted from Hirsch's dictionary. The right-hand column provides readers with another reference point, enabling them to link the bodies of information and to have a clearer and more critical reading of the facts and their raison d'être.

What every American needs to know

Government of the people, by the people, and for the people: Words from the Gettysburg Address of Abraham Lincoln, often quoted as a definition of democracy.

Indentured servant: A person under contract to work for another person for a definite period of time, usually without pay but in exchange for free passage to a new country. During the seventeenth century most of the white laborers in Maryland and Virginia came from England as indentured servants.

What Americans are not allowed to know

These words were not meant for African-Americans, since Abraham Lincoln also declared: "I will say, then, that I am not, nor ever have been in favor of bringing about in any way the social and political equality of white and black races. ... I as much as any other man am in favor of having the superior position assigned to the white race."[71]

Slavery: Although omitted from Hirsch's cultural list, slavery involved the kidnapping of Africans, breaking up their families and shipping them to the Americas to be sold to white masters to perform forced labor under duress and inhumane conditions often involving undignified and denigrating jobs. Slavery was legal and protected by U.S. laws until the Emancipation Proclamation, which freed slaves in the Confederacy, even though slavery continued unabated long after the Emancipation Proclamation.

Give me liberty or give me death: Words from a speech by Patrick Henry urging the American colonies to revolt against England. Henry spoke only a few weeks before the Revolutionary War began:

"Gentlemen may cry peace, peace, but there is no peace. The war is actually begun. The next gale that sweeps from the north will ring to our ears the clash of resounding arms. Our brethren are already in the field. ... Is life so dear, or peace so sweet, as to be purchased at the price of chains and slavery? Forbid it, Almighty God! I know not what course others may take, but for me, give me liberty or give me death!"

Navahos: A tribe of Native Americans, the most numerous in the United States. The Navahos have reservations in the Southwest.

The Navahos were forced to move by United States troops under Kit Carson in 1864. They call the march, on which many died, the Long Walk.

Today, they are known for their houses, called hogans, made of logs and earth; for their work as ranchers and shepherds; and for their skill in producing blankets and turquoise and silver jewelry.

Patrick Henry's words were never meant for African slaves or American Indians. African-Americans and American Indians continued throughout the history of the United States to experience subjugation, leading Malcolm X to pronounce in 1964 the following:

"No, I'm not an American. I'm one of the 22 million black people who are the victims of Americanism. ... One of the ... victims of democracy, nothing but disguised hypocrisy. So, I'm not standing here speaking to you as an American, or a patriot, or a flag-saluter, or a flag-waver—no, not I! I'm speaking as a victim of this American system. And I see America through the eyes of the victim. I don't see any American dream; I see an American nightmare!"[72]

As Noam Chomsky correctly stated: "The United States is founded on the destruction of the native population. Before Columbus the population north of the Rio Grande was maybe 12–15 million. At the turn of the century it was 200,000. The whole history of the conquest of the continent from the time that the saintly Pilgrims landed is the destruction of the native population by various means, sometimes just plain mass slaughter, like the Pequot Massacre by the Puritans or George Washington's destruction of the Iroquois civilization right in the middle of the War of Independence, and many later events running through the conquest of the national territory. Sometimes it was criminal expulsion like Jackson's expulsion of the Cherokees, really hard-line things. Anyway, that's the history."[73]

The landing at Plymouth rock seen through the eyes of American Indians represents the beginning of a quasi-genocide legalized by the Massachusetts legislature, which promulgated a law that provided monetary re-wards for dead Indians.

Big Stick Diplomacy characterizes U.S foreign policy, particularly in Latin America. Recent examples of such diplomacy are

- The U.S. invasion of Grenada under Ronald Reagan.
- The U.S. bombing of Libya under Ronald Reagan.
- The U.S. invasion of Nicaragua via a proxy, the Contras, under Ronald Reagan.
- The U.S. invasion of Panama under George Bush.

Plymouth Rock: The rock, in what is now Plymouth, Massachusetts, near which the Mayflower, carrying the Pilgrims, landed in 1620.

Big Stick Diplomacy: International negotiations backed by the threat of force. The phrase comes from a proverb quoted by Theodore Roosevelt, who said that the United States should "speak softly and carry a big stick."

Japanese-Americans, internment of: An action taken by the federal government in 1942, after the air force of Japan bombed Pearl Harbor and brought the United States into World War II. Government officials feared that Americans of Japanese descent living on the west coast might cooperate in an invasion of the United States by Japan. Accordingly, over 100,000 of these residents were sent into relocation camps inland, many losing their homes and jobs in the process. About two-thirds of those moved were U.S. citizens (see NISEI).

Many Japanese-Americans, including an entire army battalion, distinguished themselves in combat in World War II.

To "the Japanese who lived on the West Coast of the United States, it quickly became clear that the war against Hitler was not accompanied by a spirit of racial equality." One congressman said, "I am for catching every Japanese in America, Alaska, and Hawaii now and putting them in concentration camps. … Damn them! Let's get rid of them now!" Roosevelt, persuaded by racists in the military that the Japanese on the West Coast constituted a threat to the security of the country, signed executive Order 9066 in February 1942. This empowered the army, without warrants or indictments or hearings, to arrest every Japanese-American on the West Coast—11,000 men, women, and children—to take them from their homes, to transport them to camps far in the interior, and to keep them there under prison conditions. … Data uncovered in the 1980s by legal historian Peter Irons showed that the army falsified material in its brief to the Supreme Court. … The American press often helped to feed racism. According to *Time* magazine, "The ordinary unreasoning Jap is ignorant. Perhaps he is human. Nothing indicates it."

Ota was born in the United States. He remembered what happened in the war: "On the evening of December 7, 1941, my father was at a wedding. He was dressed in a tuxedo. When the reception was over, the FBI agents were waiting. They rounded up at least a dozen wedding guests and took 'em to county jail.

"For a few days we didn't know what happened. We

heard nothing. When we found out, my mother, my sister went to jail. ... When my father walked through the door my mother was so humiliated. ... She cried. He was in prisoner's clothing, with a denim jacket and a number on the back. The shame and humiliation just broke her down. ... Right after that day she got very ill and contracted tuberculosis. She had to be sent to a sanitarium. ... She was there till she died.

"My father was transferred to Missoula, Montana. We got letters from him—censored, of course. ... It was just my sister and myself. I was fifteen, she was twelve. School in camp was a joke. ... *One of our basic subjects was American history. They talked all the time.*"[4]

What is important to note is that the United States, in its history of expansionism and conquest, had instigated a war with Mexico so as to later claim half of Mexico's land.

Malcolm X explained the trap of racism as follows:
"There are traps that he creates. If you speak in an angry way about what has happened to our people and what is happening to our people, what does he call it? Emotionalism. Pick up on that. Here the man has got a rope around his neck and because he screams, you know, the cracker that's putting the rope around his neck accuses him of being emotional. You're supposed to have the

Remember the Alamo: A battle cry in the Texans' struggle for independence from Mexico, later used by Americans in the Mexican wars. It recalled the desperate fight of the Texan defenders of the Alamo, a besieged fort, where they died to the last man.

Malcolm X: A political leader of the twentieth century. Malcolm X, a prominent Black Muslim who explained the group's viewpoint in *The Autobiography of Malcolm X*, was assassinated in 1965.

rope around your neck and holler politely, you know. You're supposed to watch your diction, not shout and make other people——this is how you're supposed to holler. You're supposed to be respectable and responsible when you holler against what they are doing to you."[75]

Parks, Rosa: A Black seamstress from Montgomery, Alabama, who, in 1955, refused to give up her seat to a white person, as she was legally required to do. Her mistreatment after refusing to give up her seat led to a boycott of the Montgomery buses by supporters of equal rights for black people. This incident was the first major confrontation in the Civil Rights Movement.

Rosa Parks was not just mistreated. She was arrested and placed in jail. According to her: "Well, in the first place, I had been working all day on the job. I was quite tired after spending a full day working. I handled and worked on clothing that white people wear. That didn't come in my mind but this is what I wanted to know: when and how would one even determine our rights as human beings? ... It just happened that the driver made a demand and I just didn't feel like obeying his demand. He called a policeman and I was arrested and placed in jail."

Manhattan Project: The code name for the effort to develop atomic bombs for the United States during World War II. The first controlled nuclear reaction took place in Chicago in 1942, and by 1945, bombs had been manufactured that used this chain reaction to produce greater explosive force. The project was carried out in enormous secrecy. After a test explosion in July 1945, the United States dropped atomic bombs on the Japanese cities of Hiroshima and Nagasaki.

Although the American intelligence had broken the Japanese code indicating the Japanese readiness to surrender, that did not prevent President Harry Truman from going ahead and, perhaps unnecessarily, bombing two highly populated Japanese cities: "The world will note that the first atomic bomb was dropped on Hiroshima, a military base. That was because we wished in this first attack to avoid, insofar as possible, the killing of civilians."[76]

"It was a preposterous statement. Those 100,000 killed in Hiroshima were almost all civilians. The U.S. Strategic Bombing Survey said in its official report: 'Hiroshima and Nagasaki were chosen as targets because of their concentration of activities and population.'

"The dropping of the second bomb on Nagasaki seems to have been scheduled in advance, and no one has ever been able to explain why it was dropped. Was it because this was a plutonium bomb whereas the Hiroshima bomb was a uranium bomb? Were the dead and irradiated of Nagasaki victims of a scientific experiment?"[77]

"The need to 'stop communism' was used to justify the invasion of Vietnam and to carry on there a full-scale war in which over a million people died. It was used to justify the bombing of peasant villages, the chemical poisoning of crops, the 'search and destroy missions,' the laying waste of an entire country. GI Charles Hutto,

Vietnam War: A war in Southeast Asia, in which the United States fought in the 1960s and 1970s. The war was waged from 1954 to 1975 between communist North Vietnam and noncommunist South Vietnam, two parts of what was once the French colony of Indochina. Vietnamese communists attempted to take over the South, both

who participated in the massacre of Vietnamese peasants at My Lai, told army investigators: 'I remember the unit's combat assault on My Lai. The night before the mission we had a briefing by Captain Medina. He said everything in the village was communist. So we shot men, women, and children.' "78

President John F. Kennedy, who considered Vietnam "an important piece of real estate," committed "U.S. planes and U.S. pilots to undertake direct participation, not just control, in the bombing and defoliation operations in South Vietnam directed against the rural population, which was the large majority, about 80% of the population. …"

Adlai Stevenson, our UN ambassador at the time, referred to an 'internal aggression,' namely the aggression of the Vietnamese, and particularly the Vietnamese peasants, against the United States in South Vietnam. A society that can use phrases such as 'internal aggression' and can perceive the bombing of peasant villages as a defense of either us or our clients, that society has gone a long way towards a kind of operative totalitarianism."79

A large black marble memorial contains the names of over 50,000 Americans who perished in the Vietnam War.

by invasion from the North and by guerrilla warfare conducted within the South by Viet Cong. Presidents Dwight D. Eisenhower and John F. Kennedy sent increasing numbers of American military advisors to South Vietnam in the late 1950s and early 1960s. Kennedy's successor, President Lyndon Johnson, increased American military support greatly, until half a million United States soldiers were in Vietnam.

American goals in Vietnam proved difficult to achieve, and the communists' Tet Offensive was a severe setback. Report of atrocities committed by both sides in the war disturbed many Americans (see MY LAI MASSACRE). Eventually, President Richard Nixon decreased American troop strength, and sent his secretary of state, Henry Kissinger, to negotiate a cease-fire with North Vietnam. American troops were withdrawn in 1973, and South Vietnam was completely taken over by communist forces in 1975.

The involvement of the United States in the war was extremely controversial. Some supported it wholeheartedly; others opposed it in mass demonstrations and by refusing to serve in the American armed forces (see DRAFT). Still others seemed to rely on the government to decide the best course of action (see SILENT MAJORITY). A large memorial (see VIETNAM MEMORIAL) bearing the names of all members of the United States armed services who died in the Vietnam War is in Washington, D.C.

Banana republics: A term describing any of several small nations in Latin America that have economies based on a few agricultural crops.

The term "banana republic" is often used in a disparaging sense; it suggests an unstable government.

As a term, "banana republic" also refers to the puppet governments installed by the CIA to protect U.S. interests while the vast majority of the population live in dire poverty. The U.S. often installs and supports dictatorships, giving rise to political instability and periodic civil wars. What follows is a partial list of U.S. invasions of these so-called banana republics to protect the interests of U.S. companies:

- "1854: Nicaragua—invasion to avenge an insult to the American minister to Nicaragua.

- 1855: Uruguay—U.S. and European naval forces landed to protect American interests during an attempted revolution in Montevideo.

- 1954: Guatemala—a legally elected government was overthrown by invasion forces of mercenaries trained by the CIA. The government that the U.S. overthrew was the most democratic Guatemala had ever had. … What was most unsettling to American business interests was that Arbenz [the deposed president] had expropriated 234,000 acres of land owned by United Fruit, offering compensation that United Fruit called 'unacceptable.'"80

Colonialism: The control of one nation by transplanted people of another nation—often a geographically distant nation that has a different culture and dominant racial or ethnic group (see ETHNICITY).

A classic example of colonialism is the control of India by Britain from the eighteenth century to 1947. Control that is economic and cultural, rather than political, is often called Neocolonialism.

Although the United States fought for its independence against Britain, it ended up resuming the colonial role in the world by seizing control of Cuba and Puerto Rico in 1898: It established control of Canal Zone in Panama in 1903 as well as Hawaii. It also fought a war in order to subjugate the Philippines.

The United States functions as a de facto neocolonialist power because of economic and cultural control of Puerto Rico and many Latin American nations.

The United States almost always sided with the colonizers in Africa when African countries began their independence wars.

Disenfranchisement: Removal of the franchise, or right to vote.

Term often used to refer to the oppressed "minority" groups in the United States. The dominant group in the United States prefers the term "disenfranchised groups" over "oppressed groups." In the case of "disenfranchised," one can never identify the subject of the verb, whereas "oppressed" readily acknowledges an "oppressor."

Oligarchy: A system of government in which power is held by a small group.

A classic example of oligarchy is El Salvador, supported by the United States in a civil war that has cost the country 70,000 lives. The United States has spent billions of dollars maintaining a de facto oligarchy in El Salvador while ignoring outrageous human rights violations by the ultra-right and military death squads that were responsible for thousands of killings, including the massacre of six Jesuit priests.

Refugees: People who flee a nation, often to escape punishment for their political affiliations or for political dissent.

The United States adopts a double standard toward refugees. It welcomed anti-Sandinista refugees while deporting El Salvadorans who tried to escape political persecution. It welcomes Cuban refugees while it deports Haitian boat people.

Third World: The nonaligned nations—which are often developing nations—of Africa, Asia, and Latin America. They are in a "third" group of nations since they are allied with neither the United States nor the Soviet Union.

Third World also refers to underdeveloped nations. The term is misleading to the extent that we have Third World contexts in First World nations, such as ghettos, and First World realities in Third World countries.

World Court: A division of the United Nations that settles legal disputes submitted to it by member nations. The International Court of Justice, also called the World Court, meets in The Hague, Netherlands.

Although the World Court mediates legal disputes among nations, it has no power of enforcement, or execution. A classic example of its lack of execution power involves the mining of the Nicaraguan harbor by the United States. The World Court ruled in favor of Nicaragua but the United States arrogantly dismissed the ruling.

Class: A group of people sharing the same social, economic, or occupational status. The term class usually implies a social and economic hierarchy, in which those of higher class standing have greater status, privilege, prestige, and authority. Western societies have traditionally been divided into class: the upper class or leisure class, the middle class (bourgeoisie), and the lower or working class. For Marxists, the significant classes are the bourgeoisie and the Center proletariat.

The ruling elite, aided by the intelligentsia, has gone to great lengths to create mechanisms that perpetuate the myth that the United States is a classless society. That is why George Bush, during the 1988 presidential campaign, berated his Democratic opponent by saying: "I am not going to let that liberal Governor divide this nation. ... I think that's for European democracies or something else. It isn't for the United States of America. We're not going to be divided by class. ... We are the land of big dreams, of big opportunities, of fair play, and this attempt to divide America by class is going to fail because the American people realize that we are a very special country, for anybody given the opportunity can make it and fulfill the American dream."[81]

It was the same George Bush who fought hard for a capital gains tax cut for the rich while threatening to veto a tax cut for the middle class and put into place severe cuts designed to dismantle social services, including education, for the poor. It was the same George Bush who used the benefit of the capital gains tax to buy his Maine $2 million estate, arguing that his purchase "put money in the pockets of real estate agents and contractors," thus creating jobs.

George Bush would be hard put to convince residents of East L.A., Harlem, and East St. Louis that the purchase of his $2 million estate through tax cuts for the rich has made their poverty-class conditions any better. In fact, George Bush, while discouraging class struggle debate, was a principal actor in the creation of the biggest gulf between the upper class and the lower class. According to the U.S. Census Bureau statistics, as analyzed by the Center on Budget and Policy Priorities, "In 1988, the richest fifth of American families received 44 percent of the nation's total family income. That's the highest percentage ever recorded for that segment of the population. On the other hand, the poorest fifth received only 4.6 percent. That's the lowest since 1954. Second poorest fifth and the middle fifth each received the lowest ever recorded share of the nation's income." The Center on Budget and Policy Priorities stated that "while the average income for the bottom 20 percent of households fell in the 1980s, income for the top 1 percent, after taxes, rose 122 percent, from $203,000 to $451,000. The average salary of a person worth over $1 million rose from $515,499 to $770,587. The average wage of a person who earns under $20,000 rose a mere $123, from $8,528 to $8,651."

In the face of glaring evidence of class stratification, politicians and educators in the United States continue to promote the myth that the United States is a classless society. However, it would be hard to convince students in East St. Louis Senior High School that they enjoy class equity in this great land of ours: "East St. Louis Senior High School 'was awash in sewage for the second time this year. The school had to be shut because of fumes and backed-up toilets. Sewage flowed into the basement, through the floor, then up into the kitchen and the students' bathrooms. The backup, we read, 'occurred in the food preparation areas.'"[82]

The Declaration of Independence was not meant for the slaves that Thomas Jefferson owned. This is why Frederick Douglass, a well-known abolitionist not included in Hirsch's cultural list, gave the following speech on the Fourth of July, 1852:

"Fellow Citizens. Pardon me, and allow me to ask, why am I called upon to speak here today? What have I or those I represent to do with your national independence? Are the great principles of political freedom and material justice, embodied in that Declaration of Independence, extended to us? And am I, therefore, called

Declaration of Independence: The fundamental document establishing the United States as a nation, adopted on July 4, 1776. The declaration was ordered and approved by the Continental Congress, and written largely by Thomas Jefferson. It declared the Thirteen Colonies represented in the Continental Congress independent from Great Britain, offered reasons for separation, and laid out the principles for which the Revolutionary War was fought. The signers included John Adams, Benjamin Franklin, John Hancock, and Jefferson. The declaration begins (capitalization and punctuation are modernized):

"When, in the course of human events, it becomes necessary for one people to dissolve the political bands which have connected them with another, and to assume, among the powers of the earth, the separate and equal station to which the laws of nature and of nature's God entitle them, a decent respect for the opinions of mankind requires that they should declare the causes which impel them to the separation.

"We hold these truths to be self-evident: that all men are created equal; that they are endowed by their creator with certain unalienable rights; that among these are life, liberty, and the pursuit of happiness; that, to secure these rights, governments are instituted among men, deriving their powers from the consent of the governed; that whenever any form of government becomes destructive of these ends, it is the right of the people to alter or to abolish it, and to institute one government, laying its foundations on such principles, and analyzing its powers in such forms as to them shall seem most likely to effect their safety and happiness."

The day of the adoption of the Declaration of Independence is now commemorated as the Fourth of July, or Independence Day.

upon to bring our humble offering to the national altar, and to confess the benefits, and to express devout gratitude for the blessings resulting from your independence to us?

"What to the American slave is your Fourth of July? I answer, a day that reveals to him more than all other days of the year, the gross injustice and cruelty to which he is the constant victim. To him your celebration is a sham; your boasted liberty an unholy license; your national greatness, swelling vanity; your sounds of rejoicing are empty and heartless; your denunciation of tyrants, brass-fronted impotence; your shouts of liberty and equality, hollow mockery; your prayers and hymns, your sermons and thanks-givings, with all your religious parade and solemnity, are to him more bombast, fraud, deception, impiety, and hypocrisy—with a thin veil to cover up which would disgrace a nation of savages. There is no nation of the earth guilty of practices more shocking and bloody than are the people of these United States at this very hour.

"Go where you may, search where you will, roam through all the monarchies and despotisms of the Old World, travel through South America, search out every abuse and when you have found the last, lay your facts by the side of the everyday practices of this nation, and you will say with me that, for revolting barbarity and shameless hypocrisy, America reigns without a rival."[83]

The juxtaposition of the texts above reveals a pedagogy that enables readers to interlink the flux of information in order to gain a more critical reading of reality. Instead of just domestically consuming Hirsch's cultural list as facts, readers can rely on other points of reference so that they can be free to think more critically and recognize the falsehoods embedded in the various pedagogies created by the dominant class. By and large, dominant education utilizes poisonous pedagogical mechanisms to undermine independent thought, a prerequisite for the "manufacture of consent." It is only through a pedagogy that manufactures consent that a society tolerates gross distortion of realities and the rewriting of history as exemplified in an extract from *The History of the United States*, by Robert J. Field, used as a social sciences text in some of Boston's public schools:

> Vietnam is a small country near China. It is thousands of miles from the United States. Vietnam is on the other "side" of the world. But, in the 1960's, it hurt our country badly. ... The Vietnamese people fought for their freedom. Communists took advantage of the fight. Communists wanted to make Vietnam a communist country. The people of Vietnam just wanted freedom. ... The North Vietnam army fought a secret war. They hid and ambushed the Americans. Women and children helped fight against the Americans. ... Thousands of American soldiers died in Vietnam. Many Americans were against the war.[84]

What the above text clearly demonstrates is how history is distorted not only by the presentation of false historical information but also by the omission of other important historical facts that serve as a counterpoint of reference. For example, in the rewriting of the Vietnam War, Robert J. Field failed to account for the over 1 million Vietnamese who died in the war, not to mention the systematic killing of the elderly, women, and children, as evidenced in the My Lai massacre. Similar massacres were routine, as recalled by Sergeant James Daley: "'When you come into an enemy village,' we were told [by training instructors in the United States], 'you come in opening fire. You kill everything that's living—women, children, and animals.'"[85]

Sergeant James Daley's account proves that the My Lai massacre was not an isolated incident. In fact, Shad Meshad, a psychologist who served in Vietnam, described what he had heard from soldiers: "They'd been on sweeps of villages, with orders to leaving nothing living, not even chickens and [water] buffaloes. Well, what the fuck did that mean, following orders like that? Wasn't it Lieutenant Calley who created the stir in the first place? They were doing a Calley every day."[86]

The barbarism of our Western heritage civilization training proved to be lethal for the Vietnamese. Jeffrey Whitmore, a Marine, described another slaughter graphically:

> I just happened to be standing alongside the officer when the radioman said, "Look, Sir, we got children rounded up. What do you want us to do with them?" The guy says, "Goddamn it Marine, you know what to do with them: kill the bastards. If you ain't got the goddamn balls to kill them, Marine, I'll come down and kill the mother-fuckers myself." The Marine said, "Yes, Sir" and hung up the phone. About two or three minutes later I heard babies crying. I heard children crying their fucking lungs out.[87]

Although the vicious acts of violence perpetuated against innocent Vietnamese women and children by our GIs are well known and documented facts, one never reads history books in school that expose students to our crimes against humanity. Thus, it is not surprising that the cultural legionnaires such as E. D. Hirsch choose to selectively monumentalize certain aspects of our Western heritage while neglecting to report on heinous crimes that Western civilization has committed throughout its history. A more honest account of our Western cultural heritage would not only monumentalize the great deeds in museums and great books but would also look at Western civilization through a magnifying mirror so we could begin to see the grotesque and barbaric images of the Western cultural heritage. In other words, historical truth and academic and intellectual honesty would demand that for each Museum of Fine Arts we build in a given city, we should also build a museum of slavery with graphic accounts of the dehumanization of African-Americans, when entire families were split and sold on the block to the highest bidder and where pictures of lynching would remind us of our racist fabric. For each museum of science built in a given city, we should also build a museum of the quasi-genocide of American Indians, their enslavement, and the raping and expropriation of their land. Although we built a Holocaust Museum in Washington, D.C., fifty years after the Nazis' horrendous crimes against Jews, we should also build a Vietnam Museum along with the Vietnam Memorial, where graphic accounts of rape and killing of Vietnamese women by Western heritage–trained GIs would be described:

> The girls were unconscious at that point [after repeated rapes]. When they finished raping them, three of the GI's took hand flares and shoved them in the girls' vaginas. ... No one to hold them down any longer. The girls were bleeding from their mouths, noses, faces, and vaginas. Then they struck the exterior portion of the flares and they exploded inside the girls. Their stomach started bloating up and then they exploded. The stomachs exploded and their intestines were just hanging out of their bodies.[88]

Jou pt for ve?p

Although I had read a great deal about American GIs' atrocities in Vietnam, I felt revolted when reading the above quote and I immediately called a friend of mine who served in Vietnam to certify if, in fact, these crimes against humanity occurred. My friend Herman Garcia, who is now a professor at the University of New Mexico at Las Cruces, wrote an account of his experience in Vietnam in response:

> The war in Vietnam would be better characterized as "An Account of the Millions of Isolated Incidents of American-Committed Atrocities of the War." As a Chicano and a member of an oppressed cultural and linguistic-minority group in the United States, I had no political or ideological knowledge of my role in the war at the age of 19, although I intuitively knew something felt wrong. I just never had a language for expressing the feelings and intuitions I carried.
>
> One of the most vivid and horrendous accounts that I have had to live with all these years was the day a soldier in my infantry unit target practiced on a live man in an open field. We had just swept through a couple of villages in the Province of Tay Ninh, not too far from a field fire base from where we patrolled daily. The young soldier aimed his M-79 grenade launcher at the older man in the open field and fired it, hitting him on the forehead and blowing his skull off. There was a brief applause and then a couple of the soldiers walked over to get a close glimpse of the victim. As I recall the atrocious incident, I can still hear the noise the explosion made upon impact. My own dehumanized condition at the time allowed me to witness cold-blooded murder. There was no evidence to suggest the man in the field was part of any particular group considered enemy.
>
> Other violations consisted of raping women of all ages. This was a most common activity among American GIs and was not openly condoned but practiced almost daily. There seemed to be no rhyme or reason for the behaviors, it was simply a part of our own war-psychotic virus that we, as young soldiers, had been trained and brain-washed to respond in that manner. Our ability to read the world had been constructed through the rigorous training process in basic and advanced military training. It wasn't until years later that I and thousands of others like myself, began to understand the effects of the human and ecological devastation U.S. military intervention in Vietnam had caused. After I arrived home, I spent many months in therapy trying to get myself together, and finally, did but it was painful and a real inner struggle. I will always have to live and struggle with the experiences I went through in Vietnam. As we know, many Vietnam veterans did not survive civilian life and ended up taking their own lives.[89]

The Vietnam Museum would also reenact the mass killings of children in the so-called pacification operations and put human faces on disfigured children who are still suffering the aftermath of our spraying of the defoliant Agent Orange on Vietnam. It is not only Saddam Hussein who should be put on trial before an international tribunal for his use of chemicals against the Kurds. Agent Orange and napalm did no less harm to the people of Vietnam, and their use constitutes no less a crime, as graphically captured by a former soldier: "They'd be out on a mission and call in strikes. Napalm would be sprayed and the people would be burning. Sometimes they'd put them out of their misery. The guys who did that are still coming into Vet centers with it 12 years later."[90]

The presence of Slavery, Holocaust, Vietnam, and American Indian Genocide Museums alongside our Metropolitan Museums, Museums of Fine Arts, and Science Museums would create a pedagogical space that not only would keep dangerous historical memories alive but would also provide a pedagogical structure that would enable us to juxtapose historical events in order to provide a cultural collage that would force us to look at Western cultural heritage. The juxtaposition of historical events would enable us not only to develop a more critical understanding of the often mystified received historical facts but also to deconstruct these facts in order to understand the reasons behind them.

The presence of these museums of crimes against humanity also would "remind us that when we embrace the Other, we not only meet ourselves, we embrace the marginal images that the modern world, optimistic and progressive as it has been, has shunned and has paid a price for forgetting."[91]

These museums of crimes against humanity would prevent perhaps the modern world from shunning the carnage and mass rape of women, including children as young as five years of age in Bosnia. These museums could also serve as a mirror to alert us that in our social construction of the Other so as to demonize and dehumanize the Other, we also become dehumanized ourselves, as a Vietnam veteran succinctly pointed out: "When we came back after the mine sweep he [an old Vietnamese man about 80 years old] was outside his hootch. And all his relatives and friends were sitting around and crying and shit. And we laughed. And human beings don't do things like that. But we stayed there and we fucking laughed until he died. So it turns you into some sort of fucking animal."[92]

The presence of these museums of crimes against humanity, like Goya's "black paintings,"[93] would serve as a constant reminder that we should always be vigilant in order to avoid complacency and the social construction of not seeing. Perhaps, Arthur Schlesinger Jr. and E. D. Hirsch, among other Western cultural legionnaires, could learn an important lesson from Carlos Fuentes's insightful comments. If the Western cultural legionnaires honestly reflect on Fuentes's insights, they will come to the realization that the real issue is not Western culture versus multiculturalism. The fundamental issue is the recognition of humanity in us and in Others:

The art of Spain and Spanish America is a constant reminder of the cruelty that we can exercise on our fellow human beings. But like all tragic art, it asks us first to take a hard look at the consequences of our actions, and to respect the passage of time so that we can transform our experience into knowledge. Acting on knowledge, we can have hope that this time we shall prevail.

We will be able to embrace the Other, enlarging our human possibility. People and their cultures perish in isolation, but they are born or reborn in contact with other men and women, with men and women of another culture, another creed, another race. If we do not recognize our humanity in others, we shall not recognize it in ourselves.[94]

Our Uncommon Culture: The Politics of Race, Class, Gender, and Language

Our Judeo-Christian values are going to be preserved, and our
Western heritage is going to be handed down to future generations,
not dumped into some landfill called multiculturalism.

—Patrick Buchanan

DURING THE DECADE OF THE 1980s we witnessed a most reactionary political revolution in the United States, one that promised to take us back to the romanticized "good old days." This reactionary movement found its spokesman in Ronald Reagan, who preached family values while dismantling the social safety nets that could, more or less, play a role in supporting these very family values. Reagan exhorted a back-to-basics morality while his own cabinet was riddled with scandals that forced many of its members to resign. He championed an ethics of hard work and honesty only to give us what was characterized as the "decade of greed" and the "me first generation." We also witnessed wide-ranging scandals on Wall Street, the S&L debacle, and the Iran-Contra affair. On national television, Reagan, with much fanfare, excoriated a welfare mother for cheating, as proof of social-program abuse, but he remained silent about the fraud rampant within the military-industrial complex, as shown in the Pentagon's paying $700 for a toilet seat or $350 for a screwdriver. It is the same silence that surrounded the welfare for the rich in the S&L scandal, which will cost taxpayers over $250 billion. Although Charles Keating has been sentenced to ten years in jail and fined $250,000, the vast majority of the culprits in this enormous and costly scandal, including President Bush's son Neal, are shrouded in a culture of silence, leaving taxpayers once again holding the bag. The Reagan and Bush cultural legionnaires, like Patrick Buchanan, vociferously attack the "welfare state" for the poor for creating a "social catastrophe" and blame "Great Society programs not only for financial losses but also for drops in high school test scores, drug problems and 'a generation of children and youth with no fathers, no faith and no dreams other than the lure of the streets.'"[1] Patrick Buchanan and his friends remain ominously silent about the de facto social welfare for the rich, which, by and large, remains invisible and beyond public debate. For instance, according to the *Boston Globe*, the "Pentagon had a documented secret plan to fix McDonnell Douglas Corp.'s severe financial problems late in 1990, according to a confidential audit by the Department of Defense's inspector general. ... McDonnell Douglas received two questionable payments in late 1990, one for $148 million and another for $72 million."[2]

Compare the $220 million in social welfare spent to bail out McDonnell Douglas with the cuts proposed by Reagan to save less than $4 million: "The Reagan Administration's budget includes welfare cuts for pregnant women and those who get aid under the program for the aged, the blind and the disabled, government officials said today. ... The change could save $1.5 million to $3.5 million."[3] Although the cultural legionnaires urged Reagan to implement his draconian cuts, worsening the situation of the "12 million children and 8 million adults who suffer from hunger,"[4] they had kept their mouths conveniently shut in 1971 when the government, in its traditional pattern of providing welfare for the rich, generously pumped millions of dollars to bail out Lockheed. The social welfare for the rich had been unopposed by the cultural legionnaires when, in the late 1970s, the government spent billions of dollars to bail out Chrysler Corporation.

The social welfare system for the rich is more than a recent phenomenon; it has been part of the tradition of the United States. This often invisible but real social welfare for the rich was painstakingly documented by Howard Zinn, as follows:

- Alexander Hamilton provided money for bankers setting up a national bank, subsidies to manufacturers in the form of tariffs, and a government guarantee for bondholders. To pay for all those subsidies to the rich, the government began to exact taxes from poor farmers.
- In Wisconsin in 1856 the LaCrosse Milwaukee Railroad got a million acres free, after distributing about $900,000 in stocks and bonds to seventy-two state legislators and the governor.
- In the decade of the 1850s, state governments gave railroad speculators 25 million acres of public land, free of charge, along with millions of dollars in loans.
- During the Civil War, the national government gave a gift of over 100 million acres to various railroad capitalists.

- The Central Pacific, starting on the west coast, got 9 million acres of free land and $24 million in loans (after spending $200,000 in Washington for bribes).
- The Union Pacific, starting in Nebraska and going west, got 12 million acres of free land and $27 million in government loans.
- In 1954 the CIA spent millions of dollars to organize the overthrow of the elected president of Guatemala to save the properties of the United Fruit Company.
- In 1973 the U.S. government spent millions of dollars in concert with IT&T Corporation to overthrow the elected socialist leader of Chile, Salvador Allende.
- The average tax rate for the top twelve American military contractors, who made $19 billion in profits for 1981, 1982, and 1983, was 1.5 percent. Middle-class Americans paid 15 percent.[5]

This list is by no means exhaustive but could go on and on with startling examples that point to the existence of a system of social welfare for the rich. Nonetheless, we seldom hear outrage against this generous bounty for the rich. Our educational institutions, the media, and other institutional structures make sure that "thou shall not be aware" for "your own good" while they propagate the myth of rugged individualism for the poor, who should pick themselves up by their bootstraps even though, in most cases, they are bootless. It is the same hefty bounty through capital gains tax cuts that enriched George Bush while he was at the same time putting into place mechanisms to dismantle housing subsidies for the poor, thus sentencing them to the streets.

During Reagan's political revolution we were also called on to put America first, generating a highly xenophobic atmosphere, licensing the administration's "gun boat" diplomacy that violated international laws by invading Grenada, bombing Libya, and creating a proxy army to fight and inflict despair, cruelty, hunger, and death in Nicaragua. We accepted all of these calls to patriotic arms by reciting the Pledge of Allegiance even though we were violating its major principles with our very breath. We never had any doubt nor did we have any urge to question our leaders since whatever deals they made were made for our own good. We even accepted the Agriculture Department's infamous reclassification of ketchup as a vegetable in the school lunch program, going along with the Reagan administration's cutting back on funding of lunch programs for millions of children who, without them, would either go hungry or suffer from malnutrition.

While we were feeding our national ego with banal clichés and fossilized slogans, we witnessed the largest transfer of wealth ever from the working and middle class to the rich; we saw the largest increase in homelessness; and we experienced a rapid increase in the crime rate, as we became the number-one jailer in the world. The social landscape became so bleak that Reagan's successor, George Bush, promised us "a kinder and gentler nation," which would, with "one thousand points of light," rescue us from the darkness of the trickle-down theory.

The decade of the 1980s set the stage for the reappropriation of our "common culture," leading Patrick Buchanan to urge his fellow conservatives "to wage a cultural revolution in the nineties as sweeping as the political revolution of the eighties."[6] This cultural revolution is indeed moving forward with rapid speed, from the onslaught on cultural diversity and multicultural education to Patrick Buchanan's call to our national and patriotic sense to build a large wall along the Mexican border to keep Mexicans from their own land. I say "their own land" because many Mexicans (like Native Americans) did not immigrate to the United States. Mexicans inhabited the land until the U.S. government legitimized the expropriation of almost half of Mexico through the U.S.-provoked Mexican-American War. This expropriation was justified through the idea that if you fight for it and you win, you deserve the land. Could it be that this principle was in the back òf Saddam Hussein's mind when he invaded Kuwait? The attempt to reduce war for land expropriation to being the "ultima ratio" and the "unica ratio" is eloquently captured in Carl Sandburg's poem *The People, Yes:*

> *"Get off this estate."*
> *"What for?"*
> *"Because it's mine."*
> *"Where did you get it?"*
> *"From my father."*
> *"And where did he get it?"*
> *"From his father."*
> *"And where did he get it?"*
> *"He fought for it."*
> *"Well, I'll fight you for it."*[7]

The preservation of our Judeo-Christian values and the maintenance of our Western heritage represent for the conservative the ultimate excuse to rid our "common culture" of the savage contamination of other cultural values and manifestations that constitute, in reality, the cultural fabric of U.S. society. In Patrick Buchanan's own words, we have to disintoxicate our "common culture" from the "excess of democracy" of the 1960s and 1970s that attempted to put into practice the principles in the Pledge of Allegiance by creating social structures that could lead to equality, liberty, and the pursuit of happiness. Buchanan's "common culture" argument is nothing more than a racist attempt to assign supe-

.rior status to white Eurocentric values. His own testament pointed to this unfortunate fact: "I think God made all people good, but if we had to take a million immigrants in—say Zulus next year or Englishmen—and put them in Virginia, what group would be easier to assimilate and would cause less problems for the people of Virginia?"[8] What the conservative cultural agenda fails to acknowledge is that the reorganization of our "common culture" points to the existence of our "uncommon culture," for commonality is always in a dialectical relationship with uncommonality. Thus, one cannot talk about the centeredness of our "common culture" without relegating our "uncommon" cultural values and expressions to the margins, creating a de facto silent majority. It is the dominant cultural reproductive mechanisms that feed our Judeo-Christian and Western heritage myths that discourage and eradicate our "uncommon" cultural expressions, a prerequisite for those outside the cultural center to develop their own subjectivities. That is, these "uncommon" cultural values are the only means through which the de-centered cultural subject can come to consciousness, a process necessary in his or her transformation from a cultural object to a cultural subject.

It is for this reason that the dominant cultural elites continue to inculcate in us myths and beliefs about our "common culture," all the while creating mechanisms that prevent us from ever fully participating in it. This is why it has become necessary to dismantle affirmative action and other social achievements gained during the 1960s and 1970s. The preservation of these myths requires a subtle and insidious pedagogy to prevent us from ever knowing the truth. Thus, myths constitute a barrier to a true reading of reality.

What follows is a series of dialogues that I have had with Paulo Freire over the years concerning the role of culture, class, gender, and language in the development of a new anticolonial society rooted in the dynamics of cultural production. That means the creation of a radical pedagogy that will affirm and allow oppressed cultural groups to recreate their history, culture, and language, a pedagogy that will, at the same time, help lead those assimilated individuals who perceive themselves to be captive to our common-culture ideology to cease reproducing those dominant cultural values that disconfirm their lived experiences and devalue them as human beings and cultural subjects.[9]

MACEDO:
As we have seen, the reproductive mechanism of our so-called common culture is to create a center or a core of romanticized Eurocentric values while relegating other cultural expressions to the margins. Institutional mechanisms such as schooling function, by and

large, to contain and maintain these so-called subcultures submerged into a culture of silence so as to make these "silent sections of cultures" invisible or, at least, outside the parameters of public discussion or debate. This is why we can easily accept the false dichotomy encoded in the distinction between the First World and Third World contexts. What we often fail to see is that we have within the First World order Third World realities characterized by ghettos and large-scale poverty and illiteracy, while we have de facto first world realties in the form of class privileges and accumulation of capital and power by the minority ruling elite in the Third World. It is safe to assume that the ruling elite in the Third World shares a worldview that is much more in line with the cultural capital of the dominant groups of the first world. We can also safely argue that there exists a greater gulf between the first world dominant groups and the first world marginalized cultural groups than between the first and the Third World dominant groups.

Nevertheless, even liberal educators keep on insisting, for instance, that your pedagogy of the oppressed can work only in Third World countries. This is a common position taken by North American educators, one played out in a recent admission committee meeting in a prestigious university when a liberal educator argued eloquently for admitting a South African student who, according to him, "had prevailed in spite of great odds marked by a highly discriminatory society, and … the student's application showed a great commitment to social reform in her country." When it came to the evaluation of a Mexican-American student who had an extensive background working with community-based programs ranging form adult literacy to drug-prevention programs, this same liberal educator stated that "the only thing she has going for her is that she is Mexican-American." The fact that her grades and letters of recommendation were equal to or slightly better than the South African student, the fact that she had a more extensive work track record in the community, and the fact that she had demonstrated a great interest and commitment to go back and work in her community was totally ignored by our liberal educator. In the end the Mexican-American was denied admission. The South African Third World context provided the liberal educator a safe zone to exoticize liberation struggle, leaving unproblematic his inability to acknowledge the similarities (and differences as well) of oppressive structures that operate both in South Africa and in U.S. ghettos.

Our graduate school admission anecdote is not all that different from the phenomenon of some researchers who are busily writing grant proposals to go study and promote literacy in Haiti while ignoring the tens of thousands of Haitians who are experiencing failure and dropping out of our public schools. We also have heard little from those researchers who want to study Haitians in Haiti but remain silent in terms of protest and denunciation of the dehumanizing treatment that the Haitian boat people are receiving form the U.S. Immigration and Naturalization Service Bureau. Likewise, it is also more exotic to study writing difficulties of Australian aborigines than to investigate the almost critical writing crisis in our urban public schools, particularly concerning "minority" students.

For these reasons, your emancipatory literacy proposals meet with resistance even from liberal educators in the United States. A major concern in the so-called first world nations is that your literacy work is not applicable to the non–Third World context. Could you address this issue, and possibly talk about the Third World context found in the first world, and how your educational proposals may be applied in the United States?

FREIRE:
From my earliest travels throughout the world, including the First World, I have been asked these basic questions. I think, though, in the past few years this kind of questioning has diminished somewhat. First, let us talk about the issue of the Third World and the First World. From my experiences living in the United States—I was very happy in Cambridge, and I still remember Broadway, the street where I lived—I discovered the presence of the Third World in the First World, such as the ghettos in the United States. I also discovered vicious racial discrimination and linguistic chauvinism, which is a type of racism. I simultaneously found and lived this reality. I was also discriminated against—perhaps not as much as other foreigners, particularly immigrants, because many people knew me and my work. But sometimes I felt discriminated against. People thinking I was Spanish would be more courteous when I told them that I was Brazilian. I suppose that is because there were not many Brazilians in Cambridge!

Discovering the Third World in the First, I became aware of the obvious: the presence of the First World in the Third World, the ruling class. Here in the United States as elsewhere in the First World the situation is far more complex. Since the United States is not merely the First World, and since some educators, not I, say that my literacy approach is only applicable in the Third World context, they should at least apply my approach to their easily identifiable Third World.

The main problem is that these educators are dealing with the wrong issues when they say that Freire's proposals, even though they are interesting, have nothing to do with a complex society. The issues here should be defined differently. The educational proposals that I have been making for years basically derive from two rather obvious, nonsimplistic ideas.

First, education is a political act, whether at the university, high school, primary school, or adult literacy classroom. Why? Because the very nature of education has the inherent qualities to be political, as indeed politics has educational aspects. In other words, an educational act has a political nature and a political act has an educational nature. If this is generally so, it would be incorrect to say that Latin American education alone has a political nature. Education worldwide is political by nature. In metaphysical terms, politics is the soul of education, its very being, whether in the First World or in the Third World. When a teacher studies a particular subject—when Giroux, for instance, analyzes the hidden curriculum—all instances of education become political acts. There is no way I or anyone else can contradict this. The political nature of education, then, is not Paulo Freire's exoticism from the Third World.

Second, in Brazil or wherever, whether one works in literacy or postgraduate studies, education is a series of theories put into practice. We cannot escape this. Whether it be you here in Massachusetts or I in Brazil, no matter what we discuss, linguistics in your case, the relationship of educator and learner in my case, what seems to be most important is the object of knowledge posed for us as educators. Once we are involved in this educational practice, we are also engaged in a practice of knowing. We may be trying to learn a predetermined, existing knowledge, or we may be trying to create a knowledge that does not exist, like research. All these educational practices involve the act of knowing, throughout the world.

The issue to be defined now is what are our positions in these acts of knowing. What are our views in the theory of knowledge? How do we approach the object of knowledge? Do we own it? Do we carry it in our suitcases to distribute to our students? Do we use this object of knowledge to feed students or to inspire them to know? Do we stimulate students to assume the role of subjects, rather than the role of patients and recipients of our knowledge?

Well, these are not just Third World issues; they are universal issues. But I do not want to say that there are no limitations imposed by different cultures, politics, and ideologies. There are real limits on the democratic practice of knowing, in this country and elsewhere. Again, creative and critical educational experience is not an exoticism of the Third World. In literacy, learners should assume the role of subjects in the very process of mastering their language. University students should assume the role of knowing subjects in the interchange between students who know and educators who also know. Obviously, teachers are not the only subjects who know.

The point of departure in this process of knowing educators and learners focuses on the expectations and stumbling blocks that learners confront in the learning process, not on the expectations and knowledge of the educator. Again, I would point out that this is not an exoticism from the Third World.

Beyond these arguments, I am thinking about the coherence of a political position within a pedagogical outlook, which is also political by nature, and therefore, a coherence of a theoretical posture within the practice of this theory.

Sometimes educators forget to recognize that no one gets from one side of the street without crossing it! No one reaches the other side by starting from the same side. One can only reach the other side by starting from the opposite side. The level of my present knowledge is the other side to my students. I have to begin from the opposite side, that of the students. My knowledge is my reality, not theirs. So I have to begin from their reality to bring them into my reality. A teacher may say, "This is another romantic naïveté of Paulo Freire." I insist, however, that there is no romanticism in these ideas. What we find here is an epistemological coherence with a political outlook.

There seem to be fewer questions about the validity of my educational theory and practice in the First World because intellectuals and committed educators in the United States, the United Kingdom, and Europe are rigorously studying my work. Although they may not always agree with me, many see the viability of these ideas in the First World context. In the field of teaching English as a Second Language (ESL) here in the United States, there are a number of teachers and critical pedagogues who work along the general lines of my thinking. Also, Ann Berthoff and Ira Shor incorporate my ideas in both their theories and practices. About five years ago, an interesting and voluminous book, *Learning with Freire*, was published in Germany, involving a longitudinal experiment on preschool education that incorporated my methods. In *Pedagogy of the Oppressed* and *Pedagogy in Process: Letters to Guinea-Bissau*, I stressed that my experiences should be recreated, not transplanted. In sum, my educational experiments in the Third World should not be transplanted to the First World; they should be created anew.

MACEDO:
Speaking of cultural production, I would like to ask you about the relationship between education, including literacy, and culture. We have to take into account various definitions of culture, however. By

"culture" I do not mean that which is representative of those dominant elements of the elite class, that is, culture with a capital C. Culture is not an autonomous system but a system characterized by social stratification and tensions. To be precise, I have in mind Richard Johnson's definition of culture, which includes the following three main premises:

1. Cultural processes are intimately connected with social relations, especially with class relations and class formations, with sexual divisions, with the racial structuring of social relations, and with age oppressions as a form of dependency.

2. Culture involves power and helps to produce asymmetries in the abilities of individuals and social groups to define and realize their needs.

3. Culture is neither autonomous nor an externally determined field, but a site of social differences and struggles.

Given the range of factors that interact in cultural production and reproduction, how can an emancipatory literacy transcend social-class barriers to interface with all these other factors related to culture? Can you also speak about education generally and literacy in particular as factors of culture?

FREIRE:

Literacy and education in general are cultural expressions. You cannot conduct literacy work outside the world of culture because education in itself is a dimension of culture. Education is an act of knowledge—knowledge here is not to be restricted to a specific object only—on the part of the very subject who knows. Education has to take the culture that explains it as the object of a curious comprehension, as if one would use education to question itself. And every time that education questions itself, in response it finds itself in the larger body of culture. Evidently, the more it continues to interrogate itself about its purpose in culture and society, the more education discovers that culture is a totality cut across by social classes.

In Brazilian society, for example, one cannot deny certain behavior patterns characteristic of different social-class behavior. For example, taste, which is also cultural, is heavily conditioned by social-class boundaries.

MACEDO:

I did not intend to focus only on social classes in cultural production and reproduction. I think we need to investigate other cultural influences on education.

FREIRE:

When a pedagogy tries to influence other factors that could not be strictly explained by a theory of class, you still have to pass through class analysis.

Given this understanding, we must still acknowledge that social classes exist and that their presence is contradictory. That is, the existence of social classes provokes a conflict of interests. It provokes and shapes cultural ways of being and, therefore, generates contradictory expressions of culture.

In general, dominant segments of any society talk about their particular interests, their tastes, their styles of living, which they regard as concrete expressions of nationality. Thus the subordinated groups, who have their own tastes and styles of living, cannot talk about their tastes and styles as national expressions. They lack the political and economic power to do so. Only those who have power can generalize and decree their group characteristics as representative of the national culture. With this decree, the dominant group necessarily depreciates all characteristics belonging to subordinated groups, characteristics that deviate from the decreed patterns.

This is especially interesting when you understand the asymmetry generated by social institutions, and how important a role critical literacy programs play in demystifying the artificial parameters imposed on people. Critical literacy has to explicate the validity of different types of music, poetry, language, and worldviews. From this viewpoint the dominant class, which has the power to define, profile, and describe the world, begins to pronounce that the speech habits of the subordinate groups are a corruption, a bastardization of dominant discourse. It is in this sense that sociolinguists are making an enormous contribution to the demystification of these notions. What they show is that, scientifically, all languages are valid, systematic, rule-governed systems, and that the inferiority/superiority distinction is a social phenomenon. A language is developed to the degree that is reaches a certain stability in a particular area and to the extent that it is used in the comprehension and expression of the world by the groups that speak it. One cannot understand and analyze a language, then, without a class analysis. Even though we may have to go beyond class boundaries to understand certain universal properties of language, we should neither reduce the investigation of language to a mechanical comprehension, nor reduce it to only social-class analysis. But we have to do the latter to gain a global view of the total system under investigation. I think all of us ultimately speak the same language—in the abstract sense—and express ourselves in different ways.

This has to do with the question you asked concerning different discourses. If you take the Brazilian case, you have the type of language spoken by the dominant class and other types spoken by workers, peasants, and similar groups. These are part of the abstract notion we call Brazilian Portuguese. This is not language as an abstraction, but language as a concrete system spoken by different groups. It is important, then, to comprehend these different varieties of language. They involve different grammars and different syntactical and semantic representations that are conditioned and explicated by people in varying positions relative to forces of production. Language is also culture. Language is the mediating force of knowledge; but it is also knowledge itself. I believe all of this also passes through the social classes. A critical pedagogy poses this dynamic, contradictory cultural comprehension and the dynamic, contradictory nature of education as a permanent object of curiosity on the part of the learners. We find a general simplicity concerning the appreciation of these phenomena. It is as if all had been already known and decreed by the dominant groups. It is as if all that takes place at the level of culture had nothing to do with other discourses, such as the discourse of production. A pedagogy will be that much more critical and radical, the more investigative and less certain of "certainties" it is. The more "unquiet" a pedagogy, the more critical it will become. A pedagogy preoccupied with the uncertainties rooted in the issues we have discussed is, by its nature, a pedagogy that requires investigation. This pedagogy is thus much more a pedagogy of question than a pedagogy of answer.

MACEDO:

Let us clarify what you refer to as intellectual activity from the dominant point of view, so as not to preclude other intellectual activities that are generated and sustained by these students. We should emphasize that these students can, and in fact do, engage in frequent intellectual activities, but these are activities generated from their own perspective. That is, they define their own activities.

FREIRE:

It is difficult to understand these issues outside of an analysis of power relations. Only those who have power, for example, can define what is correct or incorrect. Only those who have power can decide what constitutes intellectualism. Once the intellectual parameters are set, those who want to be considered intellectuals must meet requirements of the profile dictated by the elite class. To be intellectual one must do exactly what those with the power to define intellectualism do. The intellectual activity of those without power is always characterized as nonintellectual. I think this issue should be underscored, not just as a dimension of pedagogy, but as a dimension of politics as well. This is difficult to do in a society like that of the United States, where the political nature of pedagogy is negated ideologically. It is necessary to negate the political nature of pedagogy to give the superficial appearance that education serves everyone, thus assuring that it continues to function in the interest of the dominant class.

This mythical universality of education to better serve humanity leads many to blame the students themselves for dropping out. It is their decision if they want to remain and succeed in school. Once you accept the political dimension of education, it becomes difficult to accept the dominant class's conclusion: that the dropouts are to blame. The more you deny the political dimension of education, the more you assume the moral potential to blame the victims. This is somewhat paradoxical. The many people who pass through school and come out illiterate because they resisted and refused to read the dominant word are representative of self-affirmation. This self-affirmation is, from another point of view, a process of literacy in the normal, global sense of the term. That is, the refusal to read the word chosen by the teacher is the realization on the part of the student that he or she is making a decision not to accept what is perceived as violating his or her world. In the end, what you have is a separation between teacher and student along class lines. Even though we recognize that it is very difficult to do an analysis of class in a complex society like that of the United States, we cannot deny that class division exists.

MACEDO:
In general, educators in the United States de-emphasize the issue of social class as it pertains to education. In fact, most of the studies concerning the unacceptable number of illiterates in the school system treat the problem from a technocratic perspective. And the remedies proposed tend to be technocratic as well. Although some educators may describe a possible correlation between the high dropout rate and the low socioeconomic background of students, this correlation remains at the level of description. More often than not, U.S. educators in general and literacy experts in particular fail to establish political and ideological linkages in their analyses that could illuminate the reproductive nature of schools in this society. For example, conservative educators such as Secretary of Education William Bennett call for a back-to-basics approach as they blindly embrace competency-based curricula. Although the rigidity of the competency-based approach may benefit the white and upper-class students, I doubt that it will remedy the illiteracy problem that plagues the

majority of subordinate groups in the United States. Panaceas such as more student-contact hours for reading and math and a better salary base for teachers will perpetuate those ideological elements that negate students' life experiences. As a result, students react by refusing to read what the curriculum has decided they should read.

There is no guarantee that more of the same approach, which fundamentally lacks equity and sensitivity for the culture of the subordinate groups, will diminish the resistance of students as they refuse to read the "chosen" word. When curriculum designers ignore important variables such as social-class differences, when they ignore the incorporation of the subordinate cultures' values in the curriculum, and when they refuse to accept and legitimize the students' language, their actions point to the inflexibility, insensitivity, and rigidity of a curriculum that was designed to benefit those who wrote it.

By giving teachers token salary increases, one is paternalistically placating the majority of teachers, who find themselves in an increasingly powerless position as they confront a reductionist system that aims to further de-skill them. These approaches and their related proposals tend to overlook the material conditions with which teachers struggle in their attempt to survive the overwhelming task of teaching material that is politically and ideologically at odds with the subordinate students' reality.

These approaches and proposals fail to examine the lack of time teachers have to perform a task that, by its very nature, should involve thinking and reflection. Moreover, the intellectual dimension of teaching is never celebrated by a system whose main objective is to further de-skill teachers and reduce them to mere technical agents who are destined to walk un-reflectively through a labyrinth of procedures. So my question is, do you think that these educators are aware that their proposals will exacerbate the equity gap that is already victimizing a great number of "minority" students?

FREIRE:
Let us first clarify the term "minority."

MACEDO:
I use the term in the U.S. context. I am also aware that it is contradictory in nature.

FREIRE:
Exactly. Do you see how ideologically impregnated the term "minority" is? When you use "minority" in the U.S. context to refer to the majority of people who are not part of the dominant class, you alter its semantic

value. When you refer to "minority" you are in fact talking about the "majority" who find themselves outside the sphere of political and economic dominance.

MACEDO:
If Kozol is correct, the 60 million illiterates and functional illiterates that he documents in *Illiterate America* do not constitute a minority class. These 60 million should not be added to other sizable groups who learn how to read but who are still not part of dominant political and economic spheres.

FREIRE:
In reality, as with many other words, the semantic alteration of the term "minority" serves to hide the many myths that are part of the mechanism sustaining cultural dominance.

MACEDO:
Some educators, particularly North American feminists, contend that your work tends to universalize oppression while ignoring the historical specificities of diverse and contradictory positions that characterize subordinate groups along the lines of culture, ethnicity, language, race, and gender. In particular, some feminists point out that your failure to address these historical specificities reveal "the shortcomings that emerge in the attempt to enact a pedagogy that assumes universal and abstract goals."[10] Weiler argued that "like Freirian pedagogy, feminist pedagogy is grounded in a vision of social change, and like feminist pedagogy, it rests on truth claims of primacy of experience and consciousness that are grounded in historically situated social movements."[11] She further contended that "some feminist critics feel, for instance, that you have failed to address the various forms of power held by teachers depending on their race, gender, and the historical and institutional settings in which they work."[12] Paulo, you have shared with me in various conversations that since the publication of *Pedagogy of the Oppressed* you periodically receive letters from some feminists who contend that, although your books and your theories deal with oppression and the need for social transformation so as to end all forms of domination, you tend to relegate the issue of gender to a minor position. Some of these feminists point out that not only do you not give primacy to the issue of gender, but the very language that you use, particularly in *Pedagogy of the Oppressed*, is sexist in nature. They also point out that your goals for liberation and social and political transformation are embedded in universals that, at some level, negate both your own position of

privilege as an intellectual man and the specificity of experiences which characterize conflicts among oppressed groups in general. That is to say, in theorizing about oppression as universal truth you fail to appreciate the different historical locations of oppression. For example, a Black man, although oppressed, still enjoys a privileged position vis-à-vis a Black female. For this reason you need to take into consideration that these different levels of oppression necessitate a specific analysis with a different focus that calls for a different pedagogy. An emancipatory feminist pedagogy must also, as far as Gary Olson argued:

> reject the kind of popular feminism championed by "Western white women"—the kind that posits patriarchy as the principal form of domination while ignoring race and class, the kind that frames gender relations in a simplistic us/them binary. Such a modernist, totalizing conception of gender power relations is not in keeping with the type of poststructuralist feminism championed especially by "women of color, lesbians, and poor and working-class women" and that attempts to challenge the "essentialism, separatism, and ethnocentrism that have been expressed in feminist theorizing" over the last several decades.[13]

Can you comment on these issues?

FREIRE:

I believe that the question feminists in the United States raise concerning my treatment of gender in *Pedagogy of the Oppressed* is not only valid but very timely. Given the seriousness and the complexity of the gender issue, it merits reflection in conjunction with a rigorous analysis regarding the phenomenon of oppression. It also requires new pedagogical practices so as to achieve the dream of the struggle for liberation and the victory over all forms of oppression. Early in my youth, I began to feel the pain of oppression in my country. I felt all forms of discriminatory expression ranging from the most vulgar racial oppression to the criminal theft that characterizes the unconscious appropriation of the national resources from the dispossessed class by the ruling elite to gender discrimination. Ever since the time when I was touched by the discriminatory practices that were part and parcel of the social landscape in which I was socialized, I felt angry. For example, when a black servant was verbally abused by the white ruling class discourse—a discourse that often reflected psychological violence while profiling blacks as subhuman, almost animal-like creatures. In fact, it is safe to say that, in some cases, domestic pets received better treatment by the society than the unprotected, subordinated blacks.

It was around the decade of the twenties that the verbal violence against blacks alerted my consciousness to the degree that I began not only to understand that the Brazilian society was profoundly racist and unjust but this injustice provoked in me a sense of revolt and disgust. This awareness that began to take root, as I said, during the twenties, radicalized me to take a very critical position against all forms of discrimination and expressions of oppression, including the oppressive position to which Brazilian women, particularly women of color, were relegated. But to be honest, at that time I was first struck by class and racial oppression. Being a product of the Brazilian Northeast region, a highly patriarchal and machista society, I became also, in my early developmental years, a victim of a cultural context that systematically discriminated against women. I say victim because within this framework of sexism, my sensitivities against oppression were most predominant along the lines of class and race. It is precisely through the anger which class and race oppression produced in me, that I began to open my eyes more sharply towards the total subordination of women in this highly patriarchal cultural milieu which is Northeast Brazil. It is with great satisfaction that I admit that my engagement with the feminist movements led me to take a sharper focus on the issues of gender. For this, I am indebted to the North American feminists who called gender discrimination to my attention on numerous occasions. It was during the seventies, after the publication of *Pedagogy of the Oppressed*, that I began to reflect more profoundly and learn more systematically from the work of the feminists. After the publication of *Pedagogy of the Oppressed*, I received a few letters criticizing my sexist language from some North American feminists. In fact, I received not long ago, a letter from a young woman who recently came across *Pedagogy of the Oppressed* for the first time, criticizing my machista language. This letter was very insulting and somewhat vulgar but I was not upset by it. I was not upset by her letter because, most certainly, she has only read *Pedagogy of the Oppressed* and evaluated my language as if this book were written last year. That is, she did not contextualize *Pedagogy of the Oppressed* in its historical context. But don't misunderstand me: I am not making any excuse for the sexist language of this book. I am just pointing out that during my formative years I did not escape the enveloping powers of a highly sexist culture in my country. However, since the publication of *Pedagogy of the Oppressed* I have attempted to rid my language of all those features that are demeaning to women. I have insisted that my English translators pay close attention and present my work in non-sexist English. If this young woman were to read, for example, *The Politics of Education*, which you, Donaldo, translated—you remember my insistence about the avoidance of sexist language—and *Literacy: Reading the Word and the World,* which we co-authored, she would see a marked difference in language use. Let us now turn to the central issue of sexism. During the seventies, when I began to learn with the feminists, particularly North American feminists, I must say that I was, at that time, mostly influenced by Marxist analysis, particularly the analysis of class.

When I wrote *Pedagogy of the Oppressed,* I was so influenced by Marx's class analysis, and given the incredibly cruel class oppression that characterized my developing years in Northeast Brazil, my major preoccupation was therefore class oppression. It is ironic that some Marxists even criticized me for not paying enough attention to social-class analysis. In *Pedagogy of the Oppressed,* if my memory serves me correctly, I made approximately 33 references to social-class analysis. It was exactly because of my preoccupation with the process of transformation of the world which included obviously the struggle of women, the *reivindicaçao das mulheres,* that led me to focus on what I believed to be mainly a class issue. I believed that this word *"transformation"* implied a bit of interest in class more so than individual or sex interest. In other words, liberation should take place for both men and women and not just for men or for women or along color and ethnic lines.

MACEDO:

Paulo, but here lies the problem of over-generalizing oppression and liberation. In other words, one would have to identify the specificity and location of oppression within a historical moment. You need to appreciate that both black women and men are oppressed by the white class but within this oppressive structure the position of the black man differs somewhat from that of the black woman. That is, the black woman experiences not only white racism but also male domination.

FREIRE:

But I do not disagree with that position.

MACEDO:

Yes, but the criticism leveled against your work, particularly your position concerning gender in *Pedagogy of the Oppressed,* raises the issue that you universalize oppression without appreciating the multiplicity of oppressive experiences that characterized the lived histories of individuals along race, gender ethnic, and religious lines. For this reason, a critical pedagogy must address these specificities of oppression so as to create the necessary pedagogical structures for liberation. You cannot assume that by eradicating racism, black women will automatically or magically cease to experience male oppression. The sad fact remains that the symmetrical power position to which a black woman is relegated by her male counterpart is not at all affected by the erasure of racist structures.

FREIRE:

Without avoiding the issue of gender I must say that readers have some responsibility to place my work within its historical and cultural context. That is, the person reading *Pedagogy of the Oppressed* as if it were written yesterday somehow denies its historicity. What I find absurd is to read a book like *Pedagogy of the Oppressed* and criticize it because the author did not treat all of the potential oppressive themes equally. I believe that what one needs to do is to appreciate the contribution of the work within its historical context. That I was not as acutely aware of issues of gender as I wrote *Pedagogy of the Oppressed* is an absolute fact. It is equally an absolute fact that the knowledge base with respect to gender oppression we have today, thanks to the great and comprehensive works of feminists, was not available to me then nor was it available to many women. I feel that, if I were to write *Pedagogy of the Oppressed* today and ignore the immense world of information regarding sex discrimination and the level of awareness concerning sexism that both men and women have today, some of the criticism leveled against *Pedagogy of the Oppressed* would not only be valid but would be most necessary. What I would like to think is that without wanting to universalize oppression, I did make some positive contributions to the understanding of oppressive structures and that this understanding did also contribute to the struggle of all women in their rightful quest for equality and liberation.

I believe that there are specificities in oppression without a doubt. It is interesting. For example, the other day I was making references to the mayor of São Paulo, an extraordinary woman who is also from Northeast Brazil. In a television interview she gave recently she said: "To be a woman in Brazil is very difficult. To be a woman mayor of São Paulo is something even more difficult, particularly if this woman is from the Northeast region of Brazil." That is, she is first discriminated against in her condition as woman and second in her position as a woman from the Northeast. She then added, "My difficulty as a woman mayor would be correspondingly worse if I were black and a peasant."

MACEDO:

This example you just cited captures the spirit of the criticism leveled against your work. That is to say, there exists a hierarchical structure of

Popular topic
consumers
sells books

oppression that ranges from being a white middle-class woman to an underclass black woman who may also be a peasant.

FREIRE:
Exactly. I do not disagree.

MACEDO:
You need to appreciate the fact that as a man from Northeast Brazil you would experience less discrimination than the present mayor is experiencing in her capacity as a woman from your region. Your male position privileges you to certain social acceptances which are denied her.

FREIRE:
As I said, I do not disagree with this position. However, let me ask the following question: In what ways do these specificities alter the analysis of oppression and its relations in *Pedagogy of the Oppressed*?

MACEDO:
I am not sure that these critics claim that the specificities of oppression alter your analysis of oppression and its relations. What we need to do is to understand the fact that the different historical locations of oppression necessitate a specific analysis with a different and unique focus that calls also for a different pedagogy.

FREIRE:
If you consider both men and women from Northeast Brazil, it is evident that they are more discriminated against than men and women from São Paulo. A woman from São Paulo has a more privileged condition than a woman from the Northeast. For me, one of the fundamental tactical problems in the struggle for transformation is to see how, even in view of the differences, the oppressed assume their position as such and join their forces to effectively and successfully confront a greater enemy. What I want to say is that we need to create structures of collective struggle in which the women from the Northeast who are the most discriminated against begin to learn to join forces with the less-discriminated-against women from São Paulo in a collective struggle against a greater oppression perpetrated against all women. We need to understand the extent to which the oppressed men in the Northeast will also learn to join forces with the women from the same region to struggle towards the eradication of those socio-political structures that have relegated both of them to a highly discriminated position.

MACEDO:

The joining of forces could only take place when the women from the Northeast cease to experience subordination with respect to the men of their social and cultural milieu.

FREIRE:

For me the correct pedagogical practice is for feminists to understand the different levels of male oppression, while at the same time creating pedagogical structures in which men will have to confront their oppressive position. I believe that it is not enough for women to liberate themselves from the oppression of men who are in turn oppressed by the society as a whole, but that together they simultaneously move toward cutting the chains of oppression. Obviously, both these oppressed men and women need to understand their different positions in the oppressive structures so that together they can develop effective strategies and cease to be oppressed. It may be the case that some will accuse me of being naïve. I do not believe that I am being naïve. I think that, whenever possible, the pessimists need to rectify the sexist behavior of men who are also oppressed by making them assume their position as oppressed so that, in the process, these men will also recognize their role as oppressors of women as well. And in turn, these oppressed men, by maintaining certain coherence in their struggle of liberation, will have to renounce their role as oppressors of women. I believe that through this process the struggle for liberation would envelop a collective war against all oppression. If the oppressed women choose to fight exclusively against the oppressed men when they are both in the category of oppressed they can rupture the oppressor-oppressed relations specific to men-women, the struggle will only be partial and perhaps tactically incorrect.

It is for this reason that one day while [I was] at the University of London during the seventies, a person raised the issue of gender in a debate to which I gave a shocking answer. I repeated this same answer years later in Brazil where I shocked incredibly the macho egos that predominate in my country. I said: "I too, am a woman." That is to say, this affirmation was not sexual but was an eminently political statement. What I would like to make very clear, even if my feminist friends do not agree, is that the concept of the gender struggle is political and not sexual. I do not want to have an antagonistic relationship with women. But it is possible that I may need to be reprimanded by women. If that is the case, I deserve and accept it. I do recognize the sexual differences which position both men and women in different oppressive locations, but for me, the fundamental issue is the political vision of sex, and not the sexist vision of sex. What is at stake is liberation and the creation of liberatory structures which is the overriding issue for both men and women.

MACEDO:
But, Paulo, you must recognize that there are various levels of liberation.

FREIRE:
Exactly. These levels require different tactics. In life you will not be able to accomplish much without establishing tactics with an eye towards strategies. For me the problem is the following: What is the strategy of the struggle of the oppressed? It is the utopia of liberty that severs the chains of oppression. This should be the dream of the struggle for liberation that never reaches a plenitude. In other words, when you achieve some freedom, you discover, in the process, that you need more liberation. Then, my basic strategy would have to be this utopia of freedom, that involves creativity, risks, compassion, political commitment, etc.

MACEDO:
But utopia should not undervalue the specificities of oppression.

FREIRE:
Obviously. In fact, in certain moments these differences will have to decree tactics that may even appear as not too liberating. For example, let me tell you how I recognize these differences. I remember that in the seventies, I was discussing in a seminar about the right that women have, in their initial struggle, of not accepting the presence of men during their debates. And why this tactic? It is precisely because of these specificities. That is, in the initial struggle of a group of women to coalesce a movement, the presence of men should not be permitted precisely because of the machista ideology that characterizes most societies, and gives men, at the very minimum a sarcastic and ironic air with respect to the position of women.

MACEDO:
Don't forget the power privilege that men enjoy.

FREIRE:
Yes. Precisely. For this reason, they should prohibit the presence of men in their initial debates. However, as their movement takes hold and, in the process of a critical reflection, they should also incorporate men in

their struggle. This is the undeniable process of the maturing of the struggle. You see, during the seventies the feminist movements did not criticize the treatment of gender in my work. But the feminist movements of the nineties are being very critical. Why? Because the feminists of the nineties are now seeing what in the seventies they were, perhaps, not yet aware. I think what is wrong is to criticize an author using tools that history had not given him or her. I wrote *Pedagogy of the Oppressed* twenty years ago.

MACEDO:
Some educators in North America also point out that your theory of oppression does not speak directly to the issue of race. They argue that you have failed to assign the appropriate weight to race as a fundamental factor of oppression. In their view, your class analysis oversimplifies the role of race and its historical location of oppression. Can you talk to us about your views on race issues?

FREIRE:
As I mentioned in our conversation concerning gender, I became keenly aware during the decade of the twenties of the cruel symbolic and material violence perpetrated against blacks in my country, even though some Brazilians like to think that there is no racism in Brazil. Even our own language contradicts this ignorant but never innocent position, given the verbal violence that blacks endure in their day-to-day struggle for survival. Like the issue of gender, race as an ideological category did not feature predominantly in my early work, particularly *Pedagogy of the Oppressed*. However, my critics should not use *Pedagogy of the Oppressed* as the only measure to evaluate my solidarity with subordinate racial groups, particularly Africans and African-Americans.

My involvement with literacy campaigns in various African countries, particularly Guinea-Bissau and Sao Tome e Principe, speaks of my commitment and my fight against all racial oppression and my admiration for the courage of black people in Africa in throwing out the colonizers. Obviously, the race situation in Africa is somewhat different than that of the United States and we should—and I am becoming more and more aware of this—always take into consideration the historical specificity and different forms of oppression. In other words, in Africa, the vast majority of the population is black, while the white colonizers represented only a small minority. The challenge for me in Africa, as I pointed out in *Pedagogy in Process: Letters to Guinea-Bissau*, was to always be cautious and aware of my role as an outsider who had been invited to provide some help with the transformation of the inherited colonial educational structure. In many discussions, as well as in many letters I wrote to my colleagues in Guinea-Bissau, I always stressed the importance of a thorough analysis of culture in the development of a liberatory educational plan. In fact, the importance of culture was not my idea since their leader Amilcar Cabral understood keenly well the role of culture in the struggle for liberation. As I told you in our many conversations, Donaldo, I learned immensely from Cabral's insights, particularly his analysis of culture.

The issue of race in Guinea-Bissau, as well as other African countries where I worked, is different, in my view, from that of the United States. The challenge for the liberators and educators was to understand how race as an ideological category served to legitimize the colonizers' exploitation and domination. When the colonizers used the pretext of racial inferiority to dehumanize the Africans, relegating them to subhuman status, as I said before, almost animal-like creatures, the anti-colonialist struggle had to take race as a determinant factor in their condemnation of colonialism. At least, in my denunciation of colonialism, I always felt revolted by the raw racism of the colonialist ideology. As you see, Donaldo, my collaboration in the fight against colonialism invariably involved a fight against racism. All anti-colonialist leaders and intellectuals fighting to break their countries from the yoke of colonialism were very clear about the colonizers' violent racism. From Amilcar Cabral to Frantz Fanon you find brilliant racism analyses of the cruel and tragic history of racism imperialism.

MACEDO:
I agree. Albert Memmi is a prime example of a penetrating analysis of racism as the mainstay of colonialism. For Memmi, "it is significant that racism is part of colonialism throughout the world: and it is no coincidence. Racism sums up and symbolizes the fundamental relation which unites colonialists and colonized."[14] Paulo, we need, however, to understand what happens to the role of race once the colonialists were defeated and expelled form the colonized countries.

FREIRE:
Yes. Here is when we need to understand how culture is cut across by race, gender, class, ethnicity, and languages. In the post-independence reconstruction of these African nations, where the population is all black, other factors may play a more significant role. For example, take Guinea-Bissau with its multiple cultural, linguistic, and ethnic groups. The challenge during post-independence is to understand how to reconcile the historical specificities of these differences and achieve

successfully national unity. In this complex analysis, we cannot underestimate the role of class.

MACEDO:
This is an important factor. The understanding of class as an ideological category becomes important so as to prevent the generalization that reduces all analysis to race. For instance, the petit bourgeois class of African functionaries who assimilated to the colonial cultural values are part of the same racial entity but have a very different ideological orientation and aspiration for the new nation. I think what we need to avoid is a framework of analysis that collapses all of these factors into one monolithic entity of race. The same is true of African-Americans in the United States to a degree. It would be a big mistake to view all African-Americans as one monolithic cultural group without marked differences. Although Clarence Thomas, the United States Supreme Court Justice, is black, there is a tremendous gulf of difference between him and, let us say, our friend bell hooks, even though they share the same race and class positions. They differ, however, significantly in their ideological orientation and gender issues. Similar gulfs exist between the vast mass of African-Americans who remain subordinated and reduced to ghettos and the middle-class African-Americans who, in some sense, have also partly abandoned the subordinated mass of African-Americans. I am reminded of an incident where, in a dialogue with a personal friend of Martin Luther King Jr., who had joined him in the important struggle to end black segregation and oppression during the sixties, he remarked: "Donaldo, you are right. We are using un-reflexively the dominant discourse based on euphemisms such as "economically marginal" and avoid more pointed terms such as oppression. I confess that I often feel uneasy when I am invited to discuss with various institutions issues pertaining to the community. In reality, I haven't been there in over 20 years." Having achieved great personal success and having moved to a middle-class reality, this African-American gentleman began to experience a distance with the rest of the African-Americans who remain abandoned in ghettos.

In a recent discussion with a group of students, an African-American young man who attends an Ivy League university told me that his parents usually vote with the white, middle-class interests even if, in the long run, their vote is detrimental to black people.

FREIRE:
You see, Donaldo, things have not changed much with respect to those who work for anti-racist and anti-sexist movements but oppose the

presence of class in a comprehensive social analysis. You remember the discussion we had in Boston with my wife, Nita, and an African-American friend who is a college professor and highly competent, but refused to accept class as a significant factor in social analysis of the African-American reality. You remember that we tried to point out to her that while one cannot reduce the analysis of racism to social class, we cannot understand racism fully without a class analysis, for to do one at the expense of the other is to fall into a sectarianist position which is as despicable as the racism that we need to reject.

MACEDO:

Paulo, we also need to keep in mind that the level of violent racism in the United Sates gives primacy to race in most contexts. For instance, a recent conversation I had with a taxi driver in Washington, D.C., highlights this point. During our conversation, he told me that he was from Ghana and he showed me pictures of his wife and his son who were still there. I asked him if they were going to join him in the United States and he quickly responded: "Oh, no! I don't want to expose my son to the racism I have to deal with. You see, I got a Masters' degree in business administration five years ago and the only job I got is driving this taxi. Back home, I am somebody: Here I'm just a nigger."

I think what is important is to approach race analysis through a convergent framework where race is cut across by class, gender, culture, language, and ethnicity. The brilliant work of bell hooks that unmasks the African-American male sexist orientation brings home the point that these historical specificities, even within the same race, give rise to multiple identities that should never be collapsed into one monolithic entity. However, it would also be a major mistake to give class primacy so as to diminish the urgency of analysis concerning racism. This would be a mechanism that would play into the hand of the white supremacists, who prefer to keep the ideological structure of racism unexamined. We have to always bear in mind that in a society that is so violently racist, a movement into a middle-class reality does little for African-Americans when they are outside their professional contexts. They are still followed in stores, not because they are being rendered great service, but because they are black. Being a renowned intellectual did little for Cornel West, who watched nine taxis go by and refuse to pick him up as a passenger in the streets of New York just because of the color of his skin. Henry Louis Gates Jr.'s prominence as a scholar did not lessen the racism he had to face at Duke University. bell hooks's eminence as a major feminist scholar does not lessen the pain of racism coupled with sexism that she endures. Her having written eight highly acclaimed feminist books still does not provide her access to the media and magazines as enjoyed by white feminists such as Naomi Wolf. bell hooks recently complained: "I have written eight feminist books. None of the magazines that have talked about your book, Naomi, have ever talked about my books at all. Now, that's not because there aren't ideas in my books that have universal appeal. It's because the issue that you raised in *The Beauty Myth* is still about beauty. We have to acknowledge that all of us do not have equal access."[15]

For me, the real issue is never to fall into a false dichotomy between race and class. The fundamental challenge is to accept Derrick Bell's "continuing quest for new directions in our struggle for racial justice, a struggle we must continue even if … racism is an integral, permanent, and indestructible component of this society."[16]

FREIRE:
Absolutely. It is the work of African-Americans, such as our friend bell hooks, Toni Morrison, Cornel West, Manning Marable, and Derrick Bell, among many other African-American intellectuals, that will point us to a pedagogy of hope, born from the painful experience of a dehumanizing racism.

MACEDO:
What role do cultural specificities and location play in the development of consciousness of the world in the process of literacy?

FREIRE:
The consciousness of the world is constituted in relation to the world; it is not a part of the self. The world enables me to constitute the self in relation to "you," the world. The transformation of objective reality—what I call the "writing" of reality—represents precisely the starting point where the animal that became human began to write history. It started when these animals started to use their hands differently. As this transformation was taking place, the consciousness of the "touched" world was constituting itself. It is precisely this world consciousness, touched and transformed, that bred the consciousness of the self. For a long time these beings, who were making themselves, wrote the world much more than they spoke the world. They directly touched and affected the world before they talked about it. Sometime later, though, these beings began to speak about the transformed world. And they began to speak about this transformation. After another long period of time, these beings began to register graphically the talk about the transformation. For this reason, I always say that before learners attempt to learn how to read and write they need to

read and write the world. They need to comprehend the world that involves talk about the world.

Literacy's oral dimension is important even if it takes place in a culture like that of the United States, whose memory is preponderantly written, not oral like that of Africa, for example. Considering these different moments, which took place over millennia, and also considering the modern experience, it is not viable to separate the literacy process from general educational processes. It is not viable to separate literacy from the productive process of society. The ideal is a concomitant approach in which literacy evolved in various environments, such as the workplace. But even when literacy cannot take place in various environments, I think it is impossible to dichotomize what takes place in the economic process of the world from the process of discourse. As to your question of whether economic discourse is an act of production relative to the acts of literacy, I would say that a critical pedagogy would have to stimulate students to reflect. Since this reflection should be critical, learners will begin to comprehend the relationship among different discourses. In the final analysis, these discourses are interrelated. Productive discourse and discourse about accompanying productive discourse always intersect at some level. The problem of understanding the culture in which education takes place cannot negate the presence and influence of economic production.

MACEDO:

Let us move on to another question. I think it is of paramount importance to analyze how subordinate cultures are produced in the classroom. We need to understand the antagonistic relationships between subordinate cultures and the dominant values of the curriculum. Take, for example, the resistance to speaking the required standard dialect of the curriculum. The dominant curriculum is designed primarily to reproduce the inequality of social classes, while it mostly benefits the interests of an elite minority. How can North American progressive educators capitalize on the antagonistic cultural elements produced in subordinate students' acts of resistance, and how can educators launch a literacy campaign that would enable students to comprehend their world so they can later read it? That is, is it possible to use students' rebelliousness as a platform from which they can transcend the mechanistic nature of literacy imposed on them by a curriculum that demands only the mechanical codification and de-codification of graphemes and phonemes to form words that further alienate them?

FREIRE:

Your question is absolutely fundamental. Theoretically, the answer to it is of value not only in the U.S. context, but also in the Brazilian context, as well as in other areas where there are clear class divisions and tensions. The major difference lies in how to design and implement programs that meet the different needs of each context. I would find it easier to answer your question within the Brazilian context. At any rate, theoretically your question necessarily takes us to the important issue of whether it is possible to develop a critical literacy program within the institutional space, which contradicts and neutralizes the fundamental task required by the dominant power of the schools. That is, we need to discuss the reproduction of the dominant ideology, an important issue that has been clearly and amply discussed by Henry Giroux and other North American educators, as well. Theories of reproduction tend to fall into a type of mechanical exaggeration in which they interpret the real and concrete fact that the educational system reproduces dominant ideology. Within the educational system there is another task to be executed by conscious educators, independent of the wishes of the dominant class. The educational task, from the perspective of the dominant class, is to reproduce its ideology. But the educational task that contradicts the reproductionist process cannot be carried out by anyone who opts for the status quo. This task has to be carried out by the educator, who in fact refuses to maintain the inequality inherent within the status quo. The progressive educator rejects the dominant values imposed on the school because he or she has a different dream, because he or she wants to transform the status quo. Naturally, transforming the status quo is much more difficult to do than maintaining it.

The question that you raised has to do exactly with this theory. As I have said, the educational space reproduces the dominant ideology. However, it is possible within educational institutions to contradict imposed dominant values. The reproduction of the dominant ideology necessarily implies an opaque reality. The unveiling of reality falls within the space for possible change in which progressive and politically clear educators must operate. I believe that this space for change, however small, is always available. In the United States, where society is much more complex than in Brazil, the task of emphasizing reality is more difficult. In this process it is necessary for educators to assume a political posture that renounces the myth of pedagogical neutrality. These educators cannot reduce themselves to being pure education specialists. They cannot be educators who are concerned with only the technical dimensions of bilingualism, for example, without a thorough understanding of the political and ideological implications of bilingualism and multiculturalism in the United States. Educators must become conscious individuals who live part of their dreams within their educational space. Educators cannot work successfully by themselves; they have to work collaboratively in order to succeed in integrating the cultural elements produced by the subordinate students in their educational process. Finally, these educators have to invent and create methods in which they maximize the limited space for possible change that is available to them. They need to use their students' cultural universe as a point of departure, enabling students to recognize themselves as possessing a specific and important cultural identity. The successful usage of the students' cultural universe requires respect and legitimation of students' discourses, that is, their own linguistic codes, which are different but never inferior. Educators also have to respect and understand students' dreams and expectations. In the case of black Americans, for example, educators must respect black English. It is possible to codify and de-codify black English with the same ease as standard American English. The difference is that black Americans will find it infinitely easier to codify and de-codify the dialect of their own authorship. The legitimization of black English as an educational tool does not, however, preclude the need to acquire proficiency in the linguistic code of the dominant group.

MACEDO:
Beyond the linguistic code issue, educators must understand the ways in which different dialects encode different world views. The semantic value of specific lexical items belonging to black English differs radically, in some cases, from the reading derived from the standard, dominant dialect. The first important issue is that black Americans' linguistic code not only reflects their reality, but also their lived experience in a given historical moment. Terms that encapsulate the drug culture, daily alienation, the struggle to survive the substandard and inhumane conditions of ghettos: these constitute a discourse black Americans find no difficulty in using. It is from this raw and sometimes cruel reality that black students can begin to unveil the obfuscation that characterizes their daily existence inside and outside the schools. Their language is, therefore, a powerful tool demystifying the distorted reality prepackaged for them by the dominant curriculum. Language should never be understood as a mere tool of communication. Language is packed with ideology, and for this reason it has to be given prominence in any radical pedagogy that proposes to provide space for students' emancipation.

FREIRE:

It is by the use of all dimensions of students' language, taste, and so forth that you and the students are able to arrive at the programmatic contents that attend to the immediate interests of those in power. You don't tell those in a dependent and oppressed position that, for example, they have no say in the substance of scientific study because this type of curricular requirement interests only students of the dominant class. Subordinate students also need the skills gained through studying the dominant curriculum. However, these skills should never be imposed at the sacrifice of a thorough understanding of reality, which enables students to develop a positive self-image before grappling with the type of knowledge that is outside their immediate world.

It is only after they have a firm grasp on their world that they can begin to acquire other knowledge. To acquire the selected knowledge contained in the dominant curriculum should be a goal attained by subordinate students in the process of self and group empowerment. They can use the dominant knowledge effectively in their struggle to change the material and historical conditions that have enslaved them. But they must never allow the knowledge that benefits the dominant class to domesticate themselves or, as in some cases, to turn them into little oppressors. The dominant curriculum must gradually become dominated by the dependent students so as to help them in their struggle for social equity and justice.

This vision is political and not merely epistemological. That is, in the case of black Americans, they need to master fully standard English in order to fight effectively for their preservation and their full participation in society. But that does not mean that standard American English is more beautiful or superior to Black English. The notion of linguistic superiority is artificially imposed.

MACEDO:

Then standard English can be viewed as a weapon against the oppressive forces that use this dominant dialect as a way to maintain the present social order. We should also point out that critical mastery of the standard dialect can never be achieved fully without the development of one's voice, which is contained within the social dialect that shapes one's reality.

FREIRE:

Exactly. This is what I mean by the necessary political and ideological dimensions in any pedagogy that proposes to be critical. The question of methods is directly linked to the creative and inventive capacity of political educators. Creativity obviously requires risk taking. The educational tasks that we have discussed so far can be carried out through a thorough understanding of the political and ideological nature of educators, and through a willingness to be creative and to take the risks that will allow this creativity to flourish. In highly modernized societies like that of the United States, I have noticed that people carry with them a long capitalistic historical experience that sustains a general theme of human existence always evolving from fear: the fear, for instance, of not getting tenure, the fear that conditions educators to be well behaved for many years so they can get tenure. If they are refused tenure, they become preoccupied only with trying to understand what possible misconduct led to the tenure denial. If they are granted tenure, of course, there is no reason to change the behavior for which they were bestowed the gift of tenure.

MACEDO:

There is a large body of literature in sociolinguistics on the interrelationship of language and society, analyses of the role language plays in promoting and maintaining sex differentiation, analyses of language and ethnicity, and so on. How can these language variations be used as an antagonistic force to challenge the privileged position of the so-called standard language?

FREIRE:

At a particular moment in the struggle for self-affirmation, when subordinated to and exploited by the ruling class, no social group or class or even an entire nation or people can undertake the struggle for liberation without the use of a language. At no time can there be a struggle for liberation and self-affirmation without the formation of an identity, and identity of the individual, the group, the social class, or whatever. And to the extent that conflicts increase, experience has taught us that individuals, groups, and social classes end up building walls behind which, in times of struggle or peace, they embrace their identity and protect it. Without a sense of identity, there is no need for struggle. I will only fight you if I am very sure of myself. I am definitely not you. The reasoning process is similar for groups, even at a subconscious level. In this subconscious process, which the very nature of conflict involves, we do not even recognize the significance of our elaborating a particular language while we are consciously defending ourselves in the struggle for liberation.

This is why colonized people need to preserve their native language. And the more sophisticated they make their language, the better it will be that the colonizer not understand it, and in this way they can use their language to defend themselves against the colonizer. By way of example, I am in total sympathy with women's fantastic struggle, even though I cannot fight their battle. Although I am a man, I can feel like a woman, and I am not afraid to say this. But women's liberation is their struggle. They need to elaborate their own female language. They have to celebrate the feminine characteristics of their language, which they were socialized to despise and view as weak and indecisive. In the process of their struggle, they have to use their own language, not man's language. I believe these language variations—female language, ethnic language, dialects—are intimately interconnected with, coincide with, and express identity. They help defend one's sense of identity and they are absolutely necessary in the process of struggling for liberation.

MACEDO:
How would you characterize the interrelationships of language, culture, and thought?

FREIRE:
There may be times when these interrelationships do not exist. There is a certain relationship between thought and language as an expression of the actual process of thinking and the concreteness of the reality of the one who speaks, who thinks and speaks, and who speaks and thinks. We could even invent a new verb: "to speak-think" or "to think-speak."

In a certain context of temporal space this cultural being creates itself along with other beings, similar to the way I make myself relative to that which is not me, the very world that is not me. My language and thinking, I believe, are a dialectical unity. They are deeply rooted in a context. So if there is a change of context, it will not be enough to mechanically propagate a distinct form of thinking-speaking; it will have to come about by necessity. I think one of the tasks of critical education and radical pedagogy is to help the critical thinking-speaking process to re-create itself in the re-creation of its context. Instead of assuming that this re-creation takes place at only a mechanical level, this never happens, pedagogy should assume the role of helping to reformulate this thinking.

Take Cape Verde, for example. Cape Verde has been changing radically in the past six years or so because there is no context-object anymore, as there once most definitely was in relation to the context-subject, Portugal. Cape Verde has cut the false umbilical cord. Portugal used to think that there was an umbilical cord, but there never was. For there to be a real umbilical cord there had to be an existential-historical connection, and in the case of Cape Verde there was none.

The connection was forced upon Cape Verdeans by the Portuguese. But, fortunately, the people have cut the cord. What happens after the cut? Cape Verde begins to crawl in its infant experience of being itself. Cape Verde tries to find itself. What was thought-language before independence cannot stay the same; it would be too much out of sync. But you cannot artificially change the context to any great degree, either. That is why I admire Cape Verde's president, Aristides Pereira. He gave a speech in Praia in which he made an extraordinary statement that has a lot to do with our conversation now: "We made our liberation and we drove out the colonizers. Now we need to de-colonize our minds." That is it exactly. We need to de-colonize the mind because if we do not, our thinking will be in conflict with the new context evolving from the struggle for freedom.

This new historical context, which is intertwined with culture, can only be new to the degree that it no longer is colonized. Cape Verde has a different mentality and a different culture reemerging. The repressed native culture is beginning to reemerge. Certain cultural behavior patterns that were forbidden by the colonizers, including language, expressions of the world, poetry, and music, are reappearing. People walk without having to bow any longer. They now walk upright, looking up. There is a pedagogy of walking in this new behavior, walking freely. All of these issues constitute a new way of thinking and a new way of speaking. Now you can see the tremendous problem there would be if this new thinking were not to coincide with the existing language. A new thinking expressed in the colonizer's language goes nowhere.

The issue of language, particularly in the multicultural debate in the United States, is often relegated to a secondary status. In fact, some multiculturalists, without saying so, assume that multicultural education can be effectively implemented through English only. Such an assumption neglects to appreciate how English, as a dominant language, even in a multicultural classroom, may continue to provide non-English speakers with the experience of subordination. In other words, one cannot celebrate different cultural values through the very dominant language that devalues, in many ways, the cultural experience of different cultural groups. Multiculturalists need to understand that language is the only means through which one comes to consciousness. The next chapter is an analysis of the politics of language and its role in education.

4 English Only: The Tongue-Tying of America

Monolingualism is a curable disease.
—Bumper Sticker

DURING THE PAST DECADE conservative educators such as the former secretary of education, William Bennett, and Diane Ravitch, among others, have mounted an unrelenting attack on bilingual and multicultural education. These conservative educators tend to recycle old assumptions about the "melting pot theory" and our so-called common culture, assumptions designed primarily to maintain the status quo. That status quo functions as a cultural reproduction mechanism that systematically does not allow other cultural subjects, who are considered outside of the mainstream, to be present in history. The cultural subjects who are profiled as the "other" are but palely represented in history within our purported democratic society in the form of Black History Month, Puerto Rican Day, and so forth. This historical constriction was elegantly captured by an eleventh-grade Vietnamese student in California: "I was so excited when my history teacher talked about the Vietnam War. Now at last, I thought, now we will study about my country. We didn't really study it. Just for one day, though, my country was real again."[1]

The incessant attack on bilingual education, which is based on the claim that bilingual education tongue-ties students in their native language, not only points to a xenophobic culture that blindly negates the multilingual and multicultural nature of U.S. society but also falsifies the empirical evidence in support of bilingual education, which has been amply documented. An example of a truly tongue-tied America materialized when the former foreign minister of the Soviet Union, Eduard Shevardnadze, began to deliver a speech in Russian during a recent commencement ceremony at Boston University. The silence that ensued was so overwhelming that one could hear a pin drop. Over 99 percent of the audience was saved from their monolingualism thanks to the intervention of an interpreter. In fact, the present overdose of monolingualism and Anglocentrism that dominates the current educational debate not only contributes to a type of mind-tied America, but also prevents the development of educators and leaders who can rethink what it means to prepare students to enter the ever-changing, multilingual, and multicultural world of the twenty-first century.

Simply pointing to some failures of bilingual education without examining the lack of success of linguistic-minority students within the larger context of the general failure of public education in major urban centers is both academically dishonest and misleading. Furthermore, the English Only Movement's position points to a pedagogy of exclusion that views the learning of English as education itself. What they fail to question is under what conditions will English be taught and by whom. For example, insisting on immersing non-English-speaking students in English as a Second Language Programs taught by untrained music, art, and social science teachers (as is the case in Massachusetts with the grandfather clause in English as a Second Language [ESL] certification) will do very little to accomplish the very goal of the English Only Movement. In addition, the proponents of "English only" also fail to raise two fundamental questions: First, if English is the most effective educational language, how can we explain over 60 million Americans being illiterate or functionally illiterate?[2] Second, if education in "English only" can guarantee linguistic minorities a better future, as educators like William Bennett promise, why do the majority of Black Americans, whose ancestors have been speaking English for over two hundred years, find themselves still relegated to ghettos?

I want to argue in this chapter that the answer to those fundamental questions has nothing to do with whether English is a more viable language of instruction or whether it promises non-English-speaking students "full participation first in their school and later in American society."[3] This position would point to an assumption that English is in fact a superior language and that we live in a classless, race-blind society. I want to propose that the attempt to institute proper and more effective methods of educating non-English-speaking students cannot be reduced to issues of language but rests on a full understanding of the ideological elements that generate and sustain linguistic, racial, and sex discrimination. That is, educators need to develop, as Henry Giroux has suggested, "a politics and pedagogy around a new language capable of acknowledging the multiple, contradictory, and complex subject positions people occupy within different social, cultural, and economic locations."[4]

By shifting the linguistic issue to an ideological terrain we will challenge conservative educators to confront the Berlin Wall of racism, classism, and economic deprivation that characterizes the lived experiences of minorities in U.S. public schools. For example, Anthony Lukas succinctly captured the ideological elements that promote racism and segregation in schools in his analysis of school desegregation in the Boston public schools. Lukas cited a trip to Charlestown High School, where a group of Black parents experienced firsthand the stark reality their children were destined to endure. Although the headmaster assured them that "violence, intimidation, or racial slurs would not be tolerated," they could not avoid the racial epithets on the walls: "Welcome Niggers," "Niggers Suck," "White Power," "KKK," "Bus is for Zulu," and "Be illiterate, fight busing." As those parents were boarding the bus, "they were met with jeers and catcalls 'go home niggers. Keep going all the way to Africa!'" This racial intolerance led one parent to reflect, "My god, what kind of hell am I sending my children into?" What could her children learn at a school like that, except to hate?[5] Even though forced integration of schools in Boston exacerbated the racial tensions in the Boston public schools, one should not overlook the deep-seated racism that permeates all levels of the school structure. According to Lukas:

> Even after Elvira "Pixie" Paladino's election to Boston School Committee she was heard muttering about "jungle bunnies" and "pickaninnies." And John "Bigga" Kerrigan, [also elected to the School Committee] prided himself on the unrestrained invective ("I may be a prick, but at least I'm a consistent prick"), particularly directed at Blacks ("savages") and the liberal media ("mother-fucking maggots") and Lem Tucker, a Black correspondent for ABC News, whom Kerrigan described as "one generation away from swinging in the trees," a remark he illustrated by assuming his hands upwards, and scratching his armpits.[6]

Considering this landscape of violent racism perpetrated against racial and also linguistic minorities, one can understand the reasons for the high dropout rate in the Boston public schools (approximately 50 percent). Perhaps racism and other ideological elements are part of a school reality that forces a high percentage of students to leave school, only later to be profiled by the very system as dropouts or "poor and unmotivated students." One could argue that the above incidents occurred during a tumultuous time of racial division in Boston's history, but I do not believe that we have learned a great deal from historically dangerous memories. Our leaders continue to invite racial tensions and divisiveness, as evidenced in the Willie Horton presidential campaign issue and the alleged quota for jobs.

It is very curious that this newfound concern of "English only" advocates for limited-English-proficiency students does not question those very ideological elements that psychologically and emotionally harm these students far more than the mere fact that English may present itself as a temporary barrier to an effective education. It would be more socially constructive and beneficial if the zeal that propels the U.S. English movement to spread the "English only" gospel were diverted toward the struggle to end violent racism, to alleviate the causes of poverty, homelessness, and family breakdown, among other social ills that characterize the lived experiences of minorities in the United States. If these social issues are not dealt with appropriately, it is naïve to think that the acquisition of the English language alone will, somehow, magically eclipse the raw and cruel injustices and oppression perpetrated against the dispossessed class of minorities in the United States. According to Peter McLaren, these dispossessed minority students who "populate urban settings in places such as Howard Beach, Ozone Park, El Barrio, are more likely to be forced to learn about Eastern Europe in ways set forth by neo-conservative multiculturalists than they are to learn about the Harlem Renaissance, Mexico, Africa, the Caribbean, or Aztec or Zulu culture."[7]

While arguing for the use of the students' native language in their educational development, I would like to make it very clear that the bilingual education goal should never be to restrict students to their own vernacular. This linguistic constriction inevitably leads to a linguistic ghetto. Educators must understand fully the broader meaning of the use of students' language as a requisite for their empowerment. That is, empowerment should never be limited to what Stanley Aronowitz described as "the process of appreciating and loving oneself."[8] In addition to this process, empowerment should also be a means that enables students "to interrogate and selectively appropriate those aspects of the dominant culture that will provide them with the basis for defining and transforming, rather than merely serving, the wider social order."[9] This means that educators should understand the value of mastering the standard English language of the wider society. It is through the full appropriation of the standard English language that linguistic-minority students find themselves linguistically empowered to engage in dialogue with various sectors of the wider society. What I must reiterate is that educators should never allow the limited-proficiency students' native language to be silenced by a distorted legitimation of the standard English language. Linguistic-minority students' language should never be sacrificed, since it is the only means through which they make sense of their own experience in the world.

However, given the importance of the standard English language in the education of linguistic-minority students, I must endorse the use of Antonio Gramsci's words in the brochure of the Institute for Research in English Acquisition and Development: "Without the mastery of the common standard version of the national language, one is inevitably destined to function only at the periphery of national life and, especially, outside the national and political mainstream."[10]

What these "English only" advocates fail to do is tell the other side of Antonio Gramsci's argument, which warns us: "Each time that in one way or another, the question of language comes to the fore, that signifies that a series of other problems is about to emerge, the formation and enlarging of the ruling class, the necessity to establish more 'intimate' and sure relations between the ruling groups and the popular masses, that is, the reorganization of cultural hegemony."[11]

This quoting of Gramsci's position on language out of context points to the hidden curriculum of the English Only Movement, which is designed to promote a monolithic ideology. It is also part of the present attempt toward the "reorganization of cultural hegemony," as evidenced by the unrelenting attack by conservative educators on multicultural education and curriculum diversity. The ideological force behind the call for a common culture can be measured by the words of syndicated columnist Pat Buchanan, who urged his fellow conservatives to wage a cultural revolution in the 1990s against the perceived excesses of the 1960s. In other words, as Henry Giroux has shown, the conservative cultural revolution's

> more specific expressions have been manifest on a number of cultural fronts including schools, the art world, and the more blatant attacks aimed at rolling back the benefits constructed of civil rights and social welfare reforms constructed over the last three decades. What is being valorized in the dominant language of the culture industry is an undemocratic approach to social authority and a politically regressive move to reconstruct American life within the script of Eurocentrism, racism, and patriarchy.[12]

Derrick Z. Jackson, in his brilliant article, "The End of the Second Reconstruction," bared the dominant conservative ideology that informs the present cultural hegemony when he argued that "from 1884 to 1914, more than 3,600 African-Americans were lynched. Lynching is passé today. AIDS, infant mortality, violence out of despair, and gutted public education do the same trick in inner cities neatly redlined by banks."[13] In contrast to the zeal for a common culture and "English only," these conservative educators have remained ominously silent about forms of racism, inequality, subjugation, and exploitation that daily commit symbolic and real violence against those children who by virtue of their language, race, ethnicity, class, or gender are not treated in schools with the dignity and respect all children warrant in a democracy. Instead of reconstituting education around an urban and cultural studies approach, which assumes that the social, cultural, political, and economic divisions of education and everyday life are the primary categories for understanding contemporary schooling, conservative educators have recoiled in an attempt to salvage the status quo. That is, they try to keep the present unchanged even though, as Renato Constantino pointed out: "Within the living present there are imperceptible changes which make the status quo a moving reality. ... Thus a new policy based on the present as past and not on the present as future is backward, for it is premised not on evolving conditions but on conditions that are already dying away."[14]

One such not so imperceptible change is the rapid growth of minority representation in the labor force. Therefore, the conservative leaders and educators are digging this country's economic grave by their continued failure to educate minorities. As Ferleger and Mandle convincingly argued, "Unless the educational attainment of minority populations in the United States improves, the country's hopes for resuming high rates of growth and an increasing standard of living look increasingly dubious."[15]

In addition to the real threat to the economic fabric of the United States, the persistent call for English-language only in education smacks of backwardness in our ever-changing multicultural and multilingual society. Furthermore, these conservative educators base their language-policy argument on the premise that English education in this country is highly effective. On the contrary. As Patrick Courts clearly argued in his book *Literacy and Empowerment,* English education, in general, is failing even middle-class and upper-class students. He argued that English reading and writing classes are mostly based on workbooks and grammar lessons, lessons that force student to "bark at print" or fill in the blanks. Student in such classes are too busy reading in order to learn to read. They are also too busy writing to write by engaging grudgingly in banal exercises such as practicing correct punctuation and writing business letters. Books in their classes are, Courts pointed out, too often secondary to commercially prepared ditto sheets and workbooks.[16] Courts's account suggests that in most school programs, the nature of the language experiences that the majority of students had before they reached school are not taken advantage of. These teachers become the victims of their own professional ideology when they delegitimize the language experiences that students bring with them into the classroom.

Courts's study is basically aimed at the teaching of middle-class or upper-middle-class students, those unburdened by racial discrimination and poverty, students who have done well in elementary and high school settings and are now populating the university lecture halls and seminar rooms. If schools are failing these students, the situation by implication does not bode well for those students less economically, socially, and politically advantaged. It is toward the linguistic-minority students that I would like to turn my discussion now.

The Role of Language in the Education of Linguistic-Minority Students

Within the past two decades, the issue of bilingual education has taken on a heated importance among educators. Unfortunately, the debate that has emerged tends to recycle old assumptions and values regarding the meaning and usefulness of students' native language in education. The notion that education of linguistic-minority students is a matter of learning the standard English language still informs the vast majority of bilingual programs and manifests its logic in the renewed emphasis on technical reading and writing skills.

I want to reiterate here that the education of linguistic-minority students cannot be viewed as simply the development of skills aimed at acquiring the standard English language. In other words, "English only" proponents seldom discuss the pedagogical structures that will enable these students to access other bodies of knowledge. In addition, these same proponents never question the quality of ESL instruction provided to the linguistic-minority students and the adverse material conditions under which these students learn English. The view of the teaching of English as education sustains a notion of ideology that systematically negates rather than makes meaningful the cultural experiences of the members of the subordinate linguistic groups who are, by and large, the objects of its policies. For the notion of education of linguistic-minority students to become meaningful, it has to be situated within a theory of cultural production and viewed as an integral part of the way in which people produce, transform, and reproduce meaning. Bilingual education, in this sense, must be seen as a medium that constitutes and affirms the historical and existential moments of lived culture. Hence, it is an eminently political phenomenon, and it must be analyzed within the context of a theory of power relations and an understanding of social and cultural reproduction and production. It is only through a cultural production model that we can achieve a truly democratic and liberatory educational experience. I will return to this issue later.

Although the various debates in the past two decades may differ in their basic assumptions about the education of linguistic-minority students, they all share one feature: They ignore the role of language as a major force in the construction of human subjectivities. That is, they ignore the way language may either confirm or deny the life histories and experiences of the people who use it.

The pedagogical and political implications in education programs for linguistic-minority students are far-reaching and yet largely ignored. These programs, for example, often contradict a fundamental principle of reading, namely, that students learn to read faster and with better comprehension when taught in their native tongue. The immediate recognition of familiar words and experiences enhances the development of a positive self-concept in children who are somewhat insecure about the status of their language and culture. For this reason, and to be consistent with the plan to construct a democratic society free from vestiges of oppression, a minority-literacy program should be rooted in the cultural capital of subordinate groups and have as its point of departure their own language.

Educators must develop radical pedagogical structures that provide students with the opportunity to use their own reality as a basis of literacy. This includes, obviously, the language they bring to the classroom. To do otherwise is to deny minority students the rights that lie at the core of the notion of a democratic education. The failure to base a literacy program on the minority students' language means that oppositional forces can neutralize the efforts of educators and political leaders to achieve decolonization of schooling. It is of tantamount importance that the incorporation of the minority language as the primary language of instruction in education of linguistic-minority students be given top priority. It is through their own language that linguistic-minority students will be able to reconstruct their history and their culture.

I want to argue that the minority language has to be understood within the theoretical framework that generates it. Put another way, the ultimate meaning and value of the minority language is not to be found by determining how systematic and rule governed it is. We know that already. Its real meaning has to be understood through the assumptions that govern it, and it has to be understood via the social, political, and ideological relations to which it points. Generally speaking, this issue of effectiveness and validity often hides the true role of language in the maintenance of the values and interests of the dominant class. In other words, the issue of effectiveness and validity becomes a mask that obfuscates questions about the social, political, and ideological order within which the minority language exists.

If an emancipatory and critical education program is to be developed in the United States for linguistic-minority students in which they become "subjects" rather than "objects," educators must understand the productive quality of language. James Donald put it this way:

> I take language to be productive rather than reflective of social reality. This means calling into question the assumption that we, as speaking subjects, simply use language to organize and express our ideas and experiences. On the contrary, language is one of the most important social practices

through which we come to experience ourselves as subjects. ... My point here is that once we get beyond the idea of language as no more than a medium of communication, as a tool equally and neutrally available to all parties in cultural exchanges, then we can begin to examine language both as a practice of signification and also as a site for culture struggle and as a mechanism which produces antagonistic relations between different social groups.[17]

It is to the antagonistic relationship between the minority-language and dominant-language speakers that I want to turn now. The antagonistic nature of the minority language has never been fully explored. In order to more clearly discuss this issue of antagonism, I will use Donald's distinction between oppressed language and repressed language. According to those categories, the "negative" way of posing the minority-language question is to view it in terms of oppression—that is, seeing the minority language as "lacking" the dominant standard features that usually serve as a point of reference for the minority language. By far the most common questions concerning the minority languages in the United States are posed from the oppression perspective. The alternative view of the minority language is that it is repressed in the standard dominant language. In this view, minority language as a repressed language could, if spoken, challenge the privileged standard linguistic dominance. Educators have failed to recognize the "positive" promise and antagonistic nature of the minority language. It is precisely on these dimensions that educators must demystify the standard dominant language and the old assumptions about its inherent superiority. Educators must develop liberatory and critical bilingual programs informed by a radical pedagogy so that the minority language will cease to provide its speakers the experience of subordination and, moreover, may be brandished as a weapon of resistance to the dominance of the dominant standard language of the curriculum.

In this sense, the students' language is the only means by which they can develop their own voice, a prerequisite to the development of a positive sense of self-worth. As Giroux elegantly stated, the students' voice "is the discursive means to make themselves 'heard' and to define themselves as active authors of their worlds."[18] The authorship of one's own world also implies the use of one's own language, and relates to what Mikhail Bakhtin described as "retelling a story in one's own words."[19]

A Democratic and Liberatory Education for Linguistic-Minority Students

In maintaining a certain coherence with the educational plan to reconstruct new and more-democratic educational programs for linguistic-minority students, educators and political leaders need to create a new school grounded in a new educational praxis, expressing different concepts of education consonant with the principles of a democratic, multicultural, and multilingual society. In order for this to happen, the first step is to identify the objectives of the inherently colonial education that informs the majority of bilingual programs in the United States. Next, it is necessary to analyze how colonialist methods used by the dominant schools function, legitimize the Anglocentric values and meaning and, at the same time, negate the history, culture, and language practices of the majority of linguistic-minority students. The new school, so it is argued, must also be informed by a radical bilingual pedagogy, which would make concrete such values as solidarity, social responsibility, and creativity. These values would serve the common democratic development of bilingual programs rooted in a liberatory ideology, where linguistic-minority students become "subjects" rather than mere "objects" to be assimilated blindly into an often hostile dominant "common" culture. A democratic and liberatory education needs to move away from traditional approaches, which emphasize the acquisition of mechanical basic skills while divorcing education from its ideological and historical contexts. In attempting to meet this goal, such an education must purposely reject the conservative principles embedded in the English Only Movement. Unfortunately, many bilingual programs unknowingly reproduce one common feature of the traditional approaches to education: They ignore the important relationship between language and the cultural capital of the students for whom bilingual education was developed. The result is bilingual programs whose basic assumptions are at odds with the democratic spirit that launched them.

Bilingual-program development must be largely based on the notion of a democratic and liberatory education, in which education is viewed "as one of the major vehicles by which 'oppressed' people are able to participate in the socio-historical transformation of their society."[20] Bilingual education, in this sense, is grounded in a critical reflection of the cultural capital of the oppressed. It becomes a vehicle by which linguistic-minority students are equipped with the necessary tools to reappropriate their history, culture, and language practices. It is, thus, a way to enable the linguistic-minority students to reclaim "those historical and existential experiences that are devalued in everyday life by the dominant culture in order to be both validated and critically understood."[21] To do otherwise is to deny these students their very democratic rights. In fact, the criticism that bilingual and multicultural education unwisely questions the traditions and values of our "common culture," as suggested by Kenneth T. Jackson, is both antidemocratic and academically dishonest.[22] Multicultural education and curriculum diversity did not create the S&L scandal, the Iran-Contra debacle, or the extortion of minority properties by banks, the stewards of the "common culture," who charged minorities exorbitant loan-sharking interest rates. Multicultural education and curriculum diversity did not force Joachim Maitre, the dean of public communication at Boston University, to choose the hypocritical moral high ground to excoriate the popular culture's "bleak moral content," all the while plagiarizing fifteen paragraphs of a conservative colleague's text.

The learning of English-language skills alone will not enable linguistic-minority students to acquire the critical tools "to awaken and liberate them from their mystified and distorted views of themselves and their world."[23] For example, speaking English has not enabled African-Americans to change this society's practice of jailing more Blacks than even South Africa, and this society spending over $7 billion to keep African-Americans in jail while spending only $1 billion educating them.[24]

Educators must understand the all-encompassing role that the dominant ideology has played in this mystification and distortion process of our "common culture" and our "common language." They must also recognize the antagonistic relationship between the "common culture" and those who, by virtue of their race, language, ethnicity, and gender, have been relegated to the margins. Finally, educators must develop bilingual programs based on the theory of cultural production. In other words, linguistic-minority students must be provided the opportunity to become actors in the reconstruction process of a more democratic and just society. In short, education conducted in "English only" is alienating to linguistic-minority students, since it denies them the fundamental tools for reflection, critical thinking, and social interaction. Without the cultivation of their native language, and robbed of the opportunity for reflection and critical thinking, linguistic-minority students find themselves unable to re-create their culture and history. Without the reappropriation of their culture, the valorization of their lived experiences, the vacuous promise made to students by "English only" supporters that the English language will guarantee them "full participation first in their school and later in American society"[25] can hardly be a reality.

5 *Educational Reform: Literacy and Poverty Pimps*

You just don't understand. We just want these Black kids to learn how to learn.

—Member of an Educational Reform Committee

EDUCATIONALLY, THE DECADE of the 1980s can be best characterized by an overdose of educational reform pollution controlled mostly by a conservative discourse that celebrates a language of management, competition, testing, choice, and free enterprise. What conservative educators fail to recognize is that management and free enterprise do not necessarily translate into human freedom. In fact, how can we honestly speak of human freedom in a society that produces and yet ignores the existence of ghettos, reservations, human misery, despair of poverty, hopelessness, and "savage inequalities"?[1] By ignoring these oppressive conditions, the purveyors of the present conservative educational reform discourse obviate the need to call for the creation of pedagogical spaces where issues of oppression are debated. Such a debate would enable educators to understand the intimate interrelationship between society's discriminatory practices and the "savage inequalities" in schools. Part of the reason that most educators have remained complacent before social inequalities lies in the fact that we have been subjected to a pedagogy of big lies that not only distorts and falsifies realities but also gives us "the illusion of individual freedom, ownership of our own thoughts and decisions."[2] A pedagogy of lies creates a "reality" within which we accommodate to living "within a big lie" that tranquilizes us if we adhere to the web of lies but makes us feel guilty and uncomfortable should we attempt to live in truth.[3] Thus, for example, during the Gulf War to not wear the yellow ribbon constituted an unpatriotic act.

Like signs, words have ideological power. This is why the conservative educational debate celebrates a particular discourse while discrediting other forms of language. According to Olivier Reboul, discourses are very often anchored in "shock words, terms or expressions produced by themselves, [which,] due to their strong connotations, provoke a reaction no matter what sentence within which they are inserted."[4] In other words, these terms, expressions, and words have a positive association, almost independent of their meanings. For example, in the present educational reform debate, the word "choice" provokes a positive effect that forces us to leave its meaning in different contexts unexamined. Who would be opposed to the freedom to choose a particular school? Almost everyone would support the right to choose. However, the subtext of "choice" is that although choice is theoretically possible, not all of us have the same privileged position from which we can exercise our right to choose. That is to say, middle- and upper-class White families have the means to support their choice of schools such as their ability to provide alternative transportation, their history of participation in their children's educational process, and other privileges accorded to them solely by virtue of their race and class position. An African-American family may enjoy the same class privileges but the race factor makes the matter of choice immensely more troublesome to the extent that because of the structure of racism, the probable host schools may not roll out the welcome carpet to their children. For poor non-White families, the educational choice concept is enormously problematic. Because they do not possess the cultural capital that would enable them to support their choice, they will often remain without choice, abandoned in inner-city schools with few resources and decrepit buildings.

The power of ideology is so insidious that the unanalyzed positive association of shock words such as "choice" is often accepted by the very people who are in a position to be adversely affected by such choice. Thus, many poor people, including poor people of color, are led away by the "illusion" that the shock word "choice" creates. Unfortunately, the very ideology that anchors its discourse on positive-effect shock words also prevents us from having access to the subtext that often contains the opposite meaning of the illusory "reality" created by "shock words." It is for this very reason that conservative educational reformers who promote "choice" as a panacea will not tolerate a counterdiscourse that points to the false assumption inherent in the educational choice proposal. For the right to choose to be equally exercised, we all would have to live in a classless, race-blind, and ethnic-blind society. Since we know that this is not the case, the only way we can rationalize our support for educational choice is to stay at the level of the positive effect of the shock word that often obfuscates the true reality.

Shock words, terms, and expressions do not only produce positive effects. According to Olivier Reboul, "shock words" can also "produce by themselves negative effects that disqualify those who use these shock words."[5] Thus, the use of words such as "oppression," "radical," and "activist" often provokes a negative effect that prevents a thorough analysis of the reality encoded by these terms. In other words, if "oppression" is not allowed as part of the debate, there will be no need to identify its perpetrator "oppressor." In the same vein, the dominant discourse uses the presence of these "taboo words" to dismiss the counterdiscourse that challenges the falsification of reality. The dominant discourse so acts in order to prevent the understanding of the mechanisms used as obstacles to the development of spaces for dialectical relationships. I am reminded of the former dean of the College of Arts and Sciences at my university who, when pressured by the central administration to get the college more involved in education and teacher preparation, asked my chair in the English Department to appoint a liaison with the Graduate School of Education. However, he cautioned her to avoid nominating someone who was radical. Thus, "radicalism" is a shock word that triggers a negative effect and all those involved in work that is a priori considered by the dominant discourse as radical are dismissed as political and therefore not scientific and are prevented from taking part in the discussion, particularly if the overall agenda is to maintain the status quo. In a like manner, denouncing racism with strong conviction is often considered radicalism. A moderate position is to acknowledge that racism exists but not to advocate doing anything about it, which would change the very structures that produce racism.

The term "reform" in conjunction with education produces a positive effect to the extent that, without threatening the core values of the system or the people who run it, the term announces change in a system that has been determined to be not working effectively. In this sense, reform produces a positive effect in that it tranquilizes people who consciously recognize that some cosmetic changes must occur while they adhere to those same values and mechanisms that created the need for reform in the first place. In contrast, the term "transformation" is a taboo word in that it produces a negative effect by announcing a total and radical change of a system that has been identified as not working. In the political sphere, politicians use taboo words as an effective means to control the population and dismiss any challenge presented by a counterdiscourse. For example, Michael Dukakis's challenge to Republican conservatism was totally neutralized by George Bush when he associated Dukakis with liberalism. No debate about the possible promise and values of liberalism was necessary or allowed. All Bush had to do was to call Dukakis a liberal and the little movie in people's heads filled in the proper ideological context, which did the rest. Other taboo shock words such as "socialism," "communism," and "Marxism" have the same effect and are often successfully used for ideological control.

In this chapter, I will analyze how different and contradictory ideologies are played out in the present educational reform movement. I will argue that the ambiguity in the reform movement is directly linked to the reform objective itself. In other words, the reform is being carried out by those players who have been and are part of the problem they are trying to solve. That is, given the complexity of our rapidly changing multicultural society, reform represents only a cosmetic change, leaving the inherent ideology that informs education unproblematic and unchanged. In reality, what we really need is not reform; what we need is transformation. Only through a true transformation can we incorporate into the educational debate

> issues that point to a new vision, a new language, one that combines critique and possibility with a spirit of struggle. In essence, we need to rethink what it means to educate people capable of a new vision, people who can rewrite the narrative of educational leadership by developing a public philosophy capable of animating a democratic public culture, one which prepares students to enter the ever-changing, multicultural world of the 21st century.[6]

However, transformation requires not only a thorough analysis of the structure of schooling and the ideology that informs it, but it also necessitates a critical understanding of the interdependence between schooling and the sociocultural and political reality of the society within which schools exist. This is not an easy task in the United States, particularly because of the myth that schools are very much independent of society and dislodged from the political reality that shaped them historically. By and large, schools in the United States have not been viewed as having an organic relationship with the community at large. As Peter Negroni, the superintendent of the Holyoke Public Schools in Massachusetts argued: "Americans have not made the connection between an effective quality of life in the community and the quality of public schooling in the community. The complete and total interdependence of community, schooling and democracy must be recognized by America as part of reform efforts."[7]

Unfortunately, absent from the present school reform debate is the language of democracy that points to the organic interrelationship between schooling and the community. Also missing from the present school debate is the necessary ideological shift that would prevent educators from accommodating to the deficit-orientation model and that would make them able to embrace a pedagogy of hope, one in which they can believe that all students can learn. The deficit theoretical model is so pervasive that even well-meaning educators, who would not openly or perhaps subconsciously adhere to it, are nonetheless betrayed by their discourse and practice. For instance, in a committee meeting to reform undergraduate teacher-training education at an urban university, a fellow committee member became a little annoyed at my insistence that the committee address forthrightly issues of inequality, race, gender, and ethnicity. When I kept reiterating the need for community input and the need to understand the material conditions of the community where African-American and other ethnic minorities live, my flustered fellow committee member retorted: "Donaldo, you just don't understand. We just want these Black kids to learn how to learn." Such a remark not only points to a rigid notion of the act of learning, but it also shows that this individual had become inculcated with myths and beliefs that children from certain races and cultures need to be taught how to learn.

In response to such a comment—laced with racism—I pointed out that these children show extraordinary skills of learning in order to survive the cruel and stark reality of their community. These children, in some cases, have learned how to dodge bullets on their way to school and to acquire other skills necessary for their survival. In fact, I pointed out that those children who, by accident of birth, inherit the privilege of going to "good" schools and living in a safe and "supportive" neighborhood would prove inept in negotiating the danger and obstacles many minority children face in their daily existence. The issue is not that minority children do not know how to learn. Their very survival in negotiating the oppressive conditions under which they live is the proof that they can learn. The real issues are whether they are willing to learn what mainstream educators have determined a priori they must learn, whether what they are taught is relevant and connects with their lived experiences, and whether what is being taught to them leads to an amelioration of their subordinate condition so that they can receive a more just, less paternalistic, and more dignified treatment by their teachers and the society as a whole. The total disconnection of my fellow committee member is evidenced not only in her lack of understanding of minority students' reality but also in her refusal to learn from their lived experiences, history, and the material conditions that often relegate them to a powerless position as subordinate objects.

Peter W. Cookson Jr. contended:

> The public school systems in virtually every large city are collapsing: dropout rates hover well above 50 percent, truancy is the norm rather than the exception, violence is common, students struggle for basic literacy, often without success, a great deal of teaching is uninspired, and the physical condition of schools is a disgrace. Most inner-city schools have the look of crumbling fortresses; broken windows are left unrepaired and the paint is peeling in so many places that schools appear abandoned if it were not for

the children. The playgrounds are cracked and littered with asphalt patches. These are the "Savage Inequalities."[8]

Although I consistently pushed for a more substantive debate concerning racism, sexism, and other xenophobic attitudes in schools, most of the committee members displayed discomfort with these issues and instead preferred to argue about such issues as the number of credits to be required for graduation, admissions standards, and technical curricular concerns. One should, however, not be surprised by the reluctance of some of the committee members to engage in substantive debates that would enable them to learn about the lived experiences of most minority students, since "the institution called school that is in charge of learning does not see itself as a learner. Schools and school systems see themselves solely as teacher and not as learners."[9] The refusal of most educators to learn from their students has led us to the present predicament characterized by failure. Moreover, it prompted Peter Senge to point out to educators: "Perhaps your own organization is subject to crippling learning disabilities."[10]

If it were not for the "crippling learning disabilities," educators would not only learn tremendously from their students' history and culture but they would also make their students' unveiling drama, as described below, the very core of the curriculum. Here, in an attempt to unveil that drama, I draw from an audio journal entitled "Ghetto Life 101." This program, which vividly described the raw and stark conditions of life in the inner city, aired on June 8, 1993, on the National Public Radio program *All Things Considered*. The program host, Linda Wertheimer, introduced two teenagers hired to document their lives in the ghetto, referred to in the radio transcription as Mr. Jones and Mr. Newman.

LINDA WERTHEIMER, HOST:
Life in the inner city, an audio journal, in this half-hour of *All Things Considered*.

WERTHEIMER:
LeAlan Jones and Lloyd Newman live on Chicago's south side. The two have been best friends since they were seven. Now they're teenagers. Lloyd lives in a project a few blocks from LeAlan's house. This spring, Lloyd and LeAlan were hired as reporters. Their assignment—their own lives. They were given tape machines and microphones and asked to record, for seven days, to document what it's like growing up in their neighborhood, what it's like to be them. The boys have named their documentary "Ghetto Life 101."

LEALAN JONES, CHICAGO TEENAGER:
Good morning. Day one. Walking to school, leaving out the door.
[Sounds of dog barking and growling.]
This is my dog, Ferocious. You know why he got that name if you hear him bark.
[Sounds of rock music]
I see the ghetto every day, walking to school. Guys standing on a corner, burning a fire. Be here summertime, wintertime, spring and fall, every day, their drink in their hand, probably some white port, Willie P, Jack Daniels, [unintelligible]. I live here. This is home.

PASSING TEEN:
What's up, [unintelligible]?

MR. JONES:
What's up, Voodoo?
This is my walk every day, it's going to take me on a little journey through my life. It's my life. Here's my life. My name's LeAlan Jones, and I'm 13 years old. I live in a house just outside the Otto B. Willis projects. My best friend, Lloyd Newman, live in the Otto B. This is our story. Lloyd lives about two blocks from my house, in the Otto B. Willis projects. The Otto B.'s are made up of about 3,000 units. Most of them are low-rise houses. A lot of them in miserable condition. Now, we're walking in the Otto B. Willis, which is 50 percent houses are boarded up.

MR. NEWMAN:
Now, we're going into my house. We're knocking on the door.
[Sound of knocking on door]
Kicking on the door
[Sounds of door being kicked]
I hope she hurry up and opens it.
[Sounds of door opening]

WOMAN SPEAKING:
Wipe off your feet.

MR. JONES:
Lloyd's house is kind of messed up. There's a lot of roaches sneaking around. The toilet's been stopped up off and on for years. The place is always noisy. Lloyd's mother died two years ago from drinking. His father is also an alcoholic. So, Lloyd's two older sisters have been

bringing him up since then. Lloyd's sister Sophia was the closest to their mother.

MR. NEWMAN:
[interviewing] How did you react to—to when you heard that she died?

SOPHIA:
I was very upset. I just thought my life wasn't worth living. I wanted to die, too. I just thought we wasn't going to make it without her. But, I see that we made it, and I'm very glad about it.

MR. JONES:
When I got home from our bus ride on Sunday afternoon, I found out that, in the morning, while we were eating breakfast, my cousin Tony got jumped by one of the gangs in the neighborhood. They beat him up so bad they put him in the hospital. He wouldn't let me interview him, but I recorded him while he told his friend on the phone what happened.

[Sounds of man talking on phone]

Tony's saying they beat him up until they knocked him unconscious. Then they hit him a couple more times in the mouth. That woke him up, and he got away. He says it's just a blessing that he made it back home.

[Sounds of traffic]

This is where the [unintelligible] took place last year, where the [unintelligible], exactly where we're walking now, it's a little—gangs and violence are just a way of life in this neighborhood. [unintelligible] A lot of kids we grew up with already joined gangs. When we were walking around the neighborhood, we spotted our friend, Gary, selling drugs.

MR. NEWMAN:
LeAlan asked him what he thought he would be doing in three years, since he already dropped out of school.

GARY:
I ain't going to be alive in three years, [unintelligible] he going pop my ass.

MR. JONES:
He says he won't be alive in three years because with his selling dope, someone's going to shoot him before then. I don't know why some kids just give up hope and others like me and Lloyd hold on. Maybe it's just that both me and Lloyd have at least one strong person in our families

to watch over us. But no matter what the situation, every kid who live in this neighborhood has to grow up fast.

MR. NEWMAN:
When I was nine, I knew where drugs came from. When I was 10, I seen my first automatic weapon, a Glock-9, two clips.

MR. JONES:
I seen all kinds of guns—.44, .22, tanks—

MR. NEWMAN:
Mac-10s, Mac-11s, everything. Living around here, you hear shooting all the time.

MR. JONES:
Like Vietnam, sometimes, you might hear—booga-looga-looga-sound. I remember one time, I was over at my aunt's house, spending the night, and we were playing Super Nintendo. I hear this lady out—"I heard you been looking for me, nigger." And then, she goes, boom-boom-boom-boom-boom. She let off about eight shots. Then I heard the other girl fire off. And we just stood there playing, there, like nothing happened. And then, you—Vietnam, some people term that crazy. Hell, I live in Vietnam, for what you think I'm going to be if I live [unintelligible].

MR. NEWMAN:
Living around here, man, is depressing. It's depressing.
   [Sounds of rock music]

MR. JONES:
It's not a normal childhood, by any means. Now we're walking toward the lake front. Sometimes, when we're bored and nothing else to do, we get on the bridge which goes over Lake Shore Drive, and we drop rocks on the cars below, try to crack their windshields, and then run.

MR. NEWMAN:
Moving vans are one of our favorite targets.
   [Sounds of traffic]
   Hit the white [unintelligible]. Right, right, right. Throw it now.

MR. JONES:
He's just driving the car, like—boom—I don't care about them people. Most of them are going to the suburbs.

MR. NEWMAN:
I mean, boy, you hit the [unintelligible]. Just to have some fun.

MR. JONES:
Lloyd, come on, let's start running. All I know is I bust a windshield.
   [Sounds of rock music]
   [Sounds of jazz music]
   It definitely ain't easy growing up in the ghetto. So far, me and Lloyd are okay, but it's always tough to stay out of trouble in this environment—the poverty, the drugs, the pressure, the tragedy. It gets to people.

MR. NEWMAN:
You never know who's going to get in trouble or when they're just going to give up, like LeAlan's sister, Janelle.
   [Sounds of television commercial]
   We're back at LeAlan's house.

MR. JONES:
Sister back here, asleep, in her room. What time you get in this morning? It's spooky. My older sister, Janelle, when she was my age, 13, she was an honor student. She won the spelling bee. She was the salutatorian of her class. Then when she hit 14, she started bugging out, hanging around with the wrong crowd, staying out all night, stopped going to school.

MR. NEWMAN:
The week before we did our recording, Janelle almost died. She drank too much and had to be rushed to the hospital.

MR. JONES:
Can I interview you? Come on. Janelle, tell me about yourself.

JANELLE:
Well, I'm very energetic. I like to have a lot of fun.

MR. JONES:
You like to drink a lot.

JANELLE:
No, I don't.

MR. JONES:
Yes, you do. You smoke marijuana?

JANELLE:
No, I don't.

MR. JONES:
Yes, you do, tell the truth.

JANELLE:
No, I don't.

MR. JONES:
You're seventeen?

JANELLE:
Yes.

MR. JONES:
Have a child?

JANELLE:
Yes.

MR. JONES:
How old were you when you had this child?

JANELLE:
Fifteen.

MR. JONES:
How many close friends of yours has—have got killed, through the years?

JANELLE:
I don't know. I can't count all of them. It's been a lot, though.

MR. JONES:
Do you think it's around 50?

JANELLE:
No, I don't think it's that many.

MR. JONES:
But it's around 30 or 40?

JANELLE:
Probably somewhere in that area, maybe a little less than 30.

MR. JONES:
Do you know who killed or murdered these people?

JANELLE:
I know who killed some of them.

MR. JONES:
Like who?

JANELLE:
Like Bill.

MR. JONES:
Who killed him?

JANELLE:
No, I ain't going to tell you who killed Bill.

MR. JONES:
Who else?

JANELLE:
I know who killed Slick.

MR. JONES:
Who?

JANELLE:
I don't want to tell you that, either.

MR. JONES:
Who else?

JANELLE:
C.Z.

MR. JONES:
Who killed him?

JANELLE:
I ain't going to tell you that, either.

MR. JONES:
Thank you.
  [Sounds of jazz singer]

The radio transcript captures the hopelessness, hu. an misery, and poverty found in most ghettos in the United States. Yet, middle-class, White educators are often resistant and refuse to learn from subordinate students' lived experiences, which would make the educators better prepared to intervene in the educational process of these same children. Thus, in order to uncripple these educators' "crippling learning disabilities," which are, by the way, ideologically determined, schools of education would have to rigorously adopt as an area of inquiry the sociocultural material conditions that shape and limit the dreams, aspirations, and democratic rights of an ever-increasing number of subordinate students they are entrusted to educate. A rigorous study of the sociocultural reality of subordinate students would enable educators to recognize that the lack of familiarity with the written and oral middle-class language and other cultural values of the school curriculum "does not mean ... that the lack of these experiences develop in these children a different 'nature,' that determines their absolute incompetence."[11] I am reminded of an incident when I was invited to join a group of educators who had received a Ford Foundation grant to work with Navajo students on a reservation. After a two-day visit to a number of Navajo schools, we had a debriefing session with some of the Anglo teachers, who, with obvious commitment, had opted to work with these children. After an English teacher at the reservation high school had explained the English curriculum to us, I realized that there were very few differences from the grade nine to the grade twelve curricula. All four successive years of English instruction overemphasized skills development with minimal reading of substantive works and little writing. I asked her why the skills taught in grade nine were repeated during the subsequent years. She calmly explained: "These kids have tremendous difficulty with the acquisition of English skills. They don't like to read. They try to avoid it. They are just not readers, by nature." I later learned that what we had observed at the Navajo reservation is no different from what goes on at other Indian reservations: education so as to not educate. For example, at Stewart School in Nevada, the mathematics program is similar to the English skills-banking curriculum at the Navajo high school in Arizona: "The first course for 'high school' students teaches addition and subtraction. The second level course deals with all four basic operations plus fractions. The next course is concerned with proportions for simple algebra, while the top course is finally algebra."[12] As Katherine Jensen correctly pointed out:

> Bureau teachers or administrators confronted with this evidence would undoubtedly justify it as reaching the level the students could handle. Given the eight or more years of educational retardation, not to mention personal disorganization, suffered by many of these students, the assessment may be correct. But the key to understanding boarding schools, which serve the poorest, most rural, and most reluctant students, is the epitome of colonized education.[13]

It is the same colonial model that fails most of the subordinate students in urban schools. When we returned to the university in Arizona, instead of the usual tourist account of what we had observed in the reservation schools, I pointed out the striking similarities between the colonial education practices in Cape Verde, a former Portuguese colony in Africa, and the practices we had observed on the reservation, as well as the educational approaches dominant in inner-city schools. I began by focusing on the English teacher's comment that Navajo students "are not readers, by nature." Her justification shifted the blame from the school failure to the students' "failure, not only as personal and cultural, but racial."[14] I was enthusiastically supported by two Navajo students at the university who had accompanied us on our trip and the director of the project who had invited me because of my work with Paulo Freire. Reluctantly, the rest of the group discussed not only the paternalism but also the deficit orientation with which the English teacher at the reservation had been inculcated. We also explored the probable adverse pedagogical implications inherent in both paternalism and deficit orientation.

A few months later, after my return to Boston, I learned that the director of the project who had invited me to the reservation had been removed from her position because of her aggressive intention to politicize the project. I was surprised that she was replaced, but in retrospect, I realized that I should not have been. What can you expect from a department where an English professor often boasted that in her twenty years of teaching at the university, she had never passed a Navajo student?

"Politicizing" becomes a negative "shock word" to muffle rigorous academic debate concerning both the grievances and the educational needs of subordinate students. Only through a thorough deconstruction of the ideology that prevents subordinate students' sociocultural reality from becoming an area of serious inquiry can, for example, educators like my fellow committee member and the English teacher at the reservation learn that "nature" does not determine the subordinate students' inability to learn the ABCs, which, in turn, warrants that they be taught "how to learn." These students have very little difficulty learning what the chief of psychiatry at San Diego's Children's Hospital rightly described as the "more relevant drills of the DBSs (drive-by shootings)"[15] and other survival skills, which were vividly and painfully described in the dialogue cited earlier in this section.

Teachers need to dismiss their false notion that subordinate students "can't learn" or "don't know how to learn." They also need to understand the social and cultural fabric that informs, shapes, and reproduces the despair of poverty, fatalism, and hopelessness captured in the dialogue among these youngsters. By engaging the subordinate students' text, teachers may also begin to understand that ghettos are sociopolitically constructed and that most of the ghetto people do not want to live under material conditions that sentence them to human misery, despair, and, ultimately, self-destruction. However, in order to carefully study the social construction of human misery detailed in these dialogues, schools of education would have to offer courses in, for example, "the nature of ideology," "ethics," and "cultural racism." With rare exceptions, most schools of education do not offer such courses or at least do not make these courses required. In some cases, depending on the progressive attitude of the instructor, some foundations courses may raise issues of ideology, ethics, and cultural racism but seldom as the main focus of the course. For example, if students at Harvard Graduate School of Education want to study Freire and other critical educators, they have to go to the Harvard Divinity School, where a course called "Education for Liberation" is offered. Every year, numerous students from Harvard come to ask me about where to go to pursue graduate studies in critical pedagogy.

By looking at students' cultural processes as forms of textual, social, and political analysis, educators will not only develop means to counter the dominant attempt to impose reproductive educational practices, but they will also equip themselves with the necessary tools to embrace a pedagogy of hope based on cultural production where specific groups of people produce, mediate, and confirm the mutual ideological elements that emerge from and affirm their cultural experiences. Only through experiences that are rooted in the interests of individual and collective self-determination can we create education for liberation. Cultural production, not reproduction, is the only means through which we can achieve a true cultural democracy.

Educational Reforms That Deform

A fundamental question that is rarely raised is how can schools of education provide leadership in the process of educational reform, since they are, by and large, responsible for the creation of what Senge, as we have seen, accurately called a school culture that is "subject to crippling learning disabilities"? We need to ask the following:

- ❧ Can schools of education that function as cultural reproduction models create pedagogical spaces to prepare teachers who will be agents of change and who will be committed to education for liberation?
- ❧ How can schools of education reconcile their technicist and often undemocratic approach to teacher preparation with the urgency to democratize schools?
- ❧ How can schools of education that have been accomplices to racial, cultural, gender, and ethnic discrimination create the necessary pedagogical spaces that will lead to cultural democracy?

The paradox is that although many schools of education have been "crippled with learning disabilities,"[16] they are expected to play a major role in the reform of schools. In most instances, schools of education represent the most conservative sector of university life. These faculties concentrate on reproducing values designed to maintain the status quo while de-skilling teachers through a labyrinth of how-to methods courses devoid of any substantive content. When content is incorporated into courses, it usually consists of secondary sources presented as translations from primary sources. Often, the content ignores subordinate students' culture production and the antagonistic relations generated by the discriminating school practices and the subsequent resistance of students to "savage inequalities." Schools of education cannot succeed in preparing future teachers for leadership positions and for being agents of change if they continue to advocate the use of neatly packaged instructional programs that are presented as the panacea for difficulties students face in the acquisition of prepackaged knowledge. Schools of education cannot point teachers to a truly cultural democracy if they fail to prepare teachers to both analyze and understand how subordinate cultures are produced in the classrooms and society at large.

Teachers also need to understand the antagonistic relationships between the values of subordinate cultures and the dominant values reflected in the curriculum. Take, for example, the resistance to speaking the required standard dialect of the curriculum. I believe that the dominant curriculum is designed primarily to reproduce the inequality of social classes, while it mostly benefits the interests of the dominant class. Teachers need to capitalize on the antagonistic cultural elements produced in subordinate students' acts of resistance and create a pedagogy that would enable students to comprehend their world so they read it and act upon it and, if necessary, transform it. That is, teachers need to understand how to use students' resistances and world as a platform from which they can transcend the mechanistic nature of education imposed upon them by the dominant ideology. The de-skilling of teachers is "further complicated by the fact that schools are presently organized around an industrial model rather than an informational model. Schools are traditionally organized to produce young people who are capable of working in isolation and taking directions. ... The role of the schools today is such that it attempts to extinguish the natural desire of people to gather, be inquisitive and interact."[17]

Because many schools of education train teachers to become technicists who unreflectively embrace methods and approaches, they are in some cases either unwilling or unable to prepare teachers to become intellectuals able to assume leadership through independent thought and actions. With rare exception, schools of education generally do not offer pedagogical spaces where future teachers can engage in the development of a critical attitude informed by a praxis that involves both reflection and political action. It is thus not surprising that the present school reform movement remains at the cosmetic level, dislodged from the structural reality that necessitated the call for reform in the first place. In noting that "too often meaningless changes are defined as transformation,"[18] Peter Negroni cautioned us:

> One cannot simply rearrange the chairs in a classroom into a circle and proclaim that this will help instruction. In America's public schools, historically, children have been asked to sit one behind the other and told to be still, be quiet and never to talk to each other. If the change constitutes putting the children in a circle and telling them to be still, be quiet and never talk to each other, little has been done to change the results.[19]

Negroni's words capture the drama of the present school reform debate, not only through the trivializing of reform itself in the form of cosmetic changes but also through the refusal of most educators to unveil the hidden ideology of racism and sexism that serves to devalue and disconfirm the lived experiences, culture, history, and language of subordinate students. The unwillingness to unpack the schools' hidden ideology has given rise to a plethora of methods and approaches presented as panaceas that are destined to failure and substitution by similar, faddish "teacher-proof" methods. Regardless of how progressive these methods may be, unless they are supported by the school ideology, they will inevitably fail. Methods can be effective only if teachers who adopt them understand fully both the methods' limits and possibilities in relation to the restrictions set by the school ideology. It is of paramount importance that teachers understand that the adoption of a progressive methodology will not necessarily accomplish anything if the dominant ideology within the school is diametrically opposed to the principles and values of the chosen progressive methodology. That is why Paulo Freire has often cautioned educators about the uncritical importation or exportation of methodologies. He argued that the success of any educational transformation goes hand in hand with societal transformations. A society that remains racist, undemocratic, and discriminatory will not tolerate the transformation of schools and their democratization.

In this section, I will analyze an actual reform activity of a major urban university to show how the very goals of the reform process were betrayed by the discourse and the ideology of the reformers. Language such as "we need to empower students" and "all we want to do is teach these Black kids how to learn" provides a glimpse into the hidden ideology that supports a deficit-orientation model giving rise to either paternalism or the outright delegitimation of subordinate students' culture, history, and language.

During the late 1980s, the school of education in this major urban university, whose main reason for existence is its urban mission, was staffed by an almost-all-White faculty. I believe that the percentage of White faculty was over 95 percent. In the undergraduate division 100 percent of the tenured professors were White and middle-class. The poor enrollment and retention of minority students should not come as a total surprise. For example, in 1984, the total enrollment of minority students in this urban school of education was less than 3 percent. Student teachers were mostly placed in suburban schools to do their internships, and in the early 1980s, the school offered no courses in multicultural education or bilingual education. In fact, in 1985 or 1986, a Portuguese bilingual teacher was given an English written test on her first day in an elementary methods course by her professor in order to determine if she was proficient enough in English to take the course. Since she was the wife of a faculty member in another department at the university, the issue was brought to the attention of the individual who was dean of the School of Education at the time; the dean reacted by saying that he did not believe in bilingual or multicultural education. He added that if he were to move to Portugal, he would not expect the Portuguese government to provide bilingual and bicultural education for his children. Of course he would not have to expect such services because when Americans move in great numbers to other countries, they often take along their own schools. For example, American military bases all over the world provide kindergarten through twelfth grade (K–12) schools in English. In some countries, even American university services are provided, so there is no need for Americans to bother learning the language of the host country or interact with the natives. If you were an American business person in a foreign country, you still would not have to worry about bilingual and bicultural education because most major cities with sizable American "migrant" workers offer K–12 education in English in American private schools and, in some places, American universities. What is categorically clear to me and to most of these American "migrant" workers abroad is that they do not want their children to be educated in a language other than English or to be removed from American values. Immigrants in the United States also do not want their children to lose their native language and culture. The fundamental difference is that, while the American "migrant" workers abroad are often in positions of power to choose what schools their children attend, the immigrant population in the United States is in a powerless position, which does not afford these parents with the same privilege.

Against the landscape of an almost-all-White school of education within an urban university, the central administration, following recommendations from some major reform reports, separated the undergraduate teacher training from the graduate program and placed it in the College of Arts and Sciences. The rationale at the time was that the College of Arts and Sciences had both the expertise and the resources to develop a highly successful interdisciplinary undergraduate teacher program, as called for by some of the educational reform documents. The central administration of the university correctly understood the imperative need to fracture the all-White culture of the undergraduate division and infuse it with more diversity and intellectual energy. However, the dean of the College of Arts and Sciences only reluctantly went along with the central administration's restructuring plans and appointed a small, preliminary committee to study the viability of the plan. Ironically, this committee was made up mostly of White faculty members in the College of Arts and Sciences. So much for diversity. In fact, the professor who chaired the preliminary committee was known to have recently complained about the low quality of Vietnamese students. When a professor who taught English as a Second Language courses at the university pointed out to him that many of the best students majoring in science at the university were Vietnamese students, he publicly stated: "They're all stupid now. They used to be smart. They all lie."

As a result of various pressures, the dean of the College of Arts and Sciences expanded the undergraduate teacher-training committee to include more diversity. In this process, I became one of the two minority committee members among fourteen or so professors. Even though there were a sizable number of minority faculty members at the university who had distinguished themselves in the field of education, they were not invited to participate in this endeavor. A case in point is a Puerto Rican faculty member who had chaired an important committee for the City of Boston on vocational education. Although his studies were cited in the *Boston Globe* and other major publications, our committee functioned as if he did not exist.

During the first meeting of the expanded committee under the leadership of a new chair appointed by the dean, I strongly suggested that members of the committee read all of the major educational reform reports so that we could, with more intellectual authority, analyze and determine how the structure and mission of this urban university could respond and incorporate major changes in teacher education. The objective of my suggested intensive reading and discussion was, in my view at the time, to make members of the committee more familiar with the current educational debate, since many of these professors were not educators and had little or no experience working with urban schools. My suggestion to read these educational reform reports was never intended to question my fellow committee members' technical competence in their field of specialization. My concern at that time was that no matter how competent they might be in their technical specialization, that did not necessarily make each of them a competent educator who was articulate and well versed in contemporary educational issues and challenges. Although my suggestion was never publicly rejected, it was also never implemented as part of the ongoing debate during the committee meetings. The focus of these meetings was mostly on technical issues such as resources, number of credits, number of faculty lines, student recruitment, and the state certification requirements. Even though we spent many meetings deciphering the report of the State Joint Task Force for Teacher Training (JTTP), which had made important recommendations concerning the reform of teacher-training education, the committee refused my advice to invite the principal author of the report who, incidentally, was a faculty member in this urban university. Why did we spend many precious hours trying to interpret the new requirements in the JTTP report if we had direct access to its principal author?

My participation in the committee to reform the undergraduate teacher training at this major urban university made me face the reality that my role as one of the two minority professors appointed by the dean to this committee was to legitimize the reform process and never to ask my colleagues to confront and debate the inequalities of schools concerning students from different racial, cultural, and ethnic backgrounds. My participation in the undergraduate teacher-training reform committee also made me realize that even some liberal colleagues who publicly proselytized against racism as an abstract idea resisted my pressure on them to translate this abstract idea into action.

This resistance manifested itself in various forms. For example, it was very comfortable to discuss curriculum diversity when "diversity" functioned as a positive shock word that limited the need to rigorously analyze how the various subordinate groups under the diversity umbrella occupied different historical locations in relation to the asymmetry of power maintained by the dominant ruling class. Not all subordinate groups have experienced equal level of oppression, and their asymmetrical positions vis-à-vis the dominant ruling group have varied along the lines of race, language, ethnicity, class, and gender. For example, it was important to understand that the positionality and historical specificity of White middle-class women should not constitute the only platform through which the oppression of women could be examined and analyzed. In other words, gender oppression is cut by other factors—such as culture, class, ethnicity, and race. A rigorous analysis of gender oppression must take into consideration that the subordinate position of African-American lower-class women is substantially different from that of White middle-class women, even though both groups are subjugated by the superordinate White-male order. Given the textual, social, and political differences inherent in the oppression of women, one cannot overgeneralize gender oppression as a monolithic entity, as bell hooks has so passionately and eloquently demonstrated.

Furthermore, "diversity" as a fossilized cliché does not provide space to demonstrate that, in many cases, like integration, diversity has not really increased the presence of subordinate cultural groups in institutional life. For example, after court-ordered desegregation in North Carolina, the number of African-American educational administrators in that state went from 254 to only 5 in four short years. By and large, adult education programs, literacy programs that have mostly served cultural and racial minority groups, are administered and staffed by White professionals. Thus, one cannot talk about diversity and educational success without addressing the important issues of race, gender, and economic equity. All the policies of diversity and access will not guarantee that members of subordinate racial and cultural groups or economically disadvantaged Whites will be able to finance their university education.

Diversity and access without the means of access are a form of entrapment.

Because of the intersection of factors found in the oppression of different groups, reformers who stay at the shock-word, surface level of "diversity" run the risk of relegating the term to the realm of slogans and clichés, devoid of meaningful political impact. As an empty slogan, "diversity," for instance, can provide many White liberals with a safe zone to denounce racism at the level of proclamation, thus assuaging their White guilt, as long as they are allowed to maintain their antiracist discourse as a set of abstract ideas. However, many White liberals would feel extremely uncomfortable if the curriculum diversity incorporated an antiracist pedagogy that would ask "mirror, mirror on the wall, is everyone welcome to the hall?"[20] It is this compromising ideological position on the part of may White liberals that led Carol Swain, an African-American professor at Princeton University, to observe that "white liberals are among the most racist people I know; they're so patronizing toward blacks."[21]

Sadly, not everyone is welcomed to the hall. A report entitled "Muted Voices in the Newsroom," published by the National Association of Black Journalists, revealed that 32 percent of African-American journalists fear that bringing up issues of race damages their chances for advancement. This led Derrick Z. Jackson to ask, "If African-Americans feel psychologically intimidated in the newsroom, how are we to trust the media's proclamation about racism at the corner store?"[22] It is the same question that I was trying to ask of my fellow committee members, a question that not only created tension but also raised the resistance level among many committee members. If minority students and faculty members feel psychologically intimidated in schools, how are we to trust the educators' proclamation about racism at the corner store?

Although I insisted throughout the two years of the committee's existence that community leaders, parents, and teachers be invited to give their input as to the context of the reform, only a few individuals were invited as token participants in the process. When Theresa Perry, undergraduate dean at Wheelock College and a well-known African-American educator, came to talk to the committee about the highly successful reform that she, along with her colleagues, had instituted in a mostly White private college, her discourse on racism, oppression, and her deconstruction of school inequalities did not sit well with many members of our committee. This was evidenced in the committee meeting that followed her visit. When the chair asked if committee members wanted to discuss Theresa Perry's presentation, to my surprise, no one expressed an interest and we went on discussing procedural and technical matters such as the number of positions and state certification requirements. Even though Theresa Perry had achieved great success in making race and cultural issues an integral part of the teacher-training curriculum at Wheelock, most members of our committee showed little interest in Wheelock's achievement. This was also obvious in the superficial nature of questions that were asked at her presentation, for example, How many courses deal with multicultural issues?

The issues of racism came to a head during the penultimate committee meeting during the first year when we discussed the subcommittee work on the Foundations course. Even though the Foundations course was the main vehicle through which urban issues concerning race would be raised, the subcommittee was made up entirely of White faculty members. During their presentation of the Foundations course, I pointed out that the Foundations proposal relegated urban issues to the margin as exemplified in the very language, such as "in addition, students will be encouraged to explore multicultural issues." When I kept insisting that urban, race, and gender issues should be at the core of the Foundations course, particularly because of the urban mission of the university, some members of the subcommittee became very defensive, giving rise to a very tense meeting. The chair, sensing the high level of tension in the room, tabled the discussion, which was to be continued the following academic year when the committee resumed its work.

During the second year, the committee chair was changed. To my surprise, the discussion concerning the Foundations course did not occur when we resumed our work. The second year can best be described as the continuation of the first year's technical work on procedural matters, such as certification standards and funding. I suspect that because of the tension that had characterized our meeting when we discussed the Foundations course, there was no urgency on the part of the chair and some committee members to resume discussions that touched on racial and cultural issues. For this reason, we did not return to these issues again until the very last meeting of the committee during the second year. Toward the end of the second year, a past committee member and I wrote extensive memoranda to the chair pointing out our concerns with respect to the lack of centrality of urban issues in the revised draft of the Foundations course. In response to our memoranda, the chair tried to pursue negotiation of these issues individually with dissenting members. For example, although I had urged her to distribute my colleague's memorandum to the entire committee during our individual meetings, she indicated a preference to negotiate the multicultural and urban issues separately with the subcommittee before the general discussion. The fragmentation of this discussion prevented the entire committee from debating and understanding critical issues raised in my colleague's memorandum, as indicated below:

Subject: Some comments on the draft Foundations document
Date: September 1, 1991

I'll try to put into writing some of my reactions to the draft you sent me on the Foundations portion of the teacher preparation program. A lot of what I'll write here will repeat what I said on the telephone.

I agree with you that the sections that deal with multicultural and urban issues need strengthening in this draft-in-progress. The way to do this is to state and restate in every section of the draft that case materials drawn from urban minority populations are central study matter for the course whether the topic concerns history, cognitive psychology, sociology of education, or language use. We should probably also state this concern with urban, minority case materials as a general theme at the beginning of the draft.

We also need to list somewhere a range of particular issues, like inequality, tracking, race and racism, competing models of multiculturalism, bilingualism, history of civil rights and desegregation debates in education, etc. [see the Foundations group report to the CUTP for a list of topics] that bear on the situation of urban multicultural populations. We should also make clear that we will aim to review with students some of the solutions that have been attempted and proposed to deal with urban multicultural students and their educational needs.

If we are going to deal meaningfully with and not just give lip service to, issues of urban minority people, then we have to put those at the center of our program. It will take effort and commitment, in other words, to pursue this agenda. Not everyone will be happy with it, either. It has not been the traditional way to pursue teacher preparation programs. Let's dare to do something unusual. Something brave, not safe, is what we need.

To make urban and minority issues central to the program doesn't mean that we ignore everyone else, suburban and private schools, middle class children, etc. Our program shouldn't deal only with urban, minority populations, and I think we can be assured that it won't, given the orientation of most literature in education. It just means that urban and minority concerns can't be add-ons to some sort of standard curriculum. In my view, anything less than central treatment won't work or be credible.

A related issue that also has not made it into this draft is Equity, which the Foundations group made the central issue of the course. Where urban, multicultural populations are concerned, the issue of equity is an especially appropriate one—in fact the educational situation and problems of urban multicultural populations can't be understood apart from it. Jonathan Kozol's new book, *Savage Inequalities,* is only the latest of a long line of treatments of the serious foundational inequities in American education—particularly across the race, class and urban-suburban divides. For your information, I'm enclosing a review of this book from yesterday's *New York Times.*

I don't think I or anyone else has any quibble with "Excellence" as a goal for education either, so long as we go on record as noting that Equity and Excellence are compatible, even interdependent goals. Too often people pose it as a superior goal or as one even diminished by attention to equity. We should avoid that tone, I think. The question of Equity also is linked to what the Foundations group sensed would be an appropriate ethical commitment of our program—to advocate and prepare teachers for effective, quality education of all children—a goal manifestly not being met in our society, particularly in urban systems. The material we read on the Goodlad-selected model preparation programs [I don't have my files handy to look up references here] suggested a broad ethical stance of this sort is appropriate and desirable, to lend coherence and purpose to a program.

In this same vein, in our explanation of our coverage of teaching as a role and activity, we need to deal with the idea of teachers as critics of the status quo, as critical, independent intellectuals, change agents, reflective practitioners, and the like. We need to fortify our students with professional and intellectual resources, and a sense of their own professional identities and values as educators, so that they can be innovators and resist and work to change many prevailing, bankrupt educational policies and practices.

If people want a sense of the mission of our program, why couldn't we simply say we aim to prepare students to become skilled, compassionate teachers who are committed to teaching all children well—including traditionally underserved urban, minority populations. This kind of mission would be well reflected in the core Foundations course.

I question the need at this stage to get into the specifics of listing the bodies of literature that we will cover in the course. It might be more useful at this stage of our discussion to deal with content on the level of broad topics, themes, and issues.

At this point, I regret I don't have time to suggest how the course should be divided into two sections. The material is certainly plentiful and I imagine that divisions between one semester and the next are going to be pretty arbitrary.

Yes, I think there should also be attention to education for what and for whom, and to special needs. Let's help students get some critical purchase on those issues, too. This is easy where philosophy of education is concerned, but there is also debate over the value and purpose of special needs classifications too that students should be aware of.

I hope you will change the reference to Freire as a "political educator" as if only some educators or educational thinkers are political! John Dewey, Jane Martin, Paul Gagnon, Bloom, Hirsch, DeSouza and Ravitch are pretty political, too, just to name a few. Who among educational philosophers or critics isn't political?

As an example of how urban minority issues can be mainstreamed in this course, in the section on history we could deal with the long history of bilingual education in the U.S. and controversies over it, or with the history of school segregation and desegregation among the races (extending easily into some treatment of the recent Boston controversies, now very well covered in the literature).

My colleague's memorandum was finally distributed when I publicly raised the issue with the entire committee. This was also true of my memorandum, which I will include below in part even though I may repeat some of the same arguments I made elsewhere in other chapters of this book. I believe the repetition is necessary to give readers a clear sense of how reformers often attempt to suffocate critical issues concerning race and culture, particularly if these issues call for a transformation of those structures that benefit the status quo:

Re: Foundations Coursework
Date: September 30, 1991

Let me begin by saying that I like the present draft of the Foundations Coursework to the extent that it raises some important and fundamental issues which are part of the on-going debate concerning educational reform. However, I have some concerns that, I believe, may strengthen the proposed Foundations Coursework. They are:

1. Section II.

The issues with respect to the concepts of knowledge and learning are not merely epistemological in nature. To understand the concepts of knowledge and learning we must go beyond epistemology and interrogate the relation of knowledge to power. That is, without a power relation theoretical framework, it would be extremely difficult for prospective teachers to understand the ways in which structural inequalities tend to reproduce the cultural values of the dominant White class. But more important is the ability of the Foundations Coursework to link education to the asymmetrical relations of power within the dominant society, relations of power that not only define and legitimate certain bodies of knowledge but also disempower certain groups by excluding them from such a process. We need to develop a Foundations Coursework that provides a theoretical model for empowering historical agents of change with the logic of individual and collective self-determination.

Also missing from the draft is the question of ethics. The issue of ethics was never raised and, I think, it should have preceded epistemological questions. I believe that the ethical dimension of education should be part and parcel of any attempt to create a new teacher education program grounded in a new educational praxis. The new educational praxis should express different concepts of education consonant with a plan for a more just and democratic society as a whole. In order to achieve this goal, prospective teachers must understand the ideological elements that are part of a school reality which forces a high percentage of students to experience subordination, racial discrimination, and other forms of gender and ethnic oppression. What will be the engagement of prospective teachers with social and educational struggles designed to end violent racism, structures of poverty, homelessness, and other social ills that characterize the lived experiences of minority students in our urban public schools?

If these social issues are not dealt with appropriately, it is naive to think that the acquisition of certain bodies of knowledge alone will, somehow, magically eclipse the raw and cruel injustices and oppressions perpetrated against the dispossessed class of minority students who populate our urban public schools. In short, we can either develop a teacher education program designed to celebrate the intellectual and ethical dimensions of teaching or we can develop a program designed to further de-skill teachers and reduce them to mere technical agents who are destined to walk un-reflexively through a labyrinth of methods, approaches, and procedures which reproduce the values of the status quo.

2. Section IV.

Although the proposal stresses the incorporation of different cultural and racial groups as part of the Foundations Coursework, it is still not clear to me how this multicultural dimension will be an integral part of the fabric of a new reconceptualized teacher education program. Since the issue of culture and diversity were not fully developed, I may offer the following suggestions:

a) We need to develop a truly multicultural curriculum that ceases to view other cultural and racial groups as objects of study independent from the invisible White ethnicity which is often beyond study. In other words, it is not enough to study cultural and racial groups and their learning styles outside the social and political constructs that produce antagonistic and often contradictory relations in the classroom. We need to incorporate political and ideological linkages in our analysis of cultures so as to illuminate the reproductive nature of schools in this society and the various forms of resistance minority students employ in their willful refusal to engage what the curriculum has decided they should learn.

Progressive teachers need to be part of the on-going debate on multicultural education and understand the reasons behind the unrelenting attack on cultural diversity and cultural and ethnic studies. They need to understand the conservative educators' position that tends to recycle old assumptions about the "melting pot theory" and our so-called "common culture," assumptions designed primarily to maintain the status quo. Maintained is a status quo that functions as a cultural reproduction mechanism which systematically does not allow other cultural subjects, who are considered outside of the mainstream, to be present in history. These cultural subjects (i.e. racial groups) who are profiled as the "other" are but palely represented in history in the form of Black history month, Puerto Rican week, etc.

For the notion of multicultural education to become meaningful it has to be situated within a theory of cultural production and viewed as an integral part of the way in which people produce, transform, and reproduce meaning. Multicultural education must be seen as a medium that constitutes and affirms the historical and existential moments of lived experience that produce a subordinate or a lived culture. Hence, it is an eminently political phenomenon and it must be analyzed within the context of a theory of power relations and an understanding of social and cultural reproduction and production.

By "cultural reproduction" I refer to collective experiences that function in the interest of the dominant groups, rather than in the interest of the subordinate groups that are the object of its policies. By and large, the educational landscape in the United States is characterized by a cultural reproduction context where teachers often function as cultural managers who transmit "proper" values and protect our "common culture" from ethnic and multicultural contamination. I use "cultural production" to refer to specific groups of people producing, mediating, and confirming the mutual ideological elements that emerge from and reaffirm their daily lived experiences. In this case, such experiences are rooted in the interests of individual and collective self-determination.

If we were to implement a new teacher education program based on the cultural production framework, we would have to cease to propose an acculturation model, for its counterpart is inevitably de-culturation. Prospective teachers need to fully understand how schools have served the purpose of de-culturing different cultural, racial, and ethnic groups while acculturating them into a predefined "common culture" model. ...

Given the range of factors that interact in cultural production and reproduction, the new teacher preparation program needs to transcend surface structure cultural differences (i.e. learning styles) to interface with all the other factors described above.

3. Among other issues discussed in the Foundations Course draft I am somewhat concerned about methodologies proposed to motivate students to learn. Although motivation is an important factor, it is not enough. I think the real issue is not just motivation but voice and equity. That is, how can we provide pedagogical structures which will enable students to develop their own voices so they can be present rather than merely represented in history? Since the concept of voice is intimately tied to language, we need to understand the role of language as a major force in the construction of human subjectivity. For this reason, I believe that the Foundations Coursework proposal should give more primacy to the issue of language and bilingualism. Prospective teachers need to understand the way language may either confirm or deny the life histories and experiences of the people who use it.

Also included in my memorandum was a long discussion on the role of language in education that I will not reproduce in this section since I included many of these arguments in Chapter 4. Although these two memoranda raised important critical issues, during the last committee meeting to discuss the Foundation Course, not a single committee member made any reference to the memoranda's concerns. In short, these critical urban issues of race and multiculturalism were met with deafening silence. Need I say more?

The Choiceless Choice

As I argued in the introduction of this chapter, "choice" represents a positive shock word that creates the illusion that all parents can equally exercise their democratic right to choose the best schools for their children. The illusion of choice reinforces the myth that "every American also has the right to choose where to work, sleep, and to live."[23] However, for Bill Simpson and several other African-Americans who attempted to implement the court-ordered integration of a public housing complex in Vidor, Texas, the myth became soon a nightmare: Despite his efforts to assimilate quietly, Simpson was subjected for months to Ku Klux Klan threats and racial epithets shouted from passing cars. Unable to endure the unremittingly hostile atmosphere any longer, Simpson decided to leave, as all of his fellow blacks already had.[24]

The illusion also creates a pedagogy of entrapment that makes it undemocratic to argue against school choice. Thus, school choice becomes part of a discourse that brooks no dissension or argument, for to argue against it is to deny democracy. What conservative educators such as William Bennett, Chester Finn, and John Silber fail to acknowledge is that school choice is part and parcel of a language of management that celebrates testing, privatization, and competition. Because "in the United States, all ideas about the renovation of our infrastructure, and even about education and health care, are evaluated mainly for their utility in helping us 'compete in the world economy,'"[25] our thinking and imagination are often straitjacketed in a utilitarian capitalist competition that prevents us from learning about successful experiments and experiences all over the world. A case in point is the educational transformation in São Paulo, under the leadership of Paulo Freire, a world-renowned educator. I say "transformation" and not "reform" because undemocratic education should be transformed and not left to the compromised benevolence of players who created the educational inequality problem to spearhead cosmetic reform in an attempt to solve the structural inequalities in education.

The very language of the reform movement, particularly the conservative proposals, points to an ideology that structures the education debate in terms of competition (for example, Bush's plan, America 2000, that promised that we would be best in math and science by the year 2000) and choice, which is a veiled proposal that makes us "unconsciously endorse the privatization and capitalization of every sphere of activity"[26] within the education reform movements. The actual hidden curriculum of school choice consists of taking precious resources from poor schools that are on the verge of bankruptcy to support private or well-to-do public schools. For example, at the same time that Brockton Public Schools in Massachusetts terminated the contract of 120 teachers owing to a draconian school budget cut, the system shifted approximately $1 million to support Brockton middle-class students who chose to enroll in the more affluent Avon Public Schools. Although Avon public schools benefited greatly from the school choice windfall, the system did not welcome equally all students from Brockton. When a Brockton special education student decided to defy his rejection from the Avon public schools, an Avon principal stood by the door in the first day of class to prevent this student, accompanied by his parents, from entering the school building, leading his parents to seek legal help and support from the Massachusetts Commission Against Discrimination. This episode provides a glimpse of future behavior of Avon public schools if a large number of Brockton minority students pick Avon as the schools of their choice. The school choice discourse also eclipses the more fundamental issue of educational funding inequity, as pointed out by Jonathan Kozol:

> The wealthiest and most mobile families in low-income districts are driving their children to the nearest wealthy district, in which teachers receive higher pay, classes are smaller and supplies are in abundance. Since public money follows the child, and since only those who drive or have the funds to hire drivers can exploit this advantage, the poorest districts are losing their most aggressive, affluent and vocal parents, many of their top-achieving pupils and the public money that goes with them. Low to middle-income Gloucester, for example, has already lost about $400,000. High-income Manchester-by-the-Sea, just next door to Gloucester, has gained $600,000.[27]

In cases where students choose to enroll in private schools, the private school choice is only private to the degree that it generates private profit while being supported by public funds. What is rarely discussed in the school reform debate is what is a well-known fact to most educators: The success of any school depends mostly on its student population. In other words, middle- and upper-class students generally succeed in both private and public schools, whereas lower-class students experience a greater rate of failure in school. A case in point is the quality of education and the subsequent success of students in the affluent Brookline Public Schools—in Brookline, Massachusetts—and the failure of students in the inner-city Boston Public Schools.

Unfortunately, the school reform debate centers around a discourse of not naming it for what it is: class. The taboo "c word" in American education has made educators go to great length to avoid class reality. Euphemisms such as "economically marginal," "disenfranchised students," "disadvantaged students," "at-risk students," "educational mortality," "minority" (even where they represent the majority in schools) are among the terms that have been created to obfuscate the subordinate-class position of an ever-increasing student population entering our urban schools. What school choice fails to reveal is that equal choice to unequal educational structures never leads to equality and quality education. That is to say, choice without equity represents a process whereby the system further abandons the public responsibility by allowing inner-city public schools to deteriorate further. The essence of equity was elegantly articulated by Peter Cookson when he argued that "school reform policies that are not driven by a sense of educational and social justice are bound to fail. Excellence and equity are not meaningful alternatives, because without equity there can be no excellence."[28] Unless the reformers deal head-on with the structures of poverty that characterize the lives of a large segment of students who go to inner-city public schools, the offer of school choice without the means to access it represents the ultimate pedagogy of entrapment. Put simply, by shifting more public moneys away from already decrepit schools to private and middle- and upper-class public schools, reformers are sentencing lower-class students to a de facto boot-camp minimum security detention center parading under the veil of urban public education.

Missing from the present school reform debate is a language of democracy that "reflect[s] the primacy of the ethical, social, and civic in public life."[29] Is it ethical to take precious funding from Brockton Public Schools, a district that is on the verge of bankruptcy, and give it to the more affluent Avon Public Schools? Where in Bush's America 2000 did you find references to educational equity, social justice, and liberatory education? On the contrary, America 2000 embraced a corporate ideology that promotes individualism, privatization, and competition, as seen from its goals:

1. Every child will start school ready to learn
2. The high school graduation rate will increase to 90 percent
3. Competency will be demonstrated in five core subjects in grades 4, 8, and 12
4. American students will be ranked first in the world in both math and sciences
5. Every American adult will be a literate and responsible citizen
6. Every school will be liberated from drugs and violence[30]

What the Bush plan failed to articulate is that drugs and violence in schools are directly linked to the "savage inequalities" in the society that generates the despair born of poverty, loss of dignity, dehumanization, and hopelessness, as exemplified in the dialogue "Ghetto Life 101." It would make immensely more sense if Bush's America 2000 proposed to also liberate subordinate students from the yoke of poverty, social injustices, racism, sexism, and other discriminatory practices that characterize their reality.

In contrast to the U.S. market notion of school reform that has "virtually replaced citizens or even person as the principal mode of reference to human beings,"[31] Paulo Freire put into motion an educational transformation plan whose major goals were

1. Democratization and access
2. Democratization of administration
3. New quality of teaching
4. Youth and adult education

Paulo Freire's notion of educational transformation involves the democratization of the pedagogical and educational power so that students, staff, teachers, educational specialists, and parents come together to develop a plan that is grass-roots generated, accepting the tension and contradictions that are always present in all participatory efforts, thereby searching for a democratic substantivity.[32]

This search for democratic substantivity is evidenced in the transformation of the curriculum so that when one "necessarily [teaches] the content, one teaches also how to think critically."[33] Thus, the transformation of the curriculum required rigorous analysis that led to "the identification of significant contexts from which the generative themes [were] developed."[34] These themes are as follows:

- Work and leisure: road to security
- It is possible to live without violence
- School and the interaction of humans in the occupation of space
- Work and life: How does one construct relationships?
- Citizenship: how to achieve and how to keep it
- Community: conviviality, consciousness, and transformation
- Neighborhood
- Access, occupation, and appropriation of space by humans

In emphasizing and prioritizing the democratization of schools, Paulo Freire had to decentralize power so that school administrators were divested of excessive power. At the same time he had to create structures where teachers, students, parents, school staff, and the community could empower themselves so that they could participate and contribute in the school transformation process. As Paulo Freire correctly argued: "In a really progressive, democratic, and non-authoritarian way, one does not change the 'face' of schools through the central office. One cannot decree that, from today on, the schools will be competent, serious, and joyful. One cannot democratize schools authoritarianly."[35]

Compare the goal of democratizing schools in a country that is just beginning to experience democracy after decades of a cruel military dictatorship fully supported by the United States with the proposals put forth by our educational leaders. For example, take Chester Finn's argument "against local control, and giving power to professional educators and lay governing boards."[36] Or Chubb and Moe's contention that "public schools have been pulled in too many directions by the 'excess' of democratic demands."[37] That translates as the teaching of students about "multiculturalism, environmentalism, and a thousand other world-saving crusades ... issues for which neither [students] nor teachers have even the rudiments of competence."[38] While Paulo Freire was trying to democratize schools by divesting the central administration of excessive power and proposing that even principals be democratically elected by their respective schools, in Massachusetts, the birthplace of democratic public schooling, Governor William Weld instituted draconian educational cuts and proposed the privatization of schools via school choice. In Boston, the birthplace of the first public school in the United States, Mayor Ray Flynn moved aggressively to dismantle the elected school committee and replaced it with members that he appointed.

In a short two-and-a-half years, the retention rate in the São Paulo schools went up to 81 percent, the best result obtained in the decade of the 1980s. Under Freire's administration, community councils were created and vested with real democratic power to negotiate school issues that ranged from curricular reform to school renovation. Teacher's salaries were increased dramatically, and ongoing teacher preparation was initiated. More that ninety social movements, including the unions, signed a pact with the Educational Bureau to work toward the total eradication of illiteracy in São Paulo. This is in marked contrast with the Boston Compact, formed mostly by business leaders concerned with the high failure rate in the Boston Public Schools.

The democratic spirit of Freire's administration alerted the society that

> we should not call on the people to come to the school to receive instruction, recipes, threats, reprehension and punishment, but to participate collectively in the construction of knowledge, that goes beyond the knowledge made by pure experience, that takes into consideration its needs and turns it into a tool of struggle, making it possible for them to become subjects of their own history. The people's participation in the creation of culture rup

tures with the tradition that considers that only the elites are competent and knowledgeable about the needs and interests of the entire society.[39]

This call for collective participation differs significantly from the plan proposed by Benno Schmidt Jr., who left Yale to head the first for-profit schools in the nation. Schmidt argued that "if restrictive union contracts are a burden for many school districts, Project Edison would go one better than merely hiring nonunion workers: it would get people to work for free."[40] Schmidt's notion of collective participation is that "children and parents will be volunteers, if you will, taking on much more of the burden" of running schools. He equated his plan to a Japanese model where "kids cook the meals, run the cafeteria, take care of the upkeep of the schools. Imagine a model where children are partners in the education effort."[41] Unlike Freire's concept of collective participation, Schmidt's view of educational partnership is stripped of any intellectual substance to the extent that it relegates collective participation to only utilitarian chores, a splendid curriculum to adapt poor kids to the flip-hamburgerization economy.

A democratic society that gives up its public responsibility is a democracy in crisis. A society that equates for-profit privatization with democracy is a society with confused priorities. A democratic society that falsely believes, in view of the S&L debacle and the Wall Street scandals, for example, that quality, productivity, honesty, and efficiency can be achieved only through for-profit privatization is a society characterized by a bankruptcy of ideas. If we follow the line of argument that "private" is best, we should once again consider Jack Beatty's question: "Would we set up a private Pentagon to improve our public defense establishment?"[42] Would private-is-best logic eradicate the ongoing problems in the military that range from rampant sexual harassment, as exemplified by the Tailhook scandal, and payment of over $700 for a toilet seat to billions for planes that don't fly and Pentagon officials-turned-consultants through the revolving-door effect?

Most Americans would find the privatization of the Pentagon an utter absurdity, claiming a national priority for a strong defense. I contend that the safeguarding of our democracy rests much more on the creation of an educated, smart citizenry than on the creation of smart bombs.

School choice as a reform discourse places the educational debate outside the social reality that generates discrimination, racism, sexism, and economic inequality. Thus, the present educational reform fails to address the interrelationship between schools and the sociocultural reality within which schools exist. Hence, it becomes extremely difficult to change schools without changing the society that created undemocratic schools characterized by cruel and stark inequalities.

In order to transform schools into democratic sites, we must analyze and understand the structural and causal realities that produced undemocratic and unequal schools in the first place. Thus, on the one hand, it is imperative to analyze and describe the social and historical conditions of the United States so as to explain the ideology that produced undemocratic schools and is presently reproducing education inequalities through hidden systemic mechanisms. On the other hand, educators need to also understand the students' cultural production, including their resistance, and develop pedagogies that speak to the reality of the culture produced by students.

The present school reform in the United States can be best characterized as a battle between conservative forces that aggressively want to maintain the status quo from which they have benefited greatly and liberal forces that recognize that certain changes are needed as long as they consist of the gradual incorporation of subordinate social and cultural groups into the structural reality of schools. However, the proposed incorporation of these groups should never question the asymmetrical power relations that give White liberals their privilege. Thus, many White liberals willingly call and work for curriculum diversity but are reluctant to confront issues of inequality, power, ethics, race, and ethnicity that could lead to the transformation of schools to make them more democratic, less racist, more humane, and less discriminatory.

What is rarely discussed in the present school reform debate is the total integration of diverse racial and cultural groups, leading to their active presence within the school reality so as to transcend what Lani Guinier correctly called "the triumph of tokenism." A total integration of diverse subordinate groups into an active democratic participation in schools can begin to create structures that will lead to a total decolonization of the subordinate groups so they can move from their object position in the margin to a subject position at the core of school life. This, obviously, would imply, not a curriculum diversity for inequality in the form of "triumphant tokenism," but a process that makes diversity the very core of the school reality. A total integration of subordinate students would also imply moving beyond reforms based on choice. It would require not only a total transformation of schools but also the transformation of those social and political forces that shape and maintain the present "savage inequalities." A true transformation of schools would require a political and historical project that consciously transcended the educational system created and maintained by the dominant group for its own benefit.

A total transformation of schools informed by a truly cultural democracy cannot remain paralyzed by the liberal abstraction of cultural diversity and pluralism. School transformation must speak directly to the undemocratic nature of schools that is part of a colonial legacy. Educators must realize that beneath the aura of democratic schools lies a colonial historical will that has bequeathed us the rampant social inequality along the lines of race, class, gender, language, and ethnicity. Once educators become cognizant of the colonial ideology that still informs our schools, they can begin to create pedagogical structures that will lead to a total decolonization so as to achieve democratization.

Many educators will object to my use of the term "colonialism" to characterize schools in the United States. However, as a colonized person who experienced firsthand the discriminatory practices of Portuguese colonialism, I can readily see many similarities between the colonial ideology and the dominant values that inform schooling in the United States, particularly with respect to subordinate groups. Colonialism imposes "distinction" as an ideological yardstick against which all other cultural values are measured. On the one hand, this ideological yardstick serves to overcelebrate the dominant group's values to a level of mystification, and on the other hand, it devalues other cultural expressions. It is for this reason that Portuguese colonialism tried to eradicate all manifestations of African culture by forbidding the use of African languages in institutional life and by inculcating Africans through the educational system with myths and beliefs concerning the "savage" nature of their cultures.

If we analyze closely the ideology that informs the present debate over bilingual education—spearheaded by the conservative English Only Movement—and the present polemic over the primacy of Western heritage versus multiculturalism, we can begin to see and understand that the ideological principles that sustain those debates are consonant with the structures and mechanisms of a colonial ideology as succinctly described: "Culturally, colonialism has adopted a negation to the [native culture's] symbolic systems, forgetting or undervaluing them even when they manifest themselves in action. This way, the eradication of past and the idealization and the desire to relive the cultural heritage of colonial societies constitute a situation and a system of ideas along with other elements situate the colonial society as a class."[43]

If it were not for the colonial legacy, how could we explain the U.S. educational policies in the Philippines and Puerto Rico? English was imposed as the only language of instruction in the Philippines, and the imposed American textbook presented the American culture not only as superior but as a "model par excellence for the Philippine society."[44] This type of miseducation was so prevalent that it led T. H. Pardo de Tavera, a collaborator in U.S. colonialism, to write in a letter to General Douglas MacArthur: "After Peace is established all our efforts will be directed to Americanizing ourselves, to cause a knowledge of the English language to be extended and generalized in the Philippines, in order that through its agency we may adopt its principles, its political customs, and its peculiar civilization that our redemption may be complete and radical."[45]

It is the same complete and radical redemption that the United States hoped to achieve in Puerto Rico when Theodore Roosevelt's commissioner of education in Puerto Rico, Roland P. Faulkner, mandated in 1905 that instruction in public schools had to be conducted in English and made Puerto Rican schools "agencies of Americanization in the entire country, and where [schools] would present the American ideal to our youth. Children born under the American flag and in the American soil should have constantly present this ideal, so that they can feel proud of their citizenship and have the flag that represents the true symbol of liberty."[46]

If our colonial legacy remains unexamined, the option of choosing a school where students are denied the opportunity to study their language and culture is, for all practical purposes, a choiceless choice. Instead of becoming enslaved by the management discourse of the present educational reform that enhances the economic interests of the reformers and making secure their privileged social and cultural positions, educators need to reconnect with our historical past so as to understand the colonial legacy that undermines our democratic aspirations. Although Renato Constantino was writing about the colonial legacy in the Philippines, his thoughtful words are not only apropos but also illuminating regarding the present historical juncture in education:

> We see our present with as little understanding as we view our past because aspects of the past which could illumine the present have been concealed from us. This concealment has been effected by a systemic process of miseducation characterized by a thoroughgoing inculcation of colonial values and attitudes—a process which could not have been so effective had we not been denied access to the truth and to be part of our written history. As a consequence, we have become a people without a sense of history. We accept the present as given, bereft of historicity. Because we have so little comprehension of our past, we have no appreciation of its meaningful interrelation with the present.[47]

The Method: Fetish of Reform

As the capitalist "banking model" of education generates greater and greater failure, many liberal and neoliberal educators are looking to Paulo Freire's pedagogy as an alternative. No longer can it be argued that Freire's pedagogy is appropriate only in Third World contexts. For one thing, we are experiencing a rapid "Third Worldization" of North America, where inner cities resemble more and more the shantytowns of the Third World with a high level of poverty, violence, illiteracy, human exploitation, homelessness, and human misery. The abandonment of our inner cities and the insidious decay of their respective infrastructures, including their schools, makes it very difficult to maintain the artificial division between the First World and the Third World. It is just as easy to find "Third Worldness" in the First World inner cities as it is to discover First World opulence in the oligarchies in El Salvador, Guatemala, and many other Third World nations. The Third Worldization of the North American inner cities has also produced large-scale educational failures that have created minority student dropout rates ranging from 50 to 65 percent in the Boston public schools to over 70 percent in larger metropolitan areas like New York City.

Against this landscape of educational failure, conservative educators, by and large, have drawn back in an attempt to salvage the status quo and contain the "browning" of America. These conservative educators have attempted to reappropriate the educational debate and to structure the educational discourse in terms of competition and privatization of schools.

In contrast to the market notion of school reform in the United States, many liberal and neoliberal educators have rediscovered Freire as an alternative to the conservative domestication education that equates free market ideology with democracy. Part of the problem with some of these pseudo-critical educators is that, in the name of liberation pedagogy, they reduce Freire's leading ideas to a method. According to Stanley Aronowitz, the North American fetish for method has allowed Freire's philosophical ideas to be "assimilated to the prevailing obsession of North American education, following a tendency in all human and social sciences, with methods—of verifying knowledge and, in schools, of teaching, that is, transmitting knowledge to otherwise unprepared students."[48]

This fetish for method works insidiously against educators' adhering to Freire's own pronouncement against the importation and exportation of methodology. In a long conversation I had with him about this issue he said: "Donaldo, I don't want to be imported or exported. It is impossible to export pedagogical practices without re-inventing them. Please, tell your fellow American educators not to import me. Ask them to re-create and re-write my ideas."

Freire's leading ideas concerning the act of knowing transcend the methods for which he is known. In fact, according to Linda Bimbi, "The originality of Freire's work does not reside in the efficacy of his literacy methods, but, above all, in the originality of its content designed to develop our consciousness"[49] as part of a humanizing pedagogy. Freire wrote: "A humanizing education is the path through which men and women can become conscious about their presence in the world. The way they act and think when they develop all of their capacities, taking into consideration their needs, but also the needs and aspirations of others."[50]

With that said, why is it that some educators, in their attempt to cut the chains of oppressive educational practices, blindly advocate the dialogical model, creating, in turn, a new form of methodological rigidity laced with benevolent oppression—all done under the guise of democracy, with the sole excuse that it is for the students' own good? Many of us have witnessed pedagogical contexts in which we are implicitly or explicitly required to speak, to talk about our experiences, as an act of liberation. We all have been at conferences where the speaker is chastised because he or she failed to locate himself or herself in history. In other words, he or she failed to give primacy to his or her experiences in addressing issues of critical democracy. It does not matter that the speaker had important and insightful things to say. This is tantamount to dismissing Marx because he did not entrance us with his personal lived experiences.

The appropriation of the dialogical method as a process of sharing experiences is often reduced to a form of group therapy that focuses on the psychology of the individual. Although some educators may claim that this process creates a pedagogical comfort zone, in my view, it does little beyond making the oppressed feel good about his or her own sense of victimization. In other words, the sharing of experiences should not be understood in psychological terms only. It invariably requires a political and ideological analysis as well. That is, the sharing of experiences must always be understood within a social praxis that entails both reflection and political action. In short, it must always involve a political project with the objective of dismantling oppressive structures and mechanisms.

The overdose of experiential celebration that characterizes some strands of critical pedagogy offers a reductionist view of identity and experience within, rather than outside, the problematics of power, agency, and history. By overindulging in the legacy and importance of their respective voices and experiences, these educators often fail to move beyond a notion of difference structured in polarizing binarisms and uncritical appeal to the discourse of experience.[51] For this reason, they invoke a romantic pedagogical mode that exoticizes lived experiences as a process of coming to voice. By refusing to link experiences to the politics of culture and critical democracy, these educators reduce their pedagogy to a form of middle-class narcissism. On the one hand, the dialogical method provides the participants with a group therapy space for stating their grievances, and on the other hand, it offers the educator or facilitator a safe pedagogical zone to deal with his or her class guilt.

This tension over the uncritical celebration of experience is played out in the following dialogue between two well-known feminists, bell hooks and Gloria Steinem:[52]

HOOKS:
I don't think that's dissent Gloria. I think that is something that turns me off.

STEINEM:
It's respect for individual experiences.

HOOKS:
That's exactly the model that nauseates me. I hate being in a room where we're made to feel like everybody has an equal voice. Because I've seen that model close down dissent, make it appear that all opinions are equal. It's like you've got your opinion, I've got mine.

STEINEM:
Part of the ethic of these groups was "experience." It wasn't about opinion.

HOOKS:
But I think that we were very good at hearing each other's experience. Dissent is when we can argue a point in a dialectical way.

By refusing to deal with the issue of class privilege, the pseudo-critical educator dogmatically pronounces that he or she empowers students, gives them voices. These educators are even betrayed by their own language. Instead of creating pedagogical structures that would enable oppressed students to empower themselves, they paternalistically proclaim, "We need to empower students." This position often leads to the creation of what I call literacy and poverty pimps: While proclaiming to empower students, they are in fact strengthening their own privileged position.

The following example will clarify my point: A progressive teacher who had been working with me in a community-based literacy project betrayed her liberal discourse about empowering the community when one of the agencies we work with solicited my help in writing a math-literacy proposal for them. I agreed and welcomed the opportunity. One of my goals is to develop structures so that community members and agencies can take their own initiative and chart their own course, thus eliminating the need for our continued presence and expertise. In other words, our success in creating structures that enable community members to empower themselves rests on the degree to which our presence and expertise in the community are no longer necessary. Community members will have acquired their own expertise, thus preventing a type of neocolonialism.

When this teacher heard about the math-literacy proposal she was reticent but did not show outward opposition. However, weeks later, when she learned that the community-based math-literacy grant I was writing with the community members competed with our own university-based proposal that was designed to provide literacy training to community members, my colleague reacted almost irrationally. She argued that the community agency that had written the math-literacy grant did not follow a democratic process in that it had not involved her in the development of the grant. A democratic and participatory process in her view referred to the condition that community action needed to include her, this despite the fact that she was not a member of the particular community the math-literacy grant was designed to serve. Apparently, in her mind, one can be empowered as long as the empowerment does not encroach on the "expert's" privileged, powerful position. This is a position of power designed to paternalistically empower others.

When I pointed out to this teacher the obvious ideological contradictions in her behavior, her response was quick, aggressive, and almost automatic: "I'll be very mad if they get their proposal and we don't get ours." It became very clear to me that my colleague's real political commitment to the community hinged on the extent to which her "expert" position remained unthreatened. That is, the literacy "expert," do-gooder, antiestablishment persona makes sure that his or her privileged position within the establishment as an antiestablishment "expert" is never absorbed by empowered community members.

It is this same colonizer, paternalistic attitude that led a White middle-class professor to pronounce publicly, at a major conference, that community people don't need to go to college because they know so much more than do members of the university community; thus there is little that the university can teach them. While making such public statements, this professor was busily moving from the inner-city to an affluent suburb making sure that her children attend better schools. A similar attitude emerged in a recent meeting to develop a community-university relationship grant proposal. During the meeting, a liberal, White professor rightly protested the absence of community members in the committee. However, in attempting to valorize the community knowledge base, she rapidly fell into a romantic paternalism by stating that the community people knew much more than the university professors and that they should be invited to come to teach us rather than we teaching them. This position not only discourages community members from having access to the cultural capital from which these professors have benefited greatly but it also disfigures the reality context that makes the university cultural capital indispensable for any type of real empowerment. It also smacks of a false generosity of paternalism, which Freire aggressively opposed: "The pedagogy of the oppressed animated by authentic humanism (and not humanitarianism) generously presents itself as a pedagogy of man. Pedagogy which begins with the egoistic interests of the oppressors (an egoism cloaked in the false generosity of paternalism) and makes of the oppressed the objects of its humanitarianism, itself maintains and embodies oppression. It is an instrument of dehumanization."[53] The paternalistic pedagogical attitude represents a liberal, middle-class narcissism that gives rise to pseudo-critical educators who are part of and responsible for the same social order they claim to renounce.

This is not surprising, since classical liberalism, as a school of thought and as ideology, always prioritized the right to private property while relegating human freedom and other rights to "mere epiphenomena or derivatives."[54] A rigorous analysis of thinkers such as Thomas Hobbes and John Locke will clearly show that the real essence of liberalism is the right to own property. The right to private property could only be preserved through self-conservation. This led Liubomir Tadic to pose the following question: "Isn't conservatism a more determinant characteristic for liberalism than the tendency toward freedom?"[55] He concluded that owing to this insipid ambiguity, liberalism is always positioned ideologically between revolution and reactionaryism. In other words, liberalism vacillates between two opposing poles.

It is this liberal position of vacillation that, on the one hand, propels many individuals to denounce all forms of oppression and even side with the oppressed through a form of romanticism as demonstrated by my colleague's blind celebration of the subordinate community's knowledge base. The intrinsic liberal impulse to conserve one's position of privilege (either from acquired property or other cultural capital specific to one's privileged class), on the other hand, forces liberals to always make sure that their children go to the best schools as a means to acquire the necessary cultural capital that will guarantee the children the same privileges enjoyed by their parents.

It is for this reason that many liberals prefer to go to Australia to study the causes of illiteracy among Aborigines than to attempt to analyze the oppressive structures in the United States that have generated an unacceptably high level of literacy (and poverty) among the diverse subordinate racial and cultural groups. In distant and remote areas of the world, these liberals are able to safely display their presumed benevolence toward the oppressive conditions of a particular subordinate cultural group without having to acknowledge that because of their privileged position, they are part of a social order that created the very reality of oppression they want to study. Studying and exoticizing subordinate cultural groups in remote areas of the world as well as in the United States position many liberals as tourists that can "become enamored and perhaps interested in the [groups] for a time,"[56] but always shield themselves from the reality that created the oppressive conditions they wanted to study in the first place.

The position of many liberals in the United States is similar to that of the leftist colonialists who, in not wanting to destroy their cultural privileges, found themselves in an ever-present contradiction. This contradiction surfaces often when liberals feel threatened by the legitimacy of a subordinate group's struggle—a struggle that not only may not include them but also may demand that their liberal treatment of oppression as an abstract idea must be translated into concrete political action. For example, when I was discussing some of these issues with graduate students at Harvard, a middle-class, White woman impatiently asked me if I was suggesting that she give up her job. I responded that the answer was complex but that, in some instances, giving up one's job may be necessary. I pointed out to her that as a middle-class, White Harvard graduate student she had immensely more opportunities to secure jobs than many minority women with whom she worked in the community. Her continued occupation of leadership position in a subordinate community meant that a minority woman would not occupy that position. I gave as an example the student Literacy Corps Tutor Training Program that was designed to train tutors to provide literacy in various communities. In this program, over 86 percent of coordinators are middle-class, White women. That means that if they were to hold on to their coordinatorship positions, over 90 percent of minority women and men would not have the chance to occupy such leadership positions. I also called to her attention that minority women have infinitely less opportunity outside their racial context to compete for leadership positions.

As the discussion became a little tense, another White middle-class student cited an episode that helped us come to a closure. She told us that a female friend of hers had given up a successful career in business to work in the community with battered mothers. Enthusiastic in her altruism, she went into a community center where she explained to one of the center staff how much more rewarding it would be to work helping people in need than just making money. The African-American staff member responded: "Ma'am, if you really want to help us, go back to your white folks and tell them to keep the wall of racism from crushing us." This metaphor brought home a point I had not been able to make during the discussion. That is, the issue is not to give up or not give up a job. The real issue is to understand one's privileged position in the process of helping so as not to, on the one hand, turn help into a type of missionary paternalism or, on the other hand, limit the possibilities for the creation of structures that lead to real empowerment. The metaphor also points to White teachers' responsibility to attack oppression at its very source, which is often White-racist supremacy. Otherwise, the romanticism about "empowering" subordinate students could lead to the kind of insidious paternalism that provoked a Nigerian undergraduate student enrolled in a literacy-tutor-training program to tell her White teacher while they were discussing issues of oppression: "I am tired of the oppressor always reminding the oppressed of their condition."

The understanding of one's historical and privileged positionality requires a great deal of political clarity. However, political clarity can never be achieved if one accommodates to a position of ambiguity that usually suppresses one's ideological contradictions. This process of ideological-contradiction suppression has not only been commonplace among many White liberal educators working with subordinate students, but it was also a trait of the liberal colonialist:

> While he happens to dream of tomorrow, a brand-new social state in which the colonized cease to be colonized, he certainly does not conceive, on the one hand, of a deep transformation of his own situation and his personality. In that new more harmonious state, he will go on being what he is, with his language intact and his cultural traditions dominating. Through a de facto contradiction which he either does not see in himself or refuses to see, he hopes to continue being a European by divine right in a country which would no longer be Europe chattel.[57]

This liberal colonialist contradiction is no different from that of the many White liberal educators who proselytize about empowering minorities while refusing to divest themselves of their class and whiteness privilege—a privilege that is often left unexamined, unproblematized, and accepted as a "divine right." To do otherwise is to willfully commit class and white supremacy suicide—a very difficult task, as accurately understood by Albert Memmi in his discussion of the liberal colonizer: "He vaguely hopes to be part of the future young nation, but he firmly reserves the right to remain a citizen of his native country. ... He invokes the end of colonization, but refuses to conceive that this revolution can result in the overthrow of his situation and himself. For it is too much to ask one's imagination to visualize one's own end, even if it be in order to be reborn another."[58]

The difficulty of imagining one's own end forces many White liberal educators who want to invoke the end of oppression to embrace a progressive methodology but not the leading ideas that may make one's own end a concrete reality. For this reason, many White pseudo-critical liberal educators willfully adopt Freire's methods but refuse to engage his theories. Like the White liberal pseudo-critical educator, "The colonist likes neither theory nor theorists. He who knows that he is in a bad ideological or ethical position generally boasts of being a man of action, one who draws his lessons from experience."[59]

Time and time again, I have encountered pseudo-critical educators who proclaim to be Freirian-inspired only to reject any dialogue that includes his theory, reducing his leading ideas to a fossilized dialogical method while claiming to be a "man [or a woman] of action, one who draws his [her] lessons from experience." The unwillingness to engage Freire's leading ideas while adopting his methods was pointed out to me by a graduate student in a sociolinguistics class. She asked me why most professors in our progressive graduate program talked about Freire's methods and not a single professor required her to read any of Freire's books in its entirety.

I want to end this chapter by proposing an antimethod pedagogy that refuses the rigidity of models and methodological paradigms. In other words, an antimethod pedagogy points to the impossibility of disarticulating methods from the theoretical principles that inform and shape them. An antimethod pedagogy makes it clear to educators that "a method of teaching reflects a particular view of the world and is articulated in the interest of unequal power relations. ... [and] education is involved in a complex nexus of social, cultural, and economic and political relationships that involve students, teachers, and theorists in different positions of power." By situating methods within a theoretical framework that necessarily involves a power relations analysis, educators cannot ignore their historical, racial, and privileged positions in the teaching and learning context. An antimethod pedagogy prevents the fragmentation of bodies of knowledge and requires a critical understanding of the relationship among facts and their reason for existing. It necessarily involves critical reflection followed by political action. That is, to the extent that an antipedagogy demands a high degree of political clarity, it prevents the pseudo-critical educator from romanticizing subordinate students and falling into a laissez-faire method of sharing experiences, which, in the end, may result in a new form of paternalism. Although an antimethod pedagogy would validate lived experiences, it would also require that we transcend experience so as to turn it into knowledge. Methods, divorced from the leading ideas that shape and maintain them, can never capture the complexity and contradiction inherent in a progressive and democratic pedagogy. Thus, a liberatory pedagogy should never be reduced to a method, no matter how progressive it may appear. As Lilia Bartolomé correctly argued, what is important is not the method but the process to make education more humane. She contended that teachers who use traditional methods but make the educational experience more humane achieve greater success than those teachers who adopt progressive methods but continue to devalue and disrespect their students. Bartolomé concluded that "what is important is not the method but the creation of pedagogical spaces where subordinate students move from an object to a subject position."[60]

The antimethod pedagogy calls the White liberals' attention to the fact that it is not enough to find comfort in a method that pays lip service to antiracism and social justice. It also reminds them of the enormous contradiction between their condemnation of oppression and their unwillingness to divest themselves of their received "divine" privilege from the oppressive social orders.

The antimethod pedagogy forces us to view Freire's dialogical method as a form of social praxis so that sharing of experience is always informed by reflection and political action. Dialogue as social praxis "entails that recovering the voice of the oppressed is the fundamental condition for human emancipation."[61] By "voice" I do not mean a mere exchanging of experience as a form of group therapy but rather a process that turns experience into critical reflection and political action. The antimethod pedagogy also frees us from the beaten path of certainties and specialism. It rejects the mechanization of intellectualism. It prevents the bureaucratization of the mind. The antimethod pedagogy does not allow educators to accommodate to a pedagogy of lies, but it forces them to live in truth. In short, the antimethod pedagogy calls for the illumination of Freire's leading ideas that will guide us toward the critical road of truth, toward the reappropriation of our endangered dignity, toward the reclaiming of our humanity. No one could argue more pointedly against reducing dialogue and problem posing to a mere method than Freire himself: "Problem posing education is revolutionary futurity. Hence, it is prophetic. ... Hence it corresponds to the historical nature of man. Hence it affirms men as beings who transcend themselves. ... Hence it identifies with the movement which engages men as being aware of their incompletion—an historical movement which has its point of departure, its subjects and its objective."[62]

Not only does the antimethod pedagogy adhere to Freire's view of education as revolutionary futurity, it also celebrates the eloquence of Antonio Machado's poem:

Caminante no hay camino,
se hace el camino al andar.

Traveler, there is no road.
The road is made as one walks.[63]

Notes

Chapter 1

1. Samuel Bowles, David M. Gordon, and E. Thomas Weisskopf, "An Economic Strategy for Progressives," *Nation*, Feb. 10, 1992, pp. 163–164.

2. Diego Ribadeneira, "Taking a Stand, Seated," *Boston Globe*, Nov. 14, 1991, p. 40.

3. Noam Chomsky, *Language and Politics*, ed. C. P. Otero (New York: Black Rose Books, 1988), p. 681.

4. As cited in Howard Zinn, *Declarations of Independence: Cross Examining American Ideology* (New York: Harper Collins, 1990), pp. 234–235.

5. As cited in ibid.

6. Alan Lukas, *Common Ground* (New York: Alfred A. Knopf, 1985), p. 281.

7. Herald Wire Services, *Boston Herald*, May 1, 1992, p. 2.

8. Ibid.

9. Ibid.

10. Jonathan Kozol, *Savage Inequalities: Children in America's Schools* (New York: Crown Publishers, 1991), p. 2.

11. Langston Hughes, "Montage of a Dream Deferred," *The Panther and the Lash* (New York: Alfred A Knopf Inc., 1951).

12. Chomsky, *Language and Politics*, p. 671.

13. As quoted in ibid.

14. Ibid.

15. Henry A. Giroux, *Border Crossings: Cultural Workers and the Politics of Education* (New York: Routledge, 1992), p. 3.

16. Ibid.

17. Noam Chomsky, *On Power and Ideology* (Boston: South End Press, 1987), p. 6.

18. Patrick L. Courts, *Literacy and Empowerment: The Meaning Makers* (South Hadley, Mass.: Bergin and Garvey, 1991), p. 4.

19. John Ashbery, "What Is Poetry," *Houseboat Days: Poems by John Ashbery* (New York: Penguin Books, 1977), p. 47.

20. Courts, *Literacy and Empowerment*, p. 48.

21. Personal communication, Fall 1992.

22. Personal communication, Fall 1992.

23. UNESCO, *An Asian Model of Educational Development* (Paris: UNESCO, 1966), p. 97.

24. Henry A. Giroux, *Theory and Resistance in Education: A Pedagogy for the Opposition* (South Hadley, Mass.: Bergin & Garvey, 1983), p. 87.

25. Paulo Freire, *The Politics of Education* (South Hadley, Mass.: Bergin & Garvey, 1985), p. 116.

26. Ibid., p. 114.

27. Ibid., p. 117.

28. Tom Paxton, "What Did You Learn in School Today?" Copyright © 1962 Cherry Lane Music Publishing Company, Inc. (ASCAP).

29. Jose Ortega y Gasset, *The Revolt of the Masses* (1930; reprint, New York: W. W. Norton, 1964), p. 111.

30. Ibid.

31. James Gee, *The Social Mind: Language, Ideology, and Social Practices* (South Hadley, Mass.: Bergin & Garvey, 1992), p. vii.

32. Richard Fowler, Bob Hodge, Gunter Kress, and Tony Trew, *Language and Control* (London: Routledge & Kegan Paul, 1979), p. 192.

33. Greg Myers, "Reality, Consensus, and Reform in the Rhetoric of Composition Teaching," *College English*, 48 (1986), p. 111.

34. Ortega y Gasset, *Revolt of the Masses*, p. 111

35. Giroux, *Theory and Resistance in Education*, p. 87.

36. Ortega y Gasset, *Revolt of the Masses*, p. 112.

37. Freire, *Politics of Education*, p. 131.

38. "U.S. Infant Mortality Hits Low," *Boston Globe*, Feb. 7, 1992, p. 8.

39. As cited in Paulo Freire and Donaldo Macedo, *Literacy: Reading the Word and the World* (South Hadley, Mass.: Bergin & Garvey, 1987), p. 130.

40. Ibid.

41. Paulo Freire, *Politics of Education*, p. 118.

42. Catherine Wilson, "U.S. Begins Returning Haitian Refugees," *Boston Globe*, Feb. 2, 1992, pp. 2–3; and Christopher Boyd, "Friends for Cubans Who Flee," *Boston Globe*, Feb. 2, 1992, p. 2.

43. As cited in Derrick Z. Jackson, "The Wrong Relations," *Boston Globe*, Nov. 3, 1993, p. 19.

44. Ibid.

45. As cited in Noam Chomsky, "On the Gulf Policy," *Open Magazine*, Pamphlet Series, 1991, p. 8.

46. Ibid.

47. Ibid.

48. Freire and Macedo, *Literacy*, p. 131.

49. Gee, *The Social Mind*, p. xv.

50. Freire and Macedo, *Literacy*, p. 132.

51. Ibid.

52. Gee, *The Social Mind*, p. xi.

53. Peter McLaren and Rhonda Hammer, "Media Knowledges, Warrior Citizenry, and Postmodern Literacies," *Journal of Urban and Cultural Studies* 1 (1992), p. 49.

54. William Lutz, *Doublespeak* (New York: Harper Collins, 1989), p. 1.

55. McLaren and Hammer, "Media Knowledges," p. 51.

56. Paul F. Walker and Eric Stambler, "The Surgical Myth of the Gulf War," *Boston Globe*, Apr. 16, 1991, p. 15.

57. "U.S. Ordered a Stop to Patriot Criticism MIT Professor Says," *Boston Globe*, Mar. 18, 1992, p. 3.

58. Ibid.

59. "Packaging the War," *Boston Globe*, Jan. 20, 1991, p. 74.

60. McLaren and Hammer, "Media Knowledges," p. 50.

61. Edward S. Hermon and Noam Chomsky, *Manufacturing Consent: The Political Economy of Mass Media* (New York: Pantheon Books, 1988), p. 35.

62. McLaren and Hammer, "Media Knowledges," p. 44.

63. "Packaging the War."

64. As cited in "Quayle, in Boston, Tells of U.S. Relief Effort for Iraq Refugees," *Boston Globe*, Apr. 12, 1991, p. 15.

65. Interview with Natalie Jacobson, "Nightly News at 6:00 PM," Jan. 16, 1992.

66. Ortega y Gasset, *Revolt of the Masses*, p. 130.

67. Ibid.

68. Ibid.

69. Martin A. Lee and Norman Solomon, *Unreliable Sources: A Guide to Detecting Bias in News Media* (New York: Carol Publishing Group, 1991), p. xxii.

70. Chomsky, *Language and Politics*, p. 681.

71. Ibid., p. 673.

72. Ibid., p. 708.

73. For a complete discussion of this issue, see Jonathan Kozol, *Illiterate America* (New York: Anchor Press/Doubleday, 1985), pp. 3–40.

74. Mary Jordan, "US Study Raises Alarm on Literacy Among Adults," *Boston Globe*, September 9, 1993, p. 14.

75. Giroux, *Border Crossings*, p. 111.

Chapter 2

1. Stanley Aronowitz and Henry A. Giroux, "Schooling, Culture and Literacy in the Age of Broken Dreams: A Review of Bloom and Hirsch," *Harvard Educational Review* 58, no. 2 (May 1988), p. 175.

2. Ibid., p. 178.

3. John F. Kennedy. Speech at Yale University, June 1962, cited in *Tucson Citizen*, June 16, 1981, p. 36.

4. Barbara Flores, "Language Interference or Influence: Toward a Theory for Hispanic Bilingualism," Ph.D. dissertation, University of Arizona at Tucson, 1982, p. 131.

5. Vaclav Havel, *Living in Truth* (London: Faber and Faber, 1989), p. 41.

6. Ibid.

7. Ibid., p. 42.

8. Ibid.

9. Ibid.

10. Ibid.

11. Noam Chomsky, *Language and Politics*, ed. C. P. Otero (New York: Black Rose Books, 1988).

12. Havel, *Living in Truth*, p. 42.

13. Ibid., p. 43.

14. Noam Chomsky and John Silber interview, WGBH-TV, Boston, *The Ten O'clock News,* March 13, 1986.

15. Chomsky, *Language and Politics,* p. 672.

16. An index search of the On-Line-Union-Catalog (OCLC encompasses more than 9,000 libraries worldwide and contains over 27 million bibliographical records) for John Robert Silber's academic work on the subject of philosophy revealed only two works. One was his thesis, written in 1956, entitled "The Highest Good as the Unity of Form and Content in Kant's Ethics," available only in microform in the Yale University library. The second, written in 1959, "Kant's Conception of the Highest Good as Immanent and Transcendent," was available only at the University of Texas (Austin) library. The OCLC search revealed that in 1971, a nine-page article on the topic of educational philosophy, entitled "The Pollution of Time," was published by the *National Elementary Principal.* In 1989, John Silber authored *Straight Shooting: What's Wrong with America and How to Fix It,* a detailed political plan for his candidacy for the governorship of Massachusetts. An ERIC search for recent journal articles (January 1987 through March 1993) revealed no academic work on any subject.

17. Paul Robinson, "The Chomsky Problem," review of *Language and Responsibility, New York Times Book Review,* Feb. 23, 1979, pp. 3, 37. Quote appeared on back cover of Noam Chomsky, *The Prosperous Few and the Restless Many* (Berkeley, Calif.: Odonian Press, 1993). In contrast to John Silber, Noam Chomsky has published extensively and exerted considerable influence in various fields, including linguistics, education, philosophy, and psychology.

18. Interview with John Silber by Ed Bradley, *60 Minutes,* May 2, 1993.

19. John Silber, *President's Report to the Trustees,* Boston University, Apr. 15, 1993.

20. David Nyhan, "The Truth Comes Out on a Dirty US War," *Boston Globe,* Mar. 18, 1993, p. 19. In this article, David Nyhan summarized the UN Commission's findings as follows: (1) Between 200 and 500 peasants slaughtered at El Mozote in 1981; man accused: the late Colonel Domingo Monterrosa. (2) Archbishop Oscar Romero, shot dead as he said Mass, 1980; man accused: the late Roberto D'Aubuisson. (3) Six Jesuit priests, a housekeeper, and her fifteen-year-old daughter murdered in 1989; man accused: General Rene Emilio Ponce, who until October 1993 was El Salvador's defense minister. (4) Three nuns and an American laywoman raped and killed, 1980; man accused: General Vides Casanova, a former defense minister.

In this same article, David Nyhan reported that the two American journalists, Raymond Bonner, from the *New York Times,* and Alma Guillermoprieto, from the *Washington Post,* "were attacked by name in a now-infamous *Wall Street Journal* editorial. 'Overly credulous,' said the *Journal.* That's editorial-pagese for: Those two leftie-symp journalists are in the tank to the commies. In a passage that would eventually result in getting Bonner yanked off the El Salvador beat, the *Journal* encouraged the men who ran the *Times* to mistrust their own reporter, who'd been poking around among the skeletons."

David Nyhan also reported that Elliot Abrams, assistant secretary of state for human rights under Ronald Reagan, "bragged to Congress of his truthfulness" regarding his role in Latin America, particularly Nicaragua and El Salvador. Before pleading guilty on October 7, 1991, on two counts of withholding information from Congress and lying about Iran-Contra, Abrams boldly asserted: "There are two rules which I will use to guide my efforts. The first is that we must tell the truth. ... If we corrupt the language we use to discuss liberty, we commit a grave offense against all those, including tens of thousands of Americans, who have given their lives to preserve it." After plea-bargaining with Congress for his crime of perjury, Abrams received only a two-year suspended sentence.

21. Interview with John Silber by Ed Bradley, *60 Minutes*, May 2, 1993.

22. Arthur M. Schlesinger Jr., *The Disuniting of America: Reflections on a Multicultural Society* (New York: Norton, 1992), p. 13.

23. Ibid.

24. Amilcar Cabral, *Return to the Source: Selected Speeches of Amilcar Cabral* (New York: Monthly Review Press, 1973), p. 40.

25. Ibid.

26. Ibid.

27. Schlesinger, *The Disuniting of America*, p. 15.

28. Ibid., p. 17.

29. Peter McLaren, "White Terror and Oppositional Agency: Towards a Critical Multiculturalism," *Strategies*, in press.

30. Cabral, *Return to the Source*, p. 40.

31. Schlesinger, *The Disuniting of America*, p. 17.

32. Cornel West, *Race Matters* (Boston: Beacon Press, 1993) p. x. Racist attitudes are not limited to the United States, as exemplified by the recent experience of Henry Louis Gates Jr., chairman of the department of Afro-American studies at Harvard, in Paris: "There I was standing in the lobby of my chic Latin Quarter hotel ... when this French couple comes up to me and asks whether I'm their cabdriver." See Roger Cohen, "Once Welcome, Black Artists Return to Indifferent France," *New York Times*, Feb. 7, 1994.

33. Gates was quoted in Peter Applebome, "Goal Unmet, Duke Reveals Perils in Effort to Increase Black Faculty, *New York Times*, Sept. 19, 1993, p. 34.

34. bell hooks, *Talking Back: Thinking Feminist—Thriving Black* (Boston: South End Press, 1989), pp. 63–64.

35. Andrew Hacker, *Two Nations: Black and White, Separate, Hostile, Unequal* (New York: Ballantine Books, 1992), p. 2.

36. West, *Race Matters*, p. x.

37. "Black Agents Sue Denny's," *New York Times*, May 25, 1993, p. A10.

38. Henry Louis Gates Jr., *Loose Cannons: Notes on the Culture Wars* (New York: Oxford University Press, 1992), p. xv.

39. Paulo Freire and Donaldo Macedo, *Literacy: Reading the Word and the World* (South Hadley, Mass.: Bergin and Garvey, 1987) p. 143.

40. Peter McLaren, "Collision with Otherness," *American Journal of Semiotics* 9, nos. 2–3 (1993), pp. 121–148.

41. A. P. Sanoff and S. Mimerbrook, "Race on Campus," *U.S. News and World Report*, Apr. 9, 1993, pp. 52–64.

42. "Count Division for Jeffries Raises a Host of Questions," *Boston Globe*, May 16, 1993, p. 17.

43. Sanoff and Mimerbrook, "Race on Campus," p. 57.

44. "Count Division for Jeffries."

45. Ronald Takaki, *Iron Cages: Race and Culture in 19th Century America* (New York: Oxford University Press, 1990), p. 254.

46. Aronowitz and Giroux, "Schooling, Culture and Literacy," p. 177.

47. Ibid.

48. Ibid.

49. Howard Zinn, *A People's History of the United States* (New York: Harper Perennial, 1980), p. 8.

50. Ibid.

51. Aronowitz and Giroux, "Schooling, Culture and Literacy," p. 177.

52. Sean Walmsley, "On the Purpose and Content of Secondary Reading Programs," *Curriculum Inquiry* 11 (1981), p. 78.

53. Cited in "Defense of the Tradition" memorandum included in this chapter.

54. Jonathan Kozol, *Savage Inequalities: Children in America's Schools* (New York: Crown Publishers, 1991), p. 20.

55. Aronowitz and Giroux, "Schooling, Culture and Literacy," p. 178.

56. Walter Benjamin, "Theses on the Philosophy of History," in *Illuminations*, ed. Hannah Arendt (New York: Schocken Books, 1963), pp. 253–264.

57. Aronowitz and Giroux, "Schooling, Culture and Literacy," p. 185.

58. Ibid., p. 186.

59. Alice Miller, *For Your Own Good* (New York: Noonday Press, 1990), p. 54.

60. Ibid.

61. *Boston Globe*, May 27, 1993, p. 26.

62. *Boston Globe*, Mar. 18, 1993, p. 19.

63. Miller, *For Your Own Good*, p. 13.

64. J. Sulzer, *Versuch von der Erziehung and Unterweisung der Kinder*, quoted in ibid., pp. 12–13.

65. Quoted in ibid., p. 63.

66. G. Gannaway, *The Critical Mind* (Westport, Conn.: Bergin and Garvey, 1994).

67. As cited in Richard Hofstadter, *The American Political Tradition* (New York: Vintage Press, 1974), p. 148.

68. David Stannard, "Genocide in the Americas," *Nation*, Oct. 19, 1992, p. 430.

69. Zinn, *A People's History*, p. 184.

70. E. D. Hirsch Jr., F. J. Kett, J. Tuefil, *Dictionary of Cultural Literacy: What Every American Needs to Know* (Boston: Houghton Mifflin, 1988), pp. 243–410 passim.

71. Zinn, *A People's History*, p. 184.

72. Bruce Penny, *Malcolm X: The Lost Speeches* (New York: Pathfinder, 1989), p. 41.

73. Chomsky, *Language and Politics*, pp. 683–684.

74. Zinn, *A People's History*, pp. 89–90. Emphasis mine.

75. Malcolm X speech, given on January 24, 1965.

76. President Truman, cited in Zinn, *A People's History*, p. 415.

77. Ibid.

78. Ibid., p. 267.

79. Chomsky, *Language and Politics*, p. 701.

80. Zinn, *A People's History*, pp. 430–431.

81. *Washington Post*, Oct. 30, 1988.

82. Kozol, *Savage Inequalities*, p. 23.

83. Quoted in Zinn, *A People's History*, p. 178.

84. Robert J. Fields, *The History of the United States*, vol. 2 (New Jersey: Ammanour Corp. Book-Lab, 1987), p. 135.

85. James W. Gibson, *The Perfect War* (New York: Vintage Books, 1988), p. 146.

86. Ibid., p. 158.

87. Ibid., p. 147.

88. Ibid., pp. 202–203.

89. Herman Garcia letter.

90. Gibson, *The Perfect War*, p. 146.

91. Carlos Fuentes, "The Mirror of the Other," *Nation*, Mar. 30, 1992, p. 411.

92. Gibson, *The Perfect War*, p. 204.

93. Fuentes, "The Mirror of the Other," p. 411.

94. Ibid.

Chapter 3

1. Adam Pertman, "Buchanan Annouces Presidential Candidacy," *Boston Globe*, Dec. 11, 1991, p. 1.

2. Ralph Vartabedian, "US Had Secret Plan to Bail Out Contractor," *Boston Globe*, Mar. 23, 1992, p. 3.

3. Cited in Howard Zinn, *Declarations of Independence: Cross Examining American Ideology* (New York: Harper Perennial, 1990), p. 149.

4. J. Larry Brown, "Hunger in the U.S.," *Scientific American* 256, no. 2 (Feb. 1987), pp. 37–41.

5. Cited in Zinn, *Declarations of Independence*, p. 164.

6. Cited in Henry A. Giroux, *Border Crossings: Cultural Workers and the Politics of Education* (New York: Routledge, 1992), p. 230.

7. Carl Sandburg, *The People, Yes* (New York: Harcourt, Brace & World, 1964), p. 75.

8. Pertman, "Buchanan Announces Presidential Candidancy."

9. Parts of these conversations were published in Paulo Freire and Donaldo Macedo, *Literacy: Reading the Word and the World* (South Hadley, Mass.: Bergin and Garvey, 1987).

10. Richard Johnson, "What Is Cultural Studies Anyway?" *Angistica* 26, nos. 1–2 (1983), p. 11.

11. K. Weiler, "Freire and a Feminist Pedagogy of Difference," in Peter McLaren and Colin Lankshear, eds., *Politics of Liberation* (London: Routledge, 1994), p. 12.

12. Ibid., p. xx.

13. Gary Olson, "Postcolonial Discourse and the Border Intellectual: Henry Giroux and the Politics of Hope," *Journal of Urban and Cultural Studies* 2, no. 2 (1992), p. 97.

14. Albert Memmi, *The Colonizer and the Colonized* (Boston: Beacon Press, 1991), pp. 69–70.

15. bell hooks, Gloria Steinem, Uruashi Vaid, and Naomi Wolf, "Get Real About Feminism—The Myths, the Backlash, the Movement," *Ms. Magazine*, Sept./Oct. 1993, p. 39.

16. Derrick D. Bell, *Faces at the Bottom of the Well: The Penance of Racism* (New York: Basic Books, 1992), p. xiii.

Chapter 4

1. Laurie Olsen, *Crossing the Schoolhouse Border: Immigrant Students and the California Public Schools* (San Fransisco: California Tomorrow, 1988), p. 68.

2. Jonathan Kozol, *Illiterate America* (New York: Anchor Press/Doubleday, 1985), p. 4.

3. John Silber, Boston University Commencement Program, May 1991.

4. Henry A. Giroux, *Border Crossings: Cultural Workers and the Politics of Education* (New York: Routledge 1991), p. 235.

5. Anthony J. Lucas, *Common Ground* (New York: Alfred A. Knopf, 1985), p. 282.

6. Ibid.

7. Peter McLaren, "Critical Pedagogy: Constructing an Arch of Social Dreaming and a Doorway to Hope," *Journal of Education* 173, no. 1 (1991), pp. 12–13.

8. Stanley Aronowitz, "Why Should Johnny Read," *Village Voice Literary Supplement*, May 1985, p. 13.

9. Henry A. Giroux and Peter McLaren, "Teacher Education and the Politics of Engagement: The Case for Democratic Schooling," *Harvard Educational Review* 56, no. 3 (Aug. 1986), p. 213–238.

10. Cited in a brochure published in 1990 by the now-defunct Institute for Research in English Acquisition and Development, 1990.

11. Antonio Gramsci, *Selections from Prison Notebooks*, ed. and trans. Quinten Hoare and Geoffrey Smith (New York: International Publishers, 1971), p. 52.

12. Giroux, *Border Crossings*, p. 37.

13. Derrick Z. Jackson, "The End of the Second Reconstruction," *Boston Globe*, Dec. 8, 1991, p. 27.

14. Renato Constantino, *Neocolonial Identity and Counter Consciousness* (London: Merlin Press, 1978), p. 42.

15. Lou Ferleger and Jay Mandle, typewritten manuscript, 1991.

16. Patrick L. Courts, *Literacy and Empowerment: The Meaning Makers* (Westport, Conn.: Bergen and Garvey, 1991), p. xxiii.

17. James Donald, "Language Literacy, and Schooling," in *The State and Popular Culture* (Milton Keynes: Open University Culture Unit, 1982), p. 32.

18. Giroux and McLaren, "Teacher Education and the Politics of Engagement," p. 235.

19. Mikhail Bakhtin, *The Dialogic Imagination*, trans. Caryl Emerson and Michael Holquist (Austin: University of Texas Press, 1981), p. 294.

20. S. Walmsley, "On the Purpose and Content of Secondary Reading Programs: Educational and Ideological Perspectives," *Curriculum Inquiry* 11 (1981), p. 84.

21. Henry A. Giroux, *Theory and Resistance: A Pedagogy for the Opposition* (South Hadley, Mass.: Bergin and Garvey, 1983), p. 226.

22. Kenneth T. Jackson, cited in *Boston Sunday Globe*, Editorial, July 7, 1991, p. 74.

23. Giroux, *Theory and Resistance*, p. 226.

24. Chris Black, *Boston Sunday Globe,* Jan. 13, 1991.

25. Silber, Boston University Commencement Program.

Chapter 5

1. Jonathan Kozol, *Savage Inequalities: Children in American's Schools* (New York: Crown Publishers, 1991).

2. O. Reboul, *Lenguaje e Ideologia* (Mexico: Fondo de Cultura Economica, 1986), p. 117.

3. Ibid.

4. Ibid., p. 116.

5. Ibid., p. 117.

6. Henry Giroux and Donaldo Macedo, "Editorial Comment," *Journal of Urban and Cultural Studies* 1, no. 1 (1990), p. 4.

7. Peter Negroni, "The Transformation of America's Public Schools," manuscript, p. 12.

8. Peter W. Cookson Jr., *School Choice: The Struggle for the Soul of American Education* (New Haven: Yale University Press, 1994), pp. 2–3.

9. Negroni, "The Transformation of America's Public Schools," p. 7.

10. Ibid., p. 8.

11. Paulo Freire, *Pedagogy of the City* (New York: Continuum Publishing, 1993), p. 17.

12. Katherine Jensen, "Civilization and Assimilation in the Colonized Schooling of Native Americans," in Philip Altbach and Gail Kelly, eds., *Education and the Colonial Experience* (New Brunswick, N.J.: Transaction Books, 1984), p. 170.

13. Ibid.

14. Ibid.

15. Saul Levine, "On Guns and Health Care, the U.S. Caves In to Force," *San Diego Union-Tribune,* Aug. 12, 1993, p. 11.

16. Negroni, "The Transformation of America's Public Schools," p. 9.

17. Ibid.

18. Ibid., p. 10.

19. Ibid.

20. Derrick Z. Jackson, "Muted Voices in the Newsroom," *Boston Globe,* Sept. 2, 1993, p. 15.

21. Carol Swain, *New York Times,* Sept. 19, 1993, p. 34.

22. Jackson, "Muted Voices."

23. Henry A. Giroux, *Living Dangerously: Multiculturalism and the Politics of Difference* (New York: Peter Lang, 1993), p. 134.

24. "Weary of the Hostility, a City's Blacks Will Go," *New York Times,* Aug. 29, 1993, p. 24.

25. Jeffrey F. Obser, "Even in the US, Ideology Infects Language," Letter to the Editor, *New York Times,* July 15, 1992, p. A20.

26. Ibid.

27. Jonathan Kozol, "Widening the Gap," *Boston Sunday Globe,* Nov. 3, 1991, p. 20.

28. Cookson, *School Choice,* p. xi.

29. Giroux, *Living Dangerously,* p. 128.

30. *America 2000: An Education Strategy* (Washington, D.C.: U.S. Department of Education, 1991), p. 4. (Under the Clinton administration, the program was renamed Goals 2000, but it remains essentially the same.)

31. Obser, "Even in the US, Ideology Infects Language."

32. Paulo Freire, *A Educação na Cidade* (São Paulo: Cortez Editora, 1991), pp. 14–15.

33. Freire, *Pedagogy of the City*, p. 19.

34. Ana Maria Saul, in ibid., p. 150.

35. Ibid., pp. 19–20.

36. As cited in Giroux, *Living Dangerously*, p. 131.

37. Ibid.

38. Ibid.

39. Freire, *Pedagogy of the City*, p. 20.

40. Paul Hemp, "From Whittle, a $2.3B Education Plan," *Boston Globe*, Aug. 30, 1992, p. 25.

41. Ibid.

42. Jack Beatty, "The Bankruptcy of Conservatism," *Boston Globe*, Aug. 14, 1992. p. 19.

43. Geraldo Navas Davilla, *La Dialectica del Desarrollo Nacional: El Caso de Puerto Rico* (San Juan: Editorial Universitaria, 1978), p. 27.

44. Renato Constantino, *Neocolonial Identity and Counter-Consciousness* (London: Merlin Press, 1978), p. 66.

45. Ibid., p. 67.

46. Maria M. Lopez Lagunne, *Bilingualismo en Puerto Rico: Actitudes Sociolinguisticas del Maestro* (San Juan: M.I.S.C.E.S., Corp., 1989), p. 17

47. Constantino, *Neocolonial Identity and Counter-Consciousness*, p. 1.

48. Stanley Aronowitz, "Paulo Freire's Radical Democratic Humanism," in Peter McLaren and Peter Leonard, eds., *Paulo Freire: A Critical Encounter* (London: Routledge, 1993), p. 8.

49. Cited in Moacir Gadotti, *Convite a Leitura de Paulo Freire* (São Paulo: Editora Scipione, 1989), p. 32.

50. Paulo Freire and Frei Betto, *Essa Escola Chamada Vida* (São Paulo: Editora Scipione, 1989), p. 32.

51. Henry A. Giroux, "The Politics of Difference and Multiculturalism in the Era of the Los Angeles Uprising," *Journal of the Midwest Modern Language Association*, in press.

52. bell hooks, Gloria Steinem, Uruashi Vaid, and Naomi Wolf, "Get Real About Feminism—The Myths, the Backlash, the Movement," *Ms.*, Sept./Oct. 1993, p. 41.

53. Paulo Freire, *Pedagogy of the Oppressed* (New York: Continuum Publication, 1990), p. 30.

54. Mihailo Markovic, Liubomir Tadic, Danko Grlic, *Liberalismo y Socialismo: Teoria y Praxis* (Mexico: Editorial Grijalbo, 1977), p. 19.

55. Ibid., p. 17.

56. Albert Memmi, *The Colonizer and the Colonized* (Boston: Beacon Press, 1991), p. 26.

57. Ibid., p. 40.

58. Ibid.

59. Ibid., p. 70.

60. Lilia Bartolomé, "The Methods Fetish: Towards a Humanizing Pedagogy," *Harvard Educational Review,* in press.

61. Aronowitz, "Paulo Freire's Radical Democratic Humanism," pp. 11–12.

62. Freire, *Pedagogy of the Oppressed,* p. 72.

63. Antonio Machado, *Manuel y Antonio Machado: Obras Completas* (Madrid: Editorial Plenitud, 1962), p. 826.

About the Book and Author

In Boston, twelve-year-old student David Spritzler faced disciplinary action from his school for his vocal questioning of the Pledge of Allegiance, which celebrates liberty and justice for all. The boy's concerns were not taken by the teacher as an opportunity to engage the class in a discussion of the country's problems, such as homelessness, which could be seen just outside on Boston's streets. Across the river at prestigious MIT, a linguistics student told her colleague that she could not take time to read literature outside of theoretical linguistics if she wanted to be a top scholar in her field. Even essays that linked linguistics to its historical and social context fell outside her diligent pursuit of theory.

What do these two seemingly disparate events have in common? According to Donaldo Macedo, they are part of an educational legacy that stifles critical thinking in favor of indoctrination and specialization. Our educational system has lost sight of its responsibility to prepare students in the kind of broad, critical thinking necessary for responsible citizenship.

Challenging conservatives like Allan Bloom and E. D. Hirsch, Macedo shows why so-called common culture literacy is a form of dominant cultural reproduction that undermines independent thought and goes against the best interests of our students. Offering a wide-ranging counterargument, Macedo shows why cultural literacy cannot be restricted to the acquisition of Western heritage values, which sustain an ideology that sytematically negates the cultural experiences of many members of society—not only minorities but also anyone who is poor or disenfranchised. Macedo calls on his own experience as a Cape Verdean immigrant from West Africa who had to surmount the barriers imposed by the world's most entrenched monolingual system of higher education. His eloquence in this book is testimony to the very idea that critical thinking and good education are not and must not be culturally or linguisticallly bounded.

DONALDO MACEDO is professor of English and graduate program director of bilingual and ESL (English as a Second Language) Studies at the University of Massachusetts–Boston. He is a leading authority in language and education and has published widely in the area of critical literacy. He is coauthor with Paulo Freire of *Literacy: Reading the Word and the World* and is working on a new book titled *Cultural Illiteracy Dictionary: What Americans Are Not Allowed to Know.*

Index

Abrams, Elliot, 188(n20)
Adams, John, 83
Africa, 113–115
African-Americans
    Civil Rights Movement, 75
    class differences among, 115–116
    and language, 120, 121, 126, 135
    See also Racism
All Things Considered, 142–149
American Civil Liberties Union, 10
America 2000, 165, 167–168, 194(n30)
Anesthetized consciousness, 17, 22
Anger, 4–5
Anti-Defamation League of B'nai B'rith, 52
Anti-semitism, 52
Aristide, Jean-Bertrand, 24
Aronowitz, Stanley, 174
Ashbery, John, 16
Atomic weapons, 75–76

Back-to-basics approach, 18, 103
Bakhtin, Mikhail, 133
Banana republics, 78
Banking model, 16, 18–19, 22–23, 65–66, 69, 150, 173
Barbarism
    and civilization, 30–31, 39, 68
    and radical pedagogy, 87, 88, 89–90
    Vietnam War, 86–89
Bartolomé, Lilia, 182
Beatty, Jack, 170
Beauty Myth, The (Wolf), 117
Bell, Derrick, 49, 117
Benjamin, Walter, 65
Bennett, William, 103, 125, 126, 165
Berthoff, Ann, 99
Betto, Frei, 22
Big Stick Diplomacy, 72
Bilingual education
    attacks on, 125, 127–128, 129, 154–155
    and culture, 131
    and democracy, 134

and dominant language, 120, 128–129
    importance of, 125–126
    radical pedagogy for, 131–135
    See also Language; Linguistic-minority students; Multiculturalism
Bimbi, Linda, 174
Black English, 120, 121
Bloom, Allan, 37, 39, 62, 63
Bollings, Bruce, 47
Bonner, Raymond, 188(n20)
Bosnia, 6, 89
Boston Globe, 23, 66
Boston University, 41–42
Bowles, Samuel, 9–10
Bradford, William, 68
Bradley, Ed, 42
Buchanan, Patrick, 91–92, 94–95, 129
Bush, George. *See* Gulf War; Reagan-Bush administrations
Bush, Neal, 91

Cabral, Amilcar, 43, 114
Cape Verde, 123–124, 150
Capitalism, 34, 50, 51
Carson, Kit, 71
Carter, Jimmy, 14
Casanova, Vides, 188(n20)
Cedras, Raoul, 24
Central Intelligence Agency (CIA), 78
Chemical warfare, 88–89
China, 51
Choice, 138, 165–166, 170
Chomsky, Noam, 10, 14–15, 20, 26, 34–35, 39, 40–41, 71, 188(n17)
Chrysler Corporation, 92
Chubb, 169
CIA. *See* Central Intelligence Agency
Civil Rights Movement, 75
Class
    Africa, 115
    and culture, 114–115
    and dialogical method, 176

and education, 103–104
and educational reforms, 138, 166–167
and government economic policies, 81–82, 91–93
and language, 101–102
Marxist analysis, 208
and racism, 113, 115–117
and radical pedagogy, 100–102
and sexism, 108–109
See also Economic/social inequalities
Clinton, Bill, 49, 50, 194(n30)
Closing of the American Mind, The (Bloom), 62
Coalitions, 110–112
Cole, Johnnetta B., 50–51
Collins, Marjorie, 3–4
Colonialism
and barbarism, 68
and common culture ideology, 48–49, 79
and educational reforms, 177, 179, 180–181
and Freirian pedagogy, 113–114
and language, 122–124, 134, 172–173
and oppressive education, 150, 172–173
Common culture ideology, 42, 58–63
and attacks on democracy, 94
and banking model, 65–66, 69
and colonialism, 48–49, 79
and dominant cultural hegemony, 47–48, 52, 94–96, 125, 135
and economic/social inequalities, 37, 48, 63–65
and English Only Movement, 125–126, 127–128, 129, 134
and fragmentation, 67–68
and manipulation of language, 39
melting pot theory, 43–44, 125
and racism, 44–46, 94–95, 129–130
and suppression of truth, 67–69, 70–85
See also Dominant cultural hegemony; Dominant ideology indoctrination; Multiculturalism
Competition, 165–166, 167, 174
Cone, James, 8
Conscientization, 4
Conservatives, 15, 37, 39, 42, 43–46. *See also* Common culture ideology; Dominant ideology indoctrination; Educational reforms; Reagan-Bush administrations
Constantino, Renato, 130, 173

Cookson, Peter W., Jr., 141–142, 167
Courts, Patrick, 16, 130
Creativity, 121–122
Cuba, 24, 50–51, 79
Cultural Literacy: What Every American Needs to Know (Hirsch), 65–66, 68
Cultural relativism, 37, 47. *See also* Multiculturalism
Culture
and bilingual education, 131
and class, 114–115
definitions of, 99–100
importance of, 114
and radical pedagogy, 99–100, 102
See also Common culture ideology; Multiculturalism; Subordinate cultures
Cyprus, 26

Daley, James, 86
Dangerous Place, A (Moynihan), 25
D'Aubuisson, Roberto, 42, 188(n20)
Declaration of Independence, 11, 83–84
Deficit-orientation model, 1, 3, 140–141, 149–150, 154
Democracy
and bilingual education, 134
and capitalism, 51
conservative attacks on, 15, 37, 41, 94
crisis of, 14, 15, 29
and educational reforms, 140, 167, 168
and privatization, 170
and racism, 50, 70
and U.S. foreign policy, 24, 51
See also Spritzler incident
Dialogical method, 174, 175–176, 181, 182
Dictionary of Cultural Literacy: What Every American Needs to Know, 68, 69, 70–85
"Dilettantism," 20
Disenfranchisement, 6, 79
"Diversity," 157–158
Dominant cultural hegemony
and common culture ideology, 47–48, 52, 94–96, 125, 135
and dominant ideology indoctrination, 37–38
and English Only Movement, 129
and language, 118–123, 153
and melting pot theory, 43–44
and oppressive education, 95–96, 118–123, 163

and rage, 52
Trilateral Commission perspective, 14
See also Common culture ideology;
  Dominant ideology indoctrination
Dominant ideology indoctrination
  complicity in, 12, 14, 34–35, 38, 40–41, 42–
    43, 137, 153
  and dominant cultural hegemony, 37–38
  and economic/social inequalities, 9–10,
    93–94
  and English Only Movement, 129
  and fragmentation, 25, 26–27
  and government policies, 9–11, 23–24,
    50–51, 66–67, 91–93
  and Gulf War, 29–31
  and lack of accountability, 40–43, 188(nn
    16, 17)
  and language, 5, 7–8, 132, 137–139
  and obedience, 38, 67–68
  and oppressive education, 12, 14–15, 19,
    34, 39–42, 149, 171
  and politeness, 34
  resistance to, 8, 10, 35
  and Rodney King trial, 11–12
  and specialization, 15, 17, 19–25
  and Spritzler incident, 10–11, 12, 34, 38
  and U.S. foreign policy, 23–24, 34–35, 50–
    51, 65, 93
  See also Common culture ideology;
    Dominant cultural hegemony
Donald, James, 132–133
Doublespeak, 27–29
Douglass, Frederick, 83–85
Drill-and-practice, 16
Drugs, war on, 31, 32–34
Dukakis, Michael, 139

East Timor, 25, 26
Economic/social inequalities
  and common culture ideology, 37, 48,
    63–65
  and dominant ideology indoctrination,
    9–10, 93–94
  and educational reforms, 104, 166–168
  and oppressive education, 36, 63, 64–65,
    103–105, 137, 153, 166–167
  and political system, 49–50
  and social welfare for the rich, 91–94
  suppression of truth, 81–83
  See also Racism

Education
  and class, 103–104
  and culture, 99–100
  instrumentalist approach, 15, 16–19, 130
  political nature of, 15, 39, 98, 99, 103, 121–
    122, 161
  See also Education, schools of;
    Educational reforms; Oppressive
    education; Radical pedagogy; *specific
    topics*
Education, schools of
  absence of critical tools, 12
  and oppressive education, 7–8, 151, 152–
    153
  reform attempts in, 154–164
  White dominance of, 155
Educational reforms
  and choice, 138, 165–166, 170
  and class, 138, 166–167
  and colonialism, 177, 179, 180–181
  and competition, 165–166, 167, 174
  deficit-orientation model, 154
  and economic/social inequalities, 104,
    166–168
  and methodology, 154, 174–176
  privatization, 166, 167, 169, 170, 174
  and racism, 141, 158, 159
  in schools of education, 154–164
  vs. transformation, 140, 165, 168, 171–172
  triviality of, 153–154
  See also Liberal/neoliberal educators;
    Oppressive education; Radical
    pedagogy
Eisenhower, Dwight D., 77
El Salvador, 24, 40–41, 42, 66–67, 79–80,
  100(n20)
"End of the Second Reconstruction, The"
  (Jackson), 129
English as a Second Language (ESL), 99,
  126
English Only Movement, 125, 127–128, 129,
  134, 172
ESL. *See* English as a Second Language
"Ethnic cleansing," 6

"Family values," 91
Fanon, Frantz, 114
Farrakhan, Louis, 52
Faulkner, Roland P., 173
Feminism, 105–108, 109, 123. *See also*
  Sexism

Ferleger, Lou, 130
Field, Robert J., 86
Finn, Chester, 165, 169
Flecha, Ramon, 52
Flores, Barbara, 38
Flynn, Ray, 169
Fragmentation
    and common culture ideology, 67–68
    and dominant ideology indoctrination,
        25, 26–27
    rejection of, 181
    and specialization, 17, 20–21, 22
    and U.S. government policies, 23–25
François, Michel, 24
Franklin, Benjamin, 83
Freedom of speech, 28
Freire, Paulo. *See* Freirian pedagogy
Freirian pedagogy
    on banking model, 18–19
    on class, 100–103, 115–117
    on critical reading of the world, 21–22,
        ·26, 27, 117–118
    decentralization, 168–170
    on dominant language, 118–124
    and language "clarity," 5–6, 7, 8
    and methodology, 154, 174–176, 181, 182
    on objectivity, 23
    and paternalism, 178
    as political, 161
    on racism, 106–107, 113–114, 116–117
    São Paulo, 165, 169–170
    and sexism, 105–113, 116–117
    and Third World/First World distinction,
        96–99, 173–174
    See also Radical pedagogy
Frost, Robert, 13–14
Fuentes, Carlos, 89–90

Gandhi, Mohandas, 37
Garcia, Herman, 88
Gates, Henry Louis, Jr., 46, 47, 116, 189(n32)
Gee, Jim, 26–27
Gender. *See* Sexism
Gettysburg Address, 70
"Ghetto Life 101," 142–149, 167
Giroux, Henry, 7, 15, 18, 20, 54, 57, 98, 119,
        126, 129, 133
Goals 2000, 194(n30)
Gordon, David M., 9–10
Gramsci, Antonio, 128–129
Greene, Robert, 17

Grenada, 10, 26, 32, 72, 93
Guatemala, 51, 78
Guillermoprieto, Alma, 188(n20)
Guinea-Bissau, 114–115
Guinier, Lani, 49, 50, 171
Gulf War, 10, 24–32
    and barbarism, 30–31
    and fragmentation, 24–25, 26–27
    and manipulation of language, 6, 27–29,
        39
    and oil, 32
    yellow ribbon symbol, 29, 137

Haig, Alexander M., Jr., 66–67
Haiti, 23, 24, 96–97
Hamilton, Alexander, 92
Hammer, Rhonda, 29
Hancock, John, 83
Havel, Vaclav, 38
Hawaii, 79
Helms, Jesse, 42
Henry, Patrick, 71
Hill, Anita, 49
Hiroshima/Nagasaki bombings, 30, 75–76
Hirsch, E. D., 39, 40, 65–66, 67–69, 70–85, 87
History of the United States, The (Field), 86
Hitler, Adolf, 36, 67
Hobbes, Thomas, 178
Hoff-Sommers, Christina, 52
Holocaust, 30
Homophobia, 49
hooks, bell, 20, 46, 115, 116–117, 157, 176
Horton, Willie, 11, 127
Hughes, Langston, 13–14
Hutto, Charles, 76–77

Ideology. *See* Dominant ideology
        indoctrination
Illiterate America (Kozol), 35, 105
Indentured servants, 70
Indonesia, 25, 26
Infant mortality, 22
Instrumentalist approach to education, 15,
        16–19, 130
Iran-Contra scandal, 66
Israel, 26

Jackson, Derrick Z., 24, 129, 158
Jackson, Kenneth T., 134
Japanese-American internment, 73
Jefferson, Thomas, 83

Jensen, Katherine, 150
Johnson, Lyndon B., 77
Johnson, Richard, 100

Keating, Charles, 91
Kennedy, John F., 37, 77
King, Rodney, 11–12, 17, 52
Kozol, Jonathan, 13–14, 35, 64, 105, 160, 166
Kurds, 29

Language
    "clarity," 5–8
    and class, 101–102
    and colonialism, 122–124, 134, 172–173
    and dominant cultural hegemony, 118–
        123, 153
    and dominant ideology indoctrination,
        5, 7–8, 132, 137–139
    doublespeak, 27–29
    manipulation of, 6, 27–29, 39, 77
    and multiculturalism, 124
    productive quality of, 132–133
    and sexism, 107–108, 123
    "shock words," 137–139, 151, 157, 158, 165
    and thought, 123–124
    See also Bilingual education; Linguistic-
        minority students
Learning with Freire, 99
Lebanon, 26
Liberalism, 139. *See also* Liberal/neoliberal
    educators
Liberal/neoliberal educators, 45, 174–181
    and colonialism, 177, 179, 180–181
    on culture, 48–49
    and Freirian pedagogy, 173–174, 181
    and methodology, 174–176, 181, 182
    and minority voices, 4–7
    and paternalism, 176–180, 181
    racism of, 158
    and romanticism, 178, 180, 181
    and Third World/First World distinction,
        96–97
    tokenism, 171
Libya, 10, 24, 32, 72, 93
Lincoln, Abraham, 11, 70
Linguistic-minority students
    exclusion of, 1–2, 124, 126
    radical pedagogy for, 3–4, 131–135
    See also Bilingual education
Literacy
    and consciousness, 117–118

    lack of, 35–36, 103–104, 105, 126
    See also Education; Oppressive
        education; Radical pedagogy
Literacy and Empowerment (Courts), 130
Literacy: Reading the Word and the World
    (Macedo and Freire), 5–6, 108
Locke, John, 178
Long Walk, 71
Los Angeles uprising, 52
Lukas, Anthony, 127
Lutz, William, 27

McCarthyism, 50
McDonnell Douglas, 92
Machado, Antonio, 182–183
McLaren, Peter, 29, 44–45, 48–49, 128
Maitre, Joachim, 135
Malcolm X, 71, 74–75
Mandle, Jay, 130
Manhattan Project, 75
Marable, Manning, 117
Marx, Karl, 5–6, 59, 108
"Media Knowledges, Warrior Citizenry,
    and the Postmodern Literacies"
    (McLaren and Hammer), 29
Melting pot theory, 43–44, 125
Memmi, Albert, 114, 180–181
Meshad, Shad, 86
Methodology, 154, 173–176, 181–183
Mexican-American War, 74
Mexico, 74, 94
Miller, Alice, 66
"Minorities," 104–105
Moe, 169
Monolingualism, 125–126
Monterrosa, Domingo, 188(n20)
Morocco, 26
Morrison, Toni, 117
Moynihan, Daniel Patrick, 25
Multiculturalism
    debate over, 49, 51–53, 63, 172
    importance of, 47, 104
    and language, 124
    Macedo proposal, 53–62
    and racism, 52–53
    in schools of education, 160–164
    See also Bilingual education; Common
        culture ideology; Radical pedagogy
"Muted Voices in the Newsroom"
    (National Association of Black
    Journalists), 110

My Lai massacre, 76–77, 86

National Association of Black Journalists, 158
Native Americans, 11, 30, 43, 71
Navahos, 71. *See also* Native Americans
Negroni, Peter, 140, 153
New Right, 15
Nicaragua, U.S. policy in, 72, 78
  contradictions, 10, 24, 32, 93
  World Court ruling, 26, 31, 80
Non-English speakers. *See* Linguistic-minority students
Nucci, John, 3
Nyhan, David, 188(n20)

Obedience, 38, 67–68
Objectivity, 20, 21, 23, 58
O'Bryant, John, 3, 4
Oligarchy, 79
Olson, Gary, 106
Oppression
  and coalition work, 110–112
  vs. disenfranchisement, 6, 79
  and separatism, 112–113
  as "shock word," 139
  specificity of, 108–110, 112, 116
  See also Economic/social inequalities;
    Oppressive education; Racism; Sexism
Oppressive education
  banking model, 16, 18–19, 22–23, 65–66,
    69, 150, 173
  and class, 103–104
  and colonialism, 150, 172–173
  deficit-orientation model, 1, 3, 140–141,
    149–150, 154
  and dominant cultural hegemony, 95–
    96, 118–123, 163
  and dominant ideology indoctrination,
    12, 14–15, 19, 34, 39–42, 149, 171
  and economic/social inequalities, 36, 63,
    64–65, 103–105, 137, 153, 166–167
  and exclusion, 1–2, 126
  and fragmentation, 17
  and illiteracy levels, 35–36, 103–104
  industrial model, 153
  instrumentalist approach, 15, 16–19, 130
  and obedience, 67–68
  racism, 18, 126–127, 129–130, 155–156
  refusal to learn, 142, 149, 152

and schools of education, 7–8, 151, 152–
    153
  and societal oppression, 167–168, 170
  and specialization, 22–23
  and Spritzler incident, 18, 34
  Trilateral Commission perspective, 14–15
  See also Common culture ideology
Oral literacy, 118
Ortega y Gasset, José, 19, 21, 30–31, 63
Orwell, George, 14

Panama, 10, 26, 32, 39, 72, 79
Pardo de Tavera, T. H., 172–173
Parks, Rosa, 75
Paternalism, 176–180
Patriotism, 2–3, 28, 29, 93, 137
Paxton, Tom, 19, 23
Pedagogy. *See* Education; Literacy; Radical
    pedagogy
*Pedagogy in Process: Letters to Guinea-
    Bissau* (Freire), 99, 113
Pedagogy of the Oppressed (Freire), 6, 7, 99,
    105, 106
  sexism in, 108, 109, 110, 113
Penney, Sherry, 53
People, Yes, The (Sandburg), 94
Pereira, Aristides, 124
Perry, Theresa, 158–159
Philippines, 79, 172–173
Pilgrims, 68, 71, 72
Pledge of Allegiance, 68, 93. *See also*
    Spritzler incident
Plymouth Rock, 72
Politeness, 34
Politics of Education, The (Freire), 107–108
Ponce, Rene Emilio, 188(n20)
Positivism, 21
Postal, Theodore, 28
Powell, Colin, 49
Privatization, 166, 167, 169, 170, 174
Project Edison, 170
Puerto Rico, 79, 172, 173

Quayle, Dan, 30

Racism
  Africa, 113–115
  and anesthetized consciousness, 17
  and class, 113, 115–117
  and common culture ideology, 44–46,
    94–95, 129–130

and democracy, 50, 70
and dominant ideology, 49–50
and educational reforms, 141, 158, 159
Europe, 189(n32)
extent of, 45–47, 116–117, 135
and fragmentation, 17
and Freirian pedagogy, 106–107, 113–114
and illusion of choice, 165
Japanese-American internment, 73–74
Malcolm X on, 71, 74–75
and melting pot theory, 44
and oppressive education, 18, 126–127,
    129–130, 155–156
Rodney King trial, 11–12, 17, 52
and sexism, 108–109, 116–117
U.S. history, 11, 44, 70, 71–72, 73
See also Dominant cultural hegemony;
    Economic/social inequalities
Radicalism, 139
Radical pedagogy, 86, 95
and barbarism, 87, 88, 89–90
and class, 100–102
collective participation, 169–170
and coming to voice, 4–8, 133, 182
and creativity, 121–122
and culture, 99–100, 102
dangers to educators, 13–14
decentralization, 168–169
and hope, 140, 151–152
and language, 118–123
and linguistic-minority students, 3–4,
    131–135
and literacy, 118
and methodology, 181–183
political nature of, 102–103
possibility of, 119–120
and Spritzler incident, 12–13
and subordinate cultures, 149–152
and Third World/First World distinction,
    96–99
See also Freirian pedagogy
Rape, 6, 87, 88, 89
Ravitch, Diane, 39, 40, 125
Reagan-Bush administrations
America 2000 plan, 165, 167–168
economic policies, 9–10, 81–83, 91–92, 93
Iran-Contra scandal, 66
"kinder, gentler nation" myth, 94
and liberalism, 139
racism, 11, 49–50, 95
and United Nations, 25

values under, 91
and war on drugs, 34
Willie Horton campaign, 11, 127
See also Gulf War; U.S. foreign policy
Reagan, Ronald. *See* Reagan-Bush
    administrations
Reboul, Olivier, 137–138
Refugees, 80
Relman, John, 47
Republican Party, 11
Romero, Archbishop Oscar, 42, 188(n20)
Roosevelt, Theodore, 72, 173

Salazar, Antonio, 45
Sandburg, Carl, 94
Savage Inequalities (Kozol), 64, 160
Savery, Pancho, 17
Savings and loan scandal, 91
Schlesinger, Arthur, Jr., 39, 44, 45, 46, 68
Schmidt, Benno, Jr., 170
Schools of education. *See* Education,
    schools of
Scientism, 20–21
Senge, Peter, 142, 152
Separatism, 112–113
Sexism, 105–113
and language, 107–108, 123
and other oppressions, 108–109, 110–112,
    116–117, 157
Shevardnadze, Eduard, 125
Shor, Ira, 99
Silber, John, 7, 15, 39, 40–42, 165, 188(n16)
Simpson, Bill, 165
Slavery, 30, 68, 70, 83–85
Socialism, 50
Social Mind, The (Gee), 26–27
Sociolinguistics, 122
Souljah, Sister, 52
Specialization, 15, 17, 19–25, 182
Spivak, Gayatri, 8, 20
Spritzler incident, 14, 22–23, 38
and dominant ideology indoctrination,
    10–11, 12, 34, 38
and instrumentalist approach, 18–19
and radical pedagogy, 12–13
Steinem, Gloria, 176
Stevenson, Adlai, 77
Subordinate cultures, 142–149
and class, 166–167
language of, 118–123
and radical pedagogy, 149–152

and rage, 52
See also Bilingual education; Dominant
cultural hegemony; Linguistic-
minority students; Oppression;
Racism; Sexism
Suppression of truth
and common culture ideology, 67–69,
70–85
history, 10–11, 25–26, 67–68, 70–85, 86–89
and U.S. foreign policy, 40–41, 42, 66–67,
188(n20)
See also Dominant ideology
indoctrination
Swain, Carol, 158

Tadic, Liubomir, 178
Technology, 17, 30
Third World/First World distinction, 80,
96–99, 173–174
Thomas, Clarence, 49–50, 115
Torricelli, Robert, 24
Transformation, 140, 165, 168, 171–172
Trilateral Commission, 14–15, 36
Truman, Harry S, 75–76
Turkey, 26

UNESCO, 18
United Nations, 25, 26, 31
Uruguay, 78
U.S. foreign policy
and "banana republics," 78
Big Stick Diplomacy, 72
and colonialism, 79
and dominant ideology indoctrination,
23–24, 34–35, 50–51, 65, 93
double standard, 31
lies about, 40–41, 42, 66–67, 188(n20)

and manipulation of language, 6, 27–29,
39, 77
and oligarchy, 79–80
Panama invasion, 10, 26, 32, 39, 72
Vietnam War, 34–35, 39, 76–78, 86–89
and war on drugs, 32–34
See also Gulf War; U.S. government
policies; *specific countries*
U.S. government policies
and dominant ideology indoctrination,
9–11, 66–67, 91–93
economic policy, 9–10, 81–83, 91–92
and fragmentation, 23–25
refugees, 80
scandals, 91
war on drugs, 32–34
See also Reagan-Bush administrations;
U.S. foreign policy

Vietnam War, 34–35, 39, 76–78, 86–89

Wall Street Journal, 188(n20)
Wayne, John, 29
Weisskopf, E. Thomas, 9–10
Weld, William, 169
Wertheimer, Linda, 142
West, Cornel, 45–46, 116, 117
*West Virginia State Board of Education
versus Barnett*, 10
"What Is Poetry?" (Ashbery), 16
Whitmore, Jeffrey, 87
Wiggins, Edith, 52
Wolf, Naomi, 117
World Court, 26, 31, 80
World War II, 73, 75–76

Zinn, Howard, 20, 63, 92–93